A Thousand
Sunny Days

F. JASON PHINNEY

ISBN: 1-4848-4652-4
ISBN-13: 978-1-4848-4652-0

To Deborah,

A Thousand
Sunny Days

Thanks for helping
me move on

Doug

I hunger, yet no one will feed me
I cry, yet no one comes near
I long for someone to hold me
Alone, I'm shaking with fear

Each day that passes, I weaken
Each night my spirit does wane
I'm weary searching and seeking
Yearning to come home again

I lie here watching and waiting
My life is yours to decide
I'll come without hesitating
And always be by your side

CONTENTS

Prologue

Impassively, from a comfortable position atop the king-sized bed, the dogs monitored the final stages of preparation. Perhaps they noticed I donned the same uniform as last weekend—khaki pants, blue button-down, oxford-cloth shirt, cheap, reversible brown belt, slightly scuffed brown shoes—an engineer's earnest, albeit pitiful, attempt to dress for a night on the town. I leaned forward to check the quality of my shaving effort and, in the opposite mirror, caught a glimpse of the relentlessly expanding bald spot radiating from the crown of my head. During the last decade of my forty-nine years, the bald forces had been waging a multi-front campaign against the brown forces—slowly taking territory, pushing outward from their initial encampment to join a two-pronged flanking maneuver advancing from the forehead. If and when the bald forces merged, they'd certainly annihilate the weakened brown troops remaining on the high ground.

A less noticeable guerrilla campaign was being waged by the gray forces on the sides of my head, slowly infiltrating, converting where they could, and killing where they could not. With ever-increasing numbers, no longer fearing a counterattack from the demoralized brown forces, they proudly displayed their colors, intent upon seizing the turf not yet uprooted by the bald forces. I wondered how it would play out—an entire barren landscape or a forest of gray surviving in the outer reaches? Given the relatively large and professorial shape of my head, the outcome would likely affect my chances of keeping a mate.

My thoughts were interrupted as the three dogs leaped from the bed, converged at the bedroom door, and spilled into the living room. They barreled ahead, paws working overtime on the slick tile floors, scratching and sliding as they rounded the corner, decelerating quickly as they reached the front door—tails wagging, feet dancing, bodies wriggling, their voices creating a symphony of euphoric crying and barking—*she's here!* I worried my one-hundred-pound, two-year-old, black female might be a little too excited. I held her leather collar tightly, struggling to contain the pure canine power supercharged with youthful exuberance, and opened the door.

"Hi, Pookie!" Stephanie exclaimed. "Pookie" wasn't addressed to me—it was for the eighty-pound, fur-covered male who made traveling from Midtown worthwhile. He returned the greeting with a combination of smiling, crying, and wiggling. Each time Stephanie repeated the word hi, he flashed his smile, and the tempo of wiggling doubled. His excitement level was much higher than the times other people visited or, for that matter, when I came home each day. OK, maybe I was a little jealous. After all I'd done for him—I didn't expect to be upstaged by someone he'd only known for a few months. But he had his own set of ranking criteria—and seniority couldn't trump a pretty smile.

A few moments later, the massive puppy wrestled away from my grip and raced to pick up the large cow knuckle she had temporarily abandoned in the bedroom. With the enormous bone firmly locked in her jaws, the horse-sized canine was soon upon Stephanie—one paw to the arm and the other to the rib cage.

"Well, strike up another one for her," she said. "Looks like this outfit will be going to the tailor. I guess I can cover the hole with my jacket until we're at the dinner table."

"I'm sorry, babe," I replied. "I didn't get a chance to put on her booties before you got here. We'll go shopping for a replacement with my 'Canine Casualty Allowance.'"

Stephanie laughed at my silly words. I didn't think I was all that funny, but it was nice that she humored me. My six-year-old, fifty-pound mix approached and stared soulfully into Stephanie's eyes. Responding to the gentle stroking of her head, she wagged her tail for a few moments and then retreated to her dog bed.

"I don't know why she hasn't warmed up to me yet," Stephanie said.

"No, she likes you—that's how she expresses affection," I replied. "Don't you remember how she completely ignored you in the beginning? Soon she'll be curled up next to you on the couch—always wanting to touch you."

"She is sweet—she won't look away until I do."

"Is that from my problem child?" I asked, pointing to three pale red lines on Stephanie's arm.

"Yes, my skin's real sensitive. I'll probably be bruised tomorrow."

"I'm sorry. She's so powerful and quick."

"That reminds me," Stephanie said, "I was at my doctor's this week, and she started asking some odd questions. She wondered if my boyfriend ever became angry and lost his temper. She thought the bruises on my legs and arms were from someone grabbing me too hard."

"Are you kidding?"

"No, she really thought I might be in trouble. She didn't know what to think when I told her I was attacked by a polar bear," Stephanie laughed. The polar bear analogy wasn't far from the truth. The black, heavily muscled puppy had so much power in her paws. It wasn't only the jumping or ramming that was of concern; it extended to quiet moments—just sitting on the couch or watching a movie. If she was nearby, it was a good bet at some point you'd be struck by one of her massive mitts. With surprising finesse, she punched, swatted, and threw the occasional hook. Even with my hand always prepared to fend her off, she got in a few successful shots each week.

"You know, she reminds me of one of the characters in *Of Mice and Men*," I said.

"Lenny! She's like Lenny. She doesn't know the strength of her own paws. Hey, Lenny!" Stephanie said.

The friendly giant didn't realize she was getting a new nickname.

"Lenny Paws! That's it—Lenny Paws!" she said. "It's perfect."

"It does fit her. There's absolutely no aggression—she's just clumsy."

"Oh, hey, Jason," Stephanie said playfully, turning her attention to me.

"Hey, beautiful. I can finally greet you properly now that the dogs have calmed down," I replied, holding her in my arms, becoming lost in her pretty eyes—a dark-green starburst radiating from the pupil, blending into a light-brown outer ring. I kissed her full lips longingly, feeling the romantic rush so familiar in the beginning of a relationship.

I continued, "How about a glass of wine before we go to dinner? I've got your favorite Malbec from Argentina."

"I'll have a glass of Chardonnay if you have any," she said.

"I have plenty—are you sure you want white?"

"You know how red wine changes the shade of my lips. I never like to drink it when we are going to be in public."

"Well, you always look great—even with new colors added to your smile. White it is," I said, noticing the beautiful contrast between her dark, red lips and flawless, fair skin. Not only did I have Malbec and Chardonnay, I had Cabernet, Merlot, Riesling, Pinot Grigio, and a few other styles at the ready. After only a few months of dating, I still hadn't figured out what type of wine Stephanie preferred. It changed with her mood and depended on what we planned to do. I poured the glasses and we moved to one of the few remaining pieces of furniture in the living room.

"You know, if you ever want a weekend away from this one," Stephanie said, pointing to Pookie, "I'd be glad to take him home. He's always trying to get my attention. I think he'd be very happy at my townhouse."

"Sorry, Lenny Paws would have to be part of a package deal—and my old girl would be devastated. You'll have to put up with me if you want to visit him."

"I guess it's worth it," she smiled. "I never thought I'd warm up to dogs like I have. I mean, I never thought I could fall for them like you."

"Well, there's just something about these guys," I replied, finishing the last of my wine. I left the couch and did my normal pre-departure walk-through—closing the doors to the pantry, office, bedroom, bathroom, and laundry as well as clearing the counters of any food or interesting items. Any omission in the routine could lead to an unpleasant surprise upon returning home.

"Where's Lenny Paws?" I wondered aloud.

"My question is what happened to my other shoe?" Stephanie asked, searching without success around the base of the couch.

Uh-oh. The missing shoe could mean only one thing. Lenny Paws was probably in the backyard destroying yet another "found" item.

"Gimme that shoe!" I shouted, running into the backyard to capture her. She dodged my grasp and sprinted away with her new prize. After more shouting and chasing, she brought it to me with her tail wagging and eyes bright.

"Bad dog!" I said in a tone lacking conviction and doing my best to hide the smile forcing its way out. "I guess we'll add this to the shopping list." The cork-heeled shoe, missing for only a few minutes, suffered fatal wounds.

"I'm running out of things to wear to dinner. Pretty soon we'll be ordering takeout. I guess it will be fine for tonight; they're still walkable."

"Let's go before they get your purse. You must really like these guys. I mean, I expect them to destroy my things."

"I don't think I could ever stay mad at them. Especially after hearing about all the things they went through."

"I remember when we first talked about my dogs you thought I was crazy to put up with all the chaos."

"And now I'm the one trying to talk you into adopting another. I can't get over how many dogs were at the shelter," Stephanie said. "There must've been more than two hundred. It was so sad. I still think about the little one pushing her body against the cage so I could rub her chest. She had such sweet eyes."

"She reminded me a lot of my dog that..." I hesitated. I had to change the subject quickly or risk dampening the lighthearted mood. Even after two years, the pain was right below the surface. "It's difficult to handle if you're not taking one home. I probably should've gone in by myself—it was such a long shot to find my neighbor's dog. We were more than twenty miles from where she disappeared."

"No, you did the right thing. It was only a few minutes out of our way. What if she was there and you didn't bother to check?"

"I guess you're right. At least we know—and I'm sure the little girl you played with will find a home," I added with false confidence. "If I had room for another dog, she'd be perfect. Maybe I'll get another when I buy a ranch—or get married again."

I smiled at Stephanie when those words slipped out. It was way too soon to be talking seriously about the future, though when I was with Stephanie, there was nowhere I'd rather be. I felt so alive, so renewed—so in love? After only a few months of dating, I wondered how these feelings could be real. How could I have fallen so hard for someone I barely knew? It was difficult to unravel my emotions after feeling numb for so long. Maybe the dogs and Stephanie both had it right—live in the moment. Enjoy the relationship and stop over thinking everything. I changed the subject as we headed to the car and hoped she didn't think too much about what I said.

A little behind schedule, we were seated at a table overlooking a large, tree-lined pond. The evening breeze created ripples upon which the adjacent streetlights danced. My thoughts wandered as my gaze shifted between Stephanie and the dancing lights.

"When are you going to let me read the rest of the book?" Stephanie asked.

"I can't seem to wrap it up—maybe I'll never finish."

"I'm sure it's fine the way it is," she reassured. "I'm looking forward to the parts about my little guy, Pookie."

"I think you'll be even more attached to him after and, if nothing else, you'll understand me better."

"I don't think you're hard to figure out—you love your dogs, and you're a hopeless romantic. What's not to like about that?" Stephanie smiled.

"Nothing, I suppose—except I haven't always been this way. There are a lot of things I wish I could go back and change," I unintentionally confessed. I struggled to get my mind on another topic. Nearly a year had passed since the divorce, yet I still found myself working through and, sometimes, wallowing in the tangle of emotions.

As we talked about the book, my thoughts drifted back seventeen years to one summer afternoon in Folsom, Louisiana. A relatively insignificant decision that day led to some of the most meaningful experiences of my life. A pair of adopted puppies entered my cluttered, yet lonely, existence and not only changed the course of my life, they changed me. The walls of anger and bitterness that formed after my mother's death, heavily fortified to prevent feeling anything too deeply, were shattered by the puppies' relentless affection and unconditional love. The dogs held my unshielded heart firmly in their paws, their adventures bringing unrivaled joy, their struggles testing my ability to endure. Their lives and the lives of those who followed became the canvas upon which my story was painted—the vessels into which my love was poured.

That one decision, so casually taken years before, also brought Lenny Paws and her friends into my life. Though the dogs began their lives rejected, lonely, and scared, they found love and acceptance in each other's company. Ironically, the carelessly discarded animals, unaccustomed to human kindness and affection, provided the love I desperately needed to heal my broken life.

Part One

HURRICANE CLYDE

CHAPTER ONE

Beginnings

Walliford and Pepper bounded alongside the red sedan, barking wildly as I passed the sign inscribed "Lisa Marie Oaks" and carefully made my way up the long dirt driveway. Every time I visited my sister's ranch, the same canine greeting occurred, and the same feeling of peace settled upon me. It was only ninety minutes from my small apartment on the outskirts of New Orleans, yet it felt completely isolated from the commotion of the city. Lisa's home was one of dozens of horse farms surrounding the small town of Folsom, Louisiana. Her two-story, wood-shingled house was set on two-hundred acres of rolling pasture dotted with giant oak trees under whose sprawling branches livestock escaped the sweltering south Louisiana sun.

In addition to Walliford and Pepper, Lisa's ranch was home to dozens of cows, twenty horses, a zebra donkey, a potbellied pig, and three llamas. And, a few months ago, six puppies joined what was beginning to resemble a wild-life refuge. The puppies were the reason I made the drive; it was time to choose the one I'd take home.

Walliford's dark eyes tracked my movements as I climbed from the small sedan. With ears raised slightly and long tail held upright, he craned his massive, square-shaped head slightly forward and sniffed the air between us. After a quick, but thorough, investigation, he relaxed his ears and allowed his tail to drop and move slowly, almost impercep-tibly, from side to side. Satisfied he had performed his duty, he turned and walked away. Walliford was a resident of the ranch when Lisa and her husband, Adam, acquired it. The previous owners said the dog showed up one day and never left. They made Lisa an offer she couldn't refuse—if she didn't want him, they'd take him to the pound.

I was always a little uneasy around Walliford. The hun-dred-pound, black Lab mix looked capable of inflicting serious harm if he was having a bad day. Even though I had visited the ranch dozens of times, he never warmed up to me. Pepper, Lisa's German Short-haired Pointer, was just the opposite—thin, submissive, gentle, and sweet. She craved affection and pushed her nose against my hand if I ceased petting her for even a moment. Lisa adopted her a year earlier to provide some companionship for Walliford. Soon thereafter, Pepper had her first litter—three males sporting cream-colored coats and three females dressed in black. They bore little resemblance to the parents who brought them into the world; they looked more like pure-bred Labs.

Excitedly, the puppy with bright green eyes and a dime-sized patch of white fur on the crown of his head crawled up and flipped over the one-foot steel mesh gate designed to confine him. He bounded clumsily toward me, his tiny tail wiggling joyfully, completing four strokes with each step. I found a comfortable spot in the shade of the giant oaks lining the pool area and let him crawl around on my lap.

"So, have you figured out which one you want?" Lisa inquired hopefully, eager to thin the herd.

"I'll definitely take this one," I said as the chubby, cream-colored puppy began gnawing my hand with his tiny, razor-sharp teeth. Though I spoke with confidence, I didn't have a good grasp of what was involved in caring for him. Lisa fed and cleaned up after them and did whatever else pet owners do. *How hard could it be?* He was so tiny—maybe ten pounds with a belly full of food.

"Good, he's probably the best one next to Tango." Lisa was convinced her puppy, Tango, was the pick of the litter. I didn't know much about dogs, but I was certain my little guy—so intelligent, confident, and affectionate—was the best of the bunch.

"Can you come to a party we're throwing on the fifteenth?" Lisa asked. "We're celebrating the closing of the musical I've been working. We're going to have the barbeque catered, and Adam hired a live band." Lisa enjoyed the country lifestyle despite having grown up with her two siblings in one big city after another—first Miami, then Chicago, and finally New Orleans. She wasn't living the stereotypical simple country life; she threw extravagant parties for her city friends, decorated the house with expensive art and furniture, and wore the latest designer clothes. No matter how casual the occasion, Lisa took meticulous care to choose the perfect combination of boots, buckle, hat, jeans, and shirt.

Lisa was the genetic beneficiary of a mother with the looks of a Hollywood starlet—flawless fair skin, long dirty-blonde hair, big pretty blue eyes, sweet smile and athletic figure, and a father who, in his younger days, resembled Rock Hudson. Adam was the latest in a line of wealthy men who provided the lifestyle of parties, dining, drinking, and dancing to which Lisa was accustomed.

"I'll definitely be there. I didn't know you were still doing hair and wigs for the shows. I thought you quit when you moved across the lake." Before she married, Lisa bounced from one job to another, each sharing the trait of allowing her to wake up near noon most days. When a job threatened to interfere with vacation plans, she quit and didn't lose any sleep over it.

"No, I'm still doing the big productions so I can keep my connections. By the way, there's a cute actress coming. She's looking forward to meeting you."

"What lies did you tell her?" I laughed. "I hope you didn't build me up too much."

"You just need to be yourself—she's really down-to-earth. Buying some new clothes wouldn't hurt though. You're only thirty-two and you dress like an old man."

"Thanks, Lisa, I needed the ego boost. It's because I don't know how to pick out casual clothes. Every time I go to the mall, I end up buying something ridiculous and never wear it again."

"That's because you'll buy anything as long as the sales-girl is pretty."

"I know. I think that's what they count on."

Lisa let the other puppies out of their enclosure and a black one joined her brother on my lap. She was the smallest and most docile of the bunch—the runt of the litter. They stumbled over each other for prime position near my hand and wrestled playfully, the filtered afternoon sun creating a mosaic of shapes on their hides as the warm breeze moved the large branches.

"What's going to happen to this one?" I asked, pointing to the small black creature tugging at the neck of my chosen puppy.

"We can't keep her—we have too many dogs. I've asked all my friends and no one wants her." Lisa said, turning her attention to the job of organizing the scattered lounge chairs near the pool.

"Too many dogs? What's one more on a big ranch like this?"

"Adam is getting tired of the commotion. The llamas are really getting on his nerves—they keep spitting on him."

"I hate those llamas. What possessed you to get those things?" I leaned a little to the side to get a view of the three creatures penned in the front pasture. I could understand the desire to own a dog or cat, or even a horse for that matter. *Who in their right mind likes llamas?*

"I thought they were cute. I didn't know they were so unfriendly. They don't have 'personality-plus' like Walliford," Lisa added in a childlike voice. "Right, Wally? Wally's a good boy!" Wally affectionately leaned against Lisa while she stroked his wiry, black fur. One of the puppies stumbled toward him and then thought better of it as Wally's low growl became audible.

I had only planned on one dog, but the little, black one seemed so needy and pitiful. "Well, what the hell. I'll take both of them." And because they'd have each other as playmates, I reasoned two dogs might be easier to manage than one.

"Good! Are you going to stay for dinner? Dad ought to be here soon."

"No, I think I'll pass. I need to get the little guys settled and, besides, he really gets under my skin."

"You need to be nicer to him. He doesn't have much time left. You'll be sorry when he's gone," she warned, rising to return the remaining puppies to the safety of their enclosure.

"I think he'll be around a long time. It seems the meaner you are, the longer you live." I stood and stretched my legs for the long drive home. As each foot met the ground, the two siblings launched a coordinated attack on my shoe.

"Jason, I don't know why you keep hanging onto this grudge against him. He's just a lonely, old man," Lisa said, launching into the familiar lecture.

"Lisa, I've tried to get along with him. Believe me, I've tried. I can't stand to be around someone who is a perpetual victim. Nothing is ever his fault. Someone else is always to blame. He's got a barrelful of excuses and a thimbleful of kindness," I answered, hoping to derail the sermon before it drudged up too many frustrating memories.

"It's not very Christian of you, you know."

"Well that's fine, because I'm not a Christian. Even if I were, I don't think you have to put up with someone that irritating. Are you still inviting him up every weekend? I don't know how you can stand it." I moved to one of the pool chairs while the lecture continued. The puppies were glad I was once again within reach and reinitiated their wrestling match on my lap.

"He's fine. I've learned to tune him out when he starts criticizing me about what I eat, the things I wear, how much I drink..." Lisa's voice had more than a hint of irritation as the words flowed. She returned to the puppy room, topped off the water bowls, and began shaking a box of dog bones. Pepper and Walliford sprinted to the familiar sound, anxious to get their daily allotment of the treats.

"Yeah, he's one to talk about drinking. Nothing like a reformed alcoholic to tell you how to live your life. What does Adam think about him being here every weekend?"

"He doesn't mind—and Dad really enjoys coming up here for dinner and sitting by the pool." I knew how she'd answer before I asked the question. She had no concept of the amount of irritation the old man could stimulate in others.

"Are you sure Adam doesn't mind? I don't think anyone wants their in-laws around every waking moment—especially someone as abrasive as the old man. Having him here all the time is going to be toxic. You tend to regress around him. In fact, we all do. It's like he knows just what to say to take us back to our childhood."

"I'm not going to abandon him. I don't want to live with the guilt you're going to feel," Lisa said.

"Well, I'll have to deal with it. I think it's better to ignore him than to fight with him constantly. Hey, I'm sorry we got off track talking about him. I'll work on it."

"Good. You need to." Lisa smiled, believing she had turned me around.

"I guess I need to get them loaded up. Do you have something I can put down for them?"

"Here, use this." Lisa took a towel from the washroom and made a small nest on the passenger floor for the puppies.

As I wheeled toward the gate, I saw my father's car approach from the main road. I waved halfheartedly as we passed and dropped my gaze to my new additions. The puppies snuggled against each other on the soft towel for the long ride home. After a few moments, the male began heaving and soon expelled the contents of his stomach. He laid down a few inches from the half-digested food and drifted into a peaceful slumber.

I named the male puppy Clyde in honor of the cat my brother, Rob, owned a few years before. Rob was tall and lanky with black hair and deep-set, dark-brown eyes—so dark it was hard to differentiate the pupil from the iris. Despite his good looks, he didn't make much of an effort to meet women or develop friendships after moving to Houston. It was quite a contrast from his life as a Sigma Nu at LSU where heavy drinking and parties were on the agenda most weekends. He became known as "the captain" after wet streets, alcohol, and slow reflexes left our father's Chrysler Newport submerged in the pond near the frat house. I don't know why Rob's personality and motivation both took a nosedive after graduating and moving to Houston.

My brother had the fortune or, in our case, the misfortune of being the firstborn of the siblings. My father was never a parenting role model, but his efforts with Rob set records for their destructive force. My father was easily frustrated with his clumsy, skinny namesake who was turning out to be nothing like the football player and ladies' man he had been. With few tools at his disposal, he used name-calling to help shape Rob's character. I can't remember any project, whether cutting the lawn, sweeping the sidewalk, or digging holes, completed without the generous use of "dummy" and "moron." My father probably thought he was being helpful to point out Rob's weaknesses and failings. Regardless of his intent, my father's words damaged Rob's self-confidence, and my brother became increasingly shy and isolated. Though I trailed my brother by five years, I could see the cruelty, intentional or not, in my father's words. Instead of being beaten down like my brother, I hardened myself emotionally and set out to prove I didn't need him—or anyone else for that matter.

Rob recognized the effectiveness of my father's character-building tool and employed it on me with great zeal. He knew I was insecure about my weight, so he provided me with loving monikers such as "little porker" and "tub-a-lard." Because I was much younger than Rob, I had little ammunition for a fair fight in the early days. However, I more than made up for it in my teens, hitting him wherever I thought I could do the most damage. That was how we both did it—no carpet-bombing of insults, just surgical strikes designed to hit the deepest insecurities of the other.

My father often said that being a Phinney was something special. We weren't just average people; we were a cut above everyone else. It took a while for me to realize we had little to be proud of.

Despite the dysfunctional nature of our relationship, Rob was still my brother and I'd occasionally visit his small one-bedroom apartment on the west side of Houston. Rob's cat usually ignored me during the day, yet once I settled down to sleep on the living room couch, an entirely new dimension of Clyde's personality emerged. The fifteen-pound feline ascended the nearby bookshelf, watching intently as I drifted to sleep. Once sufficiently convinced I was unconscious, he landed with a thud on my chest, then disappeared before I could react to the battering. It took a good twenty minutes for my heart rate to drop, and even longer for sleep to return. The cat's fanatic obsession with the routine added sleep deprivation to the frayed nerves and frustration usually accompanying time spent with my brother. Despite the cat's behavioral oddities, I selected the name of the tenacious, personality-rich animal for my puppy. Of course, the choice of Clyde for my little pup's name left no doubt his sister's name would be Bonnie.

It took a few hours to set up the encampment in the kitchen and begin the important task of paper training. Because Lisa had already taught the little guys to use newspaper in the penned area, they quickly transferred the skill to their new home. After a few hours of instruction and play, I turned out the lights and went to bed.

Most summer nights, heavy vibration and grinding metallic sounds, coincident with the startup of either of the shoddy air-conditioning units perched atop my bedroom ceiling, kept me from getting a decent night's sleep. Each time a unit kicked on, as they did repeatedly in the warm, humid environs one block from Lake Pontchartrain, I drifted, half-awake for two or three minutes, until the vibration and noise subsided. Add in the relentless whimpering and crying of my new charges, and there was no hope of rest. I held out as long as possible, then grabbed a blanket and joined them on the white-and-gray checkered linoleum floor. They nestled on either side of me, and I quickly fell asleep.

We awoke a little after sunrise to a loud knock at the door. The dogs barked wildly at the provocation, as I groggily stumbled toward the rapping sound.

"I see you brought a couple of dogs into your apartment," grumbled the apartment manager.

"I was going to come talk to you about them on Monday. I was thinking I could keep them on the balcony during the day. They'll be inside with me at night. No one will even know they're here."

"You're going to have to get rid of them. We don't allow pets. You should know that—it's clearly written in your lease," he said.

"I know, I know. What if I pay a couple hundred dollar pet deposit or a little extra rent every month?" I asked hopefully.

"No, we don't allow animals here. No animals means no animals. I want the dogs out immediately."

It was time for Plan B and, of course, I didn't have a Plan B. I was confronted with two unattractive options: return the dogs to Lisa or ask my father to care for them while I worked on getting a new place to live.

Even though we lived in the same city, I didn't talk to my father much and saw him even less. On the few occasions we did get together, I always left frustrated and exhausted. He could create a conflict where none existed and then remain incredibly calm while I melted down. He seemed to enjoy both the arguments and my reaction to his provocations. He could take me from a rational, logical professional to someone who appeared to be on a weekend pass from an insane asylum.

I didn't want to swallow my pride, but my affinity for the new puppies compelled me. Even after such a short time, the thought of abandoning them was more painful than facing my father. Well, maybe not face him—maybe call him on the phone.

"Hey, son! This is a surprise; I haven't talked to you in a while. I left you a few messages."

"Well, I've been busy with some things. I tried to call a few times—you must not have been home," I lied. "Anyway, I'm kind of in a bind. I took a couple of Lisa's dogs, and the apartment manager won't let me keep them."

"Well, what do you want me to do about it?" he asked guardedly.

"I was thinking since you're alone there, maybe you could let the dogs stay with you. They could keep you company, and I'll come over each day after work to take care of them."

"Why don't you just get rid of the dogs?" he asked, demonstrating his sincere concern for the animals' fate.

"Lisa doesn't have another home for them. They might end up at the pound." I didn't think she'd do it, but it was a scenario that couldn't be completely discounted.

"Well, would it be considered a favor?" he clarified, beginning the routine I had become accustomed to during my youth. Tightness gripped my chest and a nauseous feeling emanated from my stomach.

"Sure. Of course—it's a favor. I need you to do me a favor."

He deliberated a moment and conceded, "As long as you consider it a favor, I guess they can stay here."

"Yes, it is a favor."

"Because I won't do it unless it's a favor."

"IT IS A FAVOR!" I confirmed, hoping the familiar dance was drawing to a close.

"And you'll pay for the food and any damage they do, right?"

"Of course—I promise. I really appreciate you doing this."

"Come on, say it like you mean it," he chided in a voice one typically employs with a small child. The tone of my voice never quite met with his approval.

"I *really* appreciate it," I choked out.

"Thanks for calling, son. And remember, I *care* about you."

Sometime during the past few years of our relationship, I was downgraded from first class to coach when it came to the closing of our conversations. In the old days, "love" was used instead of "care about"—a subtle, yet important, distinction for my father. He told my siblings he loved them at the end of their conversations and, despite his best attempts to alienate them, Rob and Lisa always returned the affectionate words. My father, with his bizarre sense of humor, was quite adept at getting under a person's skin. He'd "encourage" my brother by introducing him with kind phrases like "This is my son Robert. He hasn't had a date in months," or "My son has a college degree and sells pagers for a living." He didn't take that approach with me—quite the opposite. He'd heap on the praise with comments like, "This is my son Jason. I'm so proud of him, he's at the top of his class at LSU," or "I'm so proud of him, he's an engineer with a big oil company." Because of the deep resentment I felt toward him, the empty words irritated me more than subtle mockery would have.

I guess I shouldn't have been surprised by the relationship downgrade as I rarely gave much encouragement the times he tried to be nice to me. Forget encouragement— all he could really count on from me was a healthy dose of hostility. Our relationship had always been adversarial, but it completely unraveled after my mother fell ill. During my sophomore year at LSU, she was diagnosed with ovarian cancer and, within months, deteriorated to the point she was hardly recognizable. Her beautiful, long, blonde hair was mostly gone, her once-athletic body weak and frail, her bright, blue eyes pale and vacant. Two years after the initial diagnosis, following several surgeries, endless radiation treatments, and sickening bouts of chemotherapy, my mother succumbed to the disease.

In the aftermath of the tragedy, I grew cold, almost emotionless, to everything in my life. I became convinced God either didn't exist or, if he did, was a cruel and heartless being. Even my mother's strong faith crumbled as the disease destroyed her body and crushed her spirit. On a particularly bad day, she asked me to pray for her because God wasn't listening to her prayers. I hadn't been to church in years, but that evening I begged him to spare her life and end the horrible suffering.

Unable, perhaps unwilling, to work through my grief and anger, I detached from my father and the rest of my family. It was the last thing my mother would have wanted. Even in the depths of her suffering, she worried about my father and made me promise to care for him. Early on, I made a few half-hearted attempts to repair the relationship, yet I was unable to get past the things he had done. I dwelt upon the problems caused by his heavy drinking, the embarrassment we experienced, the pain he put my mother through, the loneliness and disappointment she must have felt.

My cold and bitter heart stood in stark contrast to my mother's love and forgiveness. During her final days, she lay semi-conscious, struggling to draw each breath, draped in a web of plastic tubes that sustained her with food, oxygen, and a continuous flood of morphine. One evening, my father held her hand, leaned over and whispered in her ear, "Peg, I love you, I've always loved you." I watched her muscles tighten and her chest heave as she drew her final breath. It seemed as though she was hanging on just to hear those words.

Instead of being comforted by the final moments they shared, I became embittered, wondering how she could still love him after all he put her through. I catalogued his many misdeeds and used the ever-expanding list to sustain and justify my hostility.

I promised to care for my father, but it was a promise I didn't keep.

Within the first few weeks at my father's house, the pair learned to use the newspapered floor of the utility room as their bathroom, consistently sat on command for treats, and developed strategies to overcome the obstacles designed to corral them. My father, ill-equipped to handle the needy, clever, and destructive little guys, penned them in the kitchen at night in a futile attempt to curtail their mischievous pursuits. Though Clyde was barely twelve inches long, he quickly learned to scale the three-foot decorative iron fence separating the kitchen from the living room. Once atop the fence, he rolled himself onto the adjacent brown plaid, rattan couch and began his exploration of the house. Each morning, my father found Clyde roaming about a somewhat modified living area—something dragged across the room, something shredded, something broken.

They had known me only a short while, yet I was already the center of their world. With each passing visit, the dogs became more excited to see me. I could hear them barking, crying, and, in some cases, hurling themselves toward the front door, as I walked up the driveway. Upon entering the house, my arms fell victim to the sharp claws of one while I struggled to fend off the other. And, when I turned to handle the latest assailant, I was pounced on my blind side.

Despite spending most of their time with my father, they didn't form as deep a bond with him. He'd look at them, smile, wave his hand, and say, "Hello!" in a voice strangely reminiscent of Kermit the Frog. The dogs danced and wiggled, vying for physical touch, while he repeated the word, keeping his hands a secure distance from the hounds.

Within a matter of weeks, the dogs more than doubled in size to over thirty pounds. The food consumption soared and the piles of mess covered the entirety of the utility room. The dogs were now big enough and strong enough do some serious damage. During one of his nightly raids, Clyde decided the oversized, black-fabric couch needed some alterations. With great care, Clyde pulled every ounce of stuffing from the comfortable sofa, leaving its empty fabric hanging like a collection of deflated balloons. Another time, he chewed through a louvered wood cabinet, destroying a batch of poker chips and some board games. The destruction wasn't limited to midnight raids. When my father was watching television one evening, the dogs stole his wallet and mutilated his credit cards. Another time, they found his eyeglasses and turned them into monocles.

At six months and forty pounds, the back of the rattan couch, their springboard to change direction during headlong races, snapped like a twig. Then, convinced the house was still in need of renovation, they ripped out half a room of carpeting. For their crowning achievement, they ran into the sliding glass door and shattered it. Thankfully, they were unhurt and appeared completely unfazed by the time I arrived.

A few months later, my father was scheduled to have knee replacement surgery, promising to greatly impair his mobility. Caring for the powerful, energetic dogs was already difficult for him, and following surgery it would border on the impossible. The only option was to send Bonnie and Clyde to Lisa's ranch until my father regained his strength, or until I could find another place to live.

In the five months since Bonnie and Clyde left the ranch, I made little progress in the apartment search. I guess I procrastinated because the arrangement was tolerable and I wasn't thrilled about the idea of paying two concurrent apartment leases. With a new sense of urgency, I scoured the city for an apartment allowing big dogs and providing access to a yard. In a densely-packed city like New Orleans, finding such a place was no easy task. After a lengthy search, I located a two-bedroom townhouse twice the rent of my current apartment, in a relatively seedy part of town, lacking decent cycling access, and promising heavy traffic each workday. Worst of all, the apartment wasn't available for more than three months. Nevertheless, I gladly signed the lease.

After only a few weeks of Bonnie and Clyde's absence, my separation anxiety edged toward the unbearable. I knew the dogs were having a great time with their family at the ranch, yet I couldn't help worrying about them.

My instincts proved correct when I learned Clyde had been struck in the face and Tango struck in the leg by a large water moccasin. The venom caused Clyde's head to swell to nearly half again its normal size. A bad infection set in at the site of Tango's wound and the skin and muscle began to rot. Though Clyde soon began showing improvement, Tango's leg was slow to recover.

While Clyde and Tango were convalescing in the hospital, Lisa relayed more troubling news—Bonnie was embarking on search missions for her littermate. The property, fenced with horizontal lines of barbed wire strung at one-foot intervals, allowed the dogs to duck down and belly crawl under the bottom wire with little difficulty. Three days in a row, she found Bonnie wandering the streets up to a mile from the ranch. It was only a matter of time before she either lost her way in the heavily wooded area or was hit by a car.

The only way to accelerate our reunion was to pack my belongings and move in with my father. The frustrating arguments, nonsensical discussions, and tight quarters would surely challenge my patience and might, given enough time, rob me of what sanity I possessed. Despite the unpleasant future that surely awaited, I collected my friends and mentally prepared for life with my father, realizing I might lose the dogs forever if I didn't find a way to get along with him.

CHAPTER TWO

Respite

The small, red brick house stood atop a plateau of wood pilings, its foundation escaping the grip of the yard like a bruised apple pulled from a vat of warm taffy. The tiny, sunken backyard, bereft of fill for the past twelve years, formed a small, inland waterway during heavy rains. The rear oasis was hemmed by a four-foot chain link fence, bent and twisted from years of neglect, the top of which was level with the back door step—a testament to the rapidly sinking swampland filled thirty years earlier to extend the limits of the city. Each year, a dump-truck load of dirt was needed to keep pace with the subsidence. After my brother and I left home, the forces of nature soon took over, my father unwilling to replace the free labor he once enjoyed.

Tucked away in the center of Kenner, Louisiana, behind white columns and a white double front door, the experiment of living with my father was underway. The wood paneled walls, yellow linoleum floor, matching Formica table, and cheap kitchen chairs apparently hadn't been cleaned since my mother's last days. The formerly white carpet stored several pounds of dirt within the long fibers of its outdated shag—purchased on closeout, no doubt. The dart board in the game room was missing all its darts, some broken and thrown away, others lost in the yard during battles that should've resulted in a trip to the hospital. Cork covered the entirety of the wall behind it, speaking to the poor aim we employed during our childhood. The bumper pool table that once occupied the small game room was missing, sold off sometime in the past few years. It was rarely used even when the house was filled with kids. Once the art of jumping the ball over the bumper was mastered, there was little challenge to the game.

In the bedroom I once shared with my brother, pale-blue walls and dark-blue paisley curtains accented the stained and dirt-saturated, powder-blue, shag carpet upon which the twenty-year-old double bed rested. On the closet shelf was the Krewe of Okeanos doubloon collection, once treasured, now long since forgotten. In the corner lay the twisted, partly collapsed Bullworker device with its rusted tubular chrome center, cheap green plastic handles, and sagging elastic bands, purchased in my early teens when I had dreams of becoming a body builder in the mold of former Mr. Universe, Frank Zane.

The bedroom became a refuge from my father's "clever banter" or "witty repartee," as he called it. Because the non-sensical discussions usually proved inflammatory, I often called it an early night and retreated to my room with dogs in tow.

Given our history, I guess my father and I got along about as well as could be expected. He was adept at finding points of contention, and I struggled to let things go. Despite the problems, spending time with Bonnie and Clyde made it all worthwhile. Unconstrained by the need to drive home, we expanded our evening walks, taking the time to explore and enjoy new routes. At night, released from their enclosure, the dogs slept on either side of me, their bodies pinning me in place. I had never experienced anything comparable to their relentless affection and unconditional love.

Near the end of my stay with my father, Lisa and Adam took a three-week trip to Switzerland, providing me with the opportunity to care for the occupants of the wildlife refuge. Despite the punishing ninety-minute commute to work, I knew I'd enjoy the solitude, and the dogs would certainly have a great time.

Upon our arrival, Clyde, completely unfazed by Tango and Walliford's unfriendly greeting, ignored their domination attempt and turned the tables with a menacing growl. For Bonnie, the visit brought humiliation, as she was forced to roll onto her back and submit to the resident male dogs. Pepper, showing little interest in the ranking session, was ready to play from the moment we arrived. Once the chain of command was accepted, the hard feelings were forgotten, and the dogs played together as best of friends.

Soon after the pecking order was established, they raced to the pond and encircled its shoreline. With ducks flushed to the center of the pond, the dogs jumped in and converged on the fowl, sometimes chasing them in formation, but always failing to capture the elusive birds. After hours of searching the surrounding woods for mice and rabbits and several long pursuits of the resident horses, they called it a day and greedily wolfed down their dinner.

On the first night, Bonnie and Clyde, unaccustomed to Lisa's "no dogs in the house" rule, whimpered at the back door for an hour before joining their mates in the washroom. Other than coping with the guilt of leaving my distraught puppies outside, I didn't have to adjust to any hardships. Lisa left a stocked refrigerator and an incredibly comfortable bed—quite an upgrade from the decades-old mattress I was accustomed to.

The next morning I discovered, on a short excursion to the store, the property wasn't nearly as secure as I had imagined. A half mile from the ranch, I noticed one black and one cream-colored speck advancing in my rearview mirror. I pulled over and waited while the approaching dots eventually took on the form of the dogs I knew so well.

"No! Bad dogs! Get back in the yard!" I yelled. They wagged their tails and looked confounded, expecting a much warmer welcome than they received. On the way back to the main gate, I noticed dozens of possible exit points for expert belly-crawlers. Without any way to contact my sister, lining up someone else to feed the dogs and live-stock wasn't plausible. The peaceful feeling evaporated as I realized I had to train the dogs to stay on the ranch. And, with the workweek beginning in only two days, the training would have to occur in short order.

We practiced my exit dozens of times on Saturday and then dozens more on Sunday. Each time, I drove to the front gate, gave the "stay" command, drove a half mile down the side road, and waited. Undeterred, Bonnie and Clyde barreled toward me at a full sprint. I exited the car, shouted "No," swatted them on the butt with a rolled-up newspaper, and then escorted them back inside the gate. Disappointment and frustration set in as they failed to exhibit even a hint of behavior change with each succeeding trial.

Monday morning, I closed the gate, told them to stay, drove down the road, and hoped, wondering how I'd explain an absence from work spanning three weeks. Maybe the training finally struck a chord, or maybe they recognized my work clothes. Either way, it was a huge relief they didn't chase me. Heading off to the city, anxiety rose within me, remaining until I found the dogs, happy and healthy, exactly where I had left them twelve hours before.

Each night, we laid on a blanket in the bitter cold and I gazed at the sky for hours. Thousands of stars carpeted the dark expanse with the brilliance and clarity I last enjoyed on a backpacking trip to the Rocky Mountains. Clyde and Bonnie nestled astride me for warmth and growled at any of the other dogs hoping for some affection.

Each morning at sunrise, the dogs and I followed the cow trails through the tall grasses for an hour or two before venturing into the surrounding woods. A slight mist enveloped each pond, and ice crystals on the grass reflected the sunlight into its component colors. The tips of the grasses sparkled red, yellow, and blue as the soft breeze stirred the slender blades. Near the house, the sun filtered through the branches of the towering oak trees.

The large trampoline, set under the massive oaks, became my favorite place to waste away the weekend hours. Instead of joining me in some much-needed rest, Clyde always patrolled the perimeter, keeping the other dogs at bay.

One morning, Pepper spotted a pair of Canadian geese on the pond, resting and refueling for their long migration to points north. Spooked by the approaching dogs, they lumbered toward the edge of the pond, their long wings slowly providing power to take flight. Pepper intercepted the birds at the water's edge as they reached an altitude of four feet. Without breaking stride, she lunged and grabbed one of the birds by the neck. Before I could reach her, she ripped a large hole in its back, inflicting a mortal wound. Though unsettling to watch, it was the natural course of things for a Pointer. They're bred to chase birds—and, given the chance, that's what they do.

Later, I returned to the pond without the dogs to find a goose holding a vigil by his dead companion, unable to comprehend what had occurred. I watched from a distance as he brushed her lifeless body with his wing and tried to rouse her gently with his beak. After an hour or so, he took flight, circled the pond once, and continued his migration alone.

After the three-week vacation, we settled into our new living space. The townhouse was a welcome improvement over my apartment and a dramatic upgrade from the atmosphere at my dad's house. It was a much larger space than I really needed or was accustomed to. My furnishings, consisting of little more than a couch and a bed, had been along for the ride since I was in college. My only desirable possessions were a few framed pictures from national parks I visited, one high-end road bike, one fine mountain bike and another road bike held stationary by a wind-trainer. The large townhouse swallowed my possessions—the meager belongings barely making a dent in the emptiness.

Outside, the ten-foot by fifteen-foot wood deck became Bonnie and Clyde's new daytime living space. The surrounding four-foot strip of grass provided an ideal bathroom, thus house-breaking became the first order of business. The dogs were thoroughly conditioned to mess inside, but I wasn't high on the idea of hauling urine-soaked paper to the trash each evening. I hoped, with a little consistency and repetition, the smart canines would quickly learn a new routine. The training was pretty simple. If they started to go inside the house, I shouted "No!" and rushed them outside to the strip of grass. I repeated the command "Hurry up!" and heaped on the praise when they peed. Every hour, I took them out and repeated the drill. Though they mastered the system within a week or so, it was long enough for my neighbors to think I was a bit peculiar—and impatient.

Each morning before sunrise, we walked about a mile to Lafreniere Park and jogged several circuits of the paved trail. Bonnie and Clyde's matching chest harnesses alleviated the continual choking and allowed them to unleash even more power, pulling like a team of horses when they found something chase-worthy. Though they were satisfied with the length of our walks, they usually strained against the leashes to quicken the pace. To accommodate their thirst for speed, I attempted our routine on rollerblades, allowing them to really open it up and run hard. The odds, however, were clearly in their favor, and I lost the battle and my balance far too many times. It didn't take long before I hung up the blades for good, realizing sooner or later—likely sooner, I'd end up in the hospital.

The long walks should've been enough to keep them calm, yet Bonnie and Clyde experienced horrible separation anxiety when left alone for any length of time. As part of their coping mechanism, they began to systematically destroy the townhouse. The first casualty became the shingled, wood siding. They stripped off a few of the eight-foot boards and gnawed them into piles of sawdust. Later, they attacked the wood deck itself, shortening several of the planks. None of their many chew toys compared to the fine dining of a chunk of wood. Attempting to outsmart the furry termites, I bought a large bag of mesquite chips and spread the pieces around the deck. Whether the decoys worked or they had already changed their focus, the wood destruction thankfully abated.

The other coping mechanism they employed was, according to the townhouse manager, frequent, loud barking. Because they rarely made a sound while I was home, I couldn't think of any way to correct their behavior. The only thing I could do to limit their anxiety was reduce the length of time they were left alone. As a first step, I joined a gym near my office to get my weight training in at lunch. Coupled with wind trainer sessions instead of rides at the lakefront, the new routine cut several hours off my absence.

A few days after joining the gym, I met Jennifer. Her knee-length, black tights and matching halter top, made it hard not to notice her as she moved from machine to machine. She was a pretty woman—gorgeous body, shoulder-length brown hair, bright blue eyes and a sweet smile. When I finally summoned the courage to approach her, we talked for a half hour. She was small in stature at only five feet, yet her personality filled the room. She effused so much energy, so much life.

I pursued her for weeks, hitting the gym daily to enjoy our brief conversations. On the weekends, I camped out for a few hours at the gym near her home in hopes of bumping into her. When she finally agreed to go out with me, we met at her favorite coffeehouse and talked for hours. As we were about to go our separate ways, I showed her a picture of Bonnie and Clyde. Rather than an image of their current fifty-plus pound forms, I showed them when each was the size of a football. Jennifer fell in love at that moment, and getting the next date was easy.

CHAPTER THREE

Expansion

Bonnie and Clyde sniffed the ground intensely while I stretched my tired legs and looked for a number on any of the six two-story, red brick apartment buildings bordering the parking lot. As I struggled to get my bearings, Bonnie and Clyde wagged their tails and pulled against their leashes toward one of the buildings. With their heads down and their noses rapidly sampling the air, they scaled the stairs, worked the long covered hallway, and came to a halt; dancing as if they had stepped on hot coals. *What do you know? It's number 209.* I knocked at the door.

"Hey buds!" Jennifer exclaimed, smiling warmly and kneeling to stroke the faces of the oversized puppies. "I'm so glad you brought them; they're going to have so much fun on the levee!"

"I'm glad I brought them too. I might've needed to find a pay phone if they hadn't led me to your door. I think they picked up Cricket's scent. Did you know there's no number on the buildings?"

"You know, I never noticed," she laughed. "No one has ever mentioned that. Didn't I tell you it was the second one?"

"I'm sure you must have." I knew she specified the second one, but didn't think to ask whether it was second from the right or left—or even from the front for that matter. "It kinda depends on which way you're coming down the road."

Cricket stood his ground in the living room, barking aggressively at the two intruders. The dogs ignored the challenge of the pint-sized defender and followed Jennifer as she grabbed her keys and Cricket's leash. Although they were acquainted with Cricket on account of several dog outings at the lakefront, Bonnie and Clyde hadn't made the leap from tolerating to liking the little guy. He was still an outsider to their family and they were in no rush to add a new member.

Cricket was a Yorkie mix Jennifer rescued from the pound a year before we met. He had long, light-brown hair, and sometimes people assumed Jennifer dyed his hair to match her own—the color similarity was uncanny. Though he was only twelve pounds soaking wet, he projected the attitude of a much bigger dog. Jennifer warned he was skittish around men, having been hit by the previous owner who eventually dumped the little dog at the pound. Based on my first few experiences with him, I could vouch for his cautious, if not hostile, attitude toward males.

Jennifer was a dog person by nature, viewing dogs as far more than possessions—more like small, fur-covered children. She was the kind of person you'd see stopping traffic on the interstate while attempting to save a stray dog. I wasn't really a dog person until Bonnie and Clyde came into my life. My family got our first and only dog, an affectionate and playful black, Scottish terrier named Corgi, when I was about eight years old. To me, he existed only for the purposes of my enjoyment—whenever I had the time or inclination to play with him. I didn't realize he had the capacity to feel love, sadness, and other complex emotions.

Once on the levee adjacent to Jennifer's apartment, Bonnie and Clyde experienced the same freedom they enjoyed at the ranch. They ran and wrestled along the crest of the levee while Cricket walked contentedly within a few paces of Jennifer. The levee was the perfect place to cut the dogs loose—so much of their life was spent at the end of choke collars. The mile-wide Mississippi River, partially obscured by thick clusters of birch trees, bounded us thirty yards to one side and fenced yards bordered us twenty yards to the other.

Halfway through our walk, the dogs eyed a pair of ducks thirty yards off the sandy river bank. They raced to the water's edge and leaped in, swimming furiously toward their target. The ducks, recognizing the approaching threat, flew ten yards farther out and settled back in the water. The dogs increased their pace and quickly closed the gap. In response, the ducks advanced ten more. Then another ten yards. And another ten. The dogs grew increasingly frustrated and frantic with each near miss, their barking interrupted by choking as water was inhaled. My chest tightened as a feeling of helplessness swept through me. As the river's unforgiving current and their own heroic effort swiftly carried the dogs downstream, I ran along the bank desperately shouting for them to return. Then, as suddenly as they had initiated the chase, they abandoned the adventure and made their way back. By the time they returned to shore, the dogs and I were completely exhausted.

"I told you they'd come back," Jennifer laughed.

"It didn't look that way for a while. I guess I might've overreacted a little bit because of the way the ducks were drawing them out. I thought they might keep going."

"You think the ducks were doing it on purpose?"

"I think they were. I saw them do the same thing on the pond at Lisa's ranch. When the dogs chased them, the ducks could've easily flown away, but they didn't. They only flew a few yards and landed back in the water. It was almost as if the ducks teased the dogs in an effort to wear them out and drown them. Why didn't they leave if they weren't messing with the dogs?"

"I don't know, but I don't think ducks have that kind of thinking ability. Relax, you'll feel much better once I make you dinner."

"Do you still feel like cooking? I'm not feeling very hungry after all this."

"Sure, I've been promising to make you dinner for a while. I bet you'll be hungry by the time we get back, you're probably just a little nervous."

The dogs returned to the apartment with only fond memories of the chase, oblivious to the risks they faced. They stuck close to Jennifer in the small kitchen, hoping for something to fall their way during the meal preparation. After being flushed out of the kitchen, Bonnie and Clyde took up residence on Jennifer's leather sofa.

"Come on, let's go—get off the couch," I implored in a soft voice. Bonnie stretched and slowly moved to a reclining position on the soft carpet next to the couch, dutifully accepting the demotion. Clyde looked at me with confusion, as the only discernible difference between this couch and the one he commandeered at home was the color of the cushions. He rolled onto his back, pushing his arms skyward in a relaxed stretch. He peered at me from a half-open eye and wagged his tail slightly.

"Clyde, come on," I said with a little more vigor. His tail began to wiggle with increased intensity.

"Oh, don't worry about it. He's fine. That's why they're made of leather," Jennifer said.

"I'm glad you're OK with it—he already thinks he owns the place." I sat next to Clyde and laid my hand on his chest. He was every bit of seventy pounds and probably had another ten pounds of filling out to do. He and Bonnie were almost identical in their lean body structure, save the extra few pounds of muscle Clyde sported. It felt good to sit on the soft couch after the hour on the levee. The walk, run, and stress, coupled with a long bike ride earlier in the day, made my legs sink like lead weights into the plush cushions. Once Bonnie realized the coast was clear, she resumed a restful position on the couch, leaving me comfortably sandwiched between the floppy-eared bookends.

As I looked beyond the sliding glass doors leading to the balcony, a large container ship, partially obscured by a stand of birch trees, drifted by on the river. "I love the view from here," I remarked as Clyde reminded me, with a gentle touch of his paw, to continue caressing his chest.

"I know—it's so peaceful. I just absolutely love my apartment!"

Surveying the room, it took a moment to soak in the visual stimulation. I had never seen such myriad colors and shapes collected in so small a space. Every wall was covered with beautiful paintings, every shelf or counter crammed with sculptures, pottery, and glasswork.

"Jason, come sit at the bar and try some of this," she said, pointing to an appetizer of olive oil, balsamic vinegar, and Roquefort cheese, "You're going to love it." The aroma of hot Italian bread met me on the way to the counter.

"It's delicious," I said, savoring the first bite of the combination. "It's almost like the flavor of a gourmet salad without the vegetables."

"Don't worry; you'll get plenty of vegetables tonight. I'm making beet salad and we're having steamed broccoli with the main course."

"I'm really looking forward to it," I said in a feeble attempt at sincerity. I could stomach the occasional salad, but only with the aid of large quantities of bleu cheese, bacon, croutons, and a smothering of thick dressing.

"Trust me—you're going to love it. Besides, you can't have the chicken unless you eat your vegetables," she said playfully, pounding the breast meat into submission with a spiked mallet. Once sufficiently pulverized, she dipped it into an egg mixture, coated it in Italian bread crumbs, and slid it into a skillet of hot olive oil. A few seconds after it was fished out of the pan, she pushed a small piece toward me to sample. It was by far the best chicken I had ever tasted. In fact, the entire meal was incredible—even the vegetables deserved second helpings. I had never met anyone like Jennifer—spunky, energetic, funny, and beautiful. And, of course, it didn't hurt that she knew how to put together an incredible meal.

Until the levee incident, I didn't realize how attached I had become to the little guys. I redoubled my training efforts, working on the four basics every day: sit, stay, come, and no. Progress was minimal because the two littermates consistently distracted one another. They were impossible for Jennifer to walk, and they expressed only a limited desire to obey me.

Needing professional help, we arrived at the obedience class with Bonnie and Clyde, their six-foot leather leashes, and choke collars. We walked the dogs in a circle, keeping each dog at heel by repeated choking. Then we made the dogs sit, again relying on the choking technique. As the tough love continued for the dogs, the trainer critiqued the way Jennifer handled Bonnie. *Pull up harder—keep her on your right—hold the leash like this.* Bonnie, confused by the harsh treatment she was receiving, did her best to follow the commands. Clyde, on the other hand, made no effort to comply. He was a dominant male and, given any opportunity, confidently asserted his superior status. He hadn't been around other dogs much and perhaps wasn't socially well adjusted. As a result, I had to correct him quite a bit during the ordeal.

"We aren't going back for another session," I said to Jennifer as we walked our remedial students back to the car. "I'm not going to choke my dogs into submission and turn them into robots. We'll just have to work harder to train them on our own."

"Thank God," Jennifer said with a sigh of relief. "It was all I could do to make it through the session without giving her a piece of my mind."

"Yeah, I noticed you were getting a lot of attention from her."

"That woman was ridiculous. You don't need to choke an animal to train them."

"I figured that out about halfway through. Well, we're not going back. Hey, do you want to come over for dinner Saturday evening? I want to try to cook for you."

"Oh, that's so sweet. I'd love that."

"Can you leave Cricket home though?"

"Why would I want to do that?" Jennifer asked, her tone instantly shifting from playful to defensive.

"The apartment manager is getting complaints about barking. You know how Cricket barks at everything—and nothing at all."

"I think they all bark at the same things. What's wrong with me bringing my little dog? You really think the barking of a ten-pound dog is something to worry about?"

"Well, the bigger problem is my dogs don't like him much."

"Let me set you straight, Jason—Cricket and I are a package deal. It's your choice: either he comes along, or you can eat alone."

So, of course, I caved and invited the little guy, and he, surprisingly, kept the barking to a minimum. From then on, Cricket was accepted as an equal member of the group. Maybe Bonnie and Clyde could sense I was friendlier toward him, or maybe they had finally worked out the pecking order.

Months later, we camped out with the dogs on the beach in Destin, Florida. We spent the days walking along the shore while the dogs played in the water and chased the seagulls. We passed the evenings gazing at the stars, talking, and enjoying something off the grill. We fell asleep each night listening to the sound of waves crashing rhythmically along the shore. The combination of sun, sand, good times, and good food was more than I could take. I looked deeply into Jennifer's blue eyes, told her I loved her and, without hesitation, asked her to move in with me and the puppies.

The day Jennifer moved in, I wandered from room to room exploring the new environment. Though I found my bikes where I'd left them and my pictures still decorated the walls, nothing else remained of the former landscape.

"Where'd you store my furniture?" I asked.

"Oh, I didn't store it. I gave it to the moving guys," she replied calmly.

"Why the hell did you do that?"

"I felt sorry for the guys. They had nothing and they were thrilled when I offered to give it to them."

"Jennifer, it was my stuff."

"Come on, Jason, the furniture was junk. Did you have it when you were in high school?"

"Yeah, but that's not the point." Though the furniture was indeed junk, I wasn't raised to give things away. Her actions struck me irresponsible and downright bizarre. "I don't understand why you gave my stuff away without asking."

"Come on, relax, it was old junky stuff. It's not like they were family heirlooms or something."

After reflecting on it for a few minutes, I realized the cheap, worn-out furniture wasn't worth fighting over. It was hard to stay mad at her for being generous—even if she was being generous with my possessions.

Without the commute separating us, Jennifer and I began spending more active time with the dogs. Our favorite thing was to pile into the car at five in the morning, drive two miles to the lake, and walk the levee. It was pitch dark except for the moon and an occasional backyard light. I attached red strobe lights to the dogs' harnesses, which appeared to float above the ground as the dogs ran ahead. Occasionally, we passed joggers who seemed spooked by their surprise encounter with the flashing hounds. The lake was fairly safe for the dogs; traffic was blocks away, and most of the houses were fenced. Actually, Jennifer and I were probably more at risk than the dogs. Crime was a part of life in the suburbs of New Orleans. Yet, in the stillness before dawn, it felt safe enough for us.

As the weeks passed, I noticed Bonnie becoming increasingly agitated when I returned from work. She was more aggressive with other animals and, on rare occasions, even growled at us. As I removed her collar one evening, I noticed the light flash, signaling the delivery of an electric shock. She began wearing the device a few months earlier when the apartment manager threatened eviction if we didn't control the barking. The collar was delivering a jolt unprovoked by Bonnie's bark—all it took was a slight tilt of her head. How agonizing it must have been for her—no way to draw a connection between the pain and the random activity preceding it. I removed the batteries and put the collars back on to keep up appearances with the manager. It only took a few weeks before the complaints rolled in again. After some negotiation, they gave us two months to relocate.

It was just as well; it was time to move on. I had grown weary of the townhouse management and tired of the small yard and lack of privacy. The dogs didn't know it, but I was about to buy a house for them.

Jennifer was the kind of person who, when she set her mind to it, could make something happen quickly. Within a week, she found a thirty-year-old house in the Bucktown area of New Orleans perfectly suited to our lifestyle; close to work, walking distance to the lake, and I could ride my bike for miles along the lakefront. As an added bonus, the house had a huge backyard by New Orleans standards—about fifty feet by ninety feet—with a carport, an attached shed and an overhang to keep the dogs shaded and dry during the day. The inside of the house, however, was decrepit, covered in thirty years of accumulated dirt and grime. The heavy smoking of the previous occupants saturated the rooms with a stale smoke odor and left the walls stained a sickly yellowish-brown hue.

Knowing almost nothing about home renovation, we dove in anyway. We made a number of rookie mistakes; hiring unqualified contractors, replacing perfectly good paneling with sheet rock, moving walls, and so on. We learned the hard way that each modification, however small, created a cascade of unplanned, expensive work. Despite the many unforced errors, we muddled through and turned the old, broken-down structure into a beautiful home.

The peaceful beauty of the lake drew us like a magnet each day. It wasn't out of the ordinary for us to walk four or five miles with the three dogs. I was always amazed Cricket could hang with the big dogs for the entire walk—taking three steps for each one of Clyde's. The long walks gave us plenty of time to talk, connect and, from time to time, discuss where our relationship was heading. Jennifer wasn't satisfied with the informal nature of our living arrangement and often reminded me she didn't move in to merely be my girlfriend. I delayed the decision as long as her patience allowed, but the time had come to either walk away or ask Jennifer to be my wife.

The night Jennifer accepted my proposal, I was truly elated. But soon, as the details of the event were nailed down and the reality sunk in, I began to have doubts. With each passing day and task accomplished, my anxiety continued to build. One evening, after our walk with the dogs, I couldn't contain my feelings any longer.

"I can't go through with the wedding. I'm not…"

"What? Are you kidding me?"

"I just can't do it. I'm not ready yet."

"How dare you! I already bought my dress. We've already sent the invitations," she cried.

"I'm sorry, Jennifer. I didn't mean to hurt you. I'm just not ready."

"Please don't do this Jason," she begged. "How can you do this? You're going to humiliate me in front of everyone."

"I'm sorry. I wish I could handle it."

"I'm done with this—you're a mess. Give me a call when you grow up. No, on second thought, don't ever call me again!" Her anger faded to sadness as she added, "I'll be moving my things out. You made me give up my beautiful apartment on the river. Now, I don't know where I'll end up."

"Can we at least still be friends?"

"Sure, Jason. Why not? Why don't I just move down the street from you? Then I can say hi to Bonnie and Clyde every day on the lakefront—and I can tell you to go screw yourself!"

"Please don't be mad, hon."

"Don't call me 'hon' anymore," she warned. "I hope you'll be happy here alone." Then she began to sing in an overly-dramatic, Judy Garland style as she walked toward the door. "Home—alone—again, having bah-ba-cues no one attends…"

"C'mon Jennifer, please try to understand."

"Home—alone—again, having bah-ba-cues no one attends," she repeated as she closed the car door and drove away.

After Jennifer moved out, the house was quiet—and empty. All of her nice things were gone and my junk was in someone else's home.

As the weeks passed, I found myself unable to move on. I missed her smile, her kindness, and her love.

"Jennifer, I have something I need to talk to you about—it's urgent,"

"What's wrong? Are you hurt?"

"I'm fine. I just need to talk to you. Can you meet me at the coffee shop near your office?"

"What's going on? Why are you being so mysterious?"

"Please, Jennifer. Let's just have a talk."

"OK, I'll see you in a bit."

A half hour later, I met up with her on the sidewalk in front of Tulane Hospital, dropped to one knee, and asked, "Will you marry me tonight? We'll go to the justice of the peace—there'll be no chance of me backing out."

"Yes," she said, tears welling in her eyes. "I love you."

A few hours later, I waited nervously in the front courtyard of a small, run-down, dull-blue, wood-shingled building. At six-thirty, I looked at my watch and wondered aloud where Jennifer was.

In his usual sensitive way, my father said, "Maybe she changed her mind."

"Very funny. She'll be here." Though I still had some raw feelings toward my father, I wanted to share the moment with him. He put up with a lot of chaos and destruction caused by my two hounds. I doubt many people would've tolerated the imposition.

Twenty minutes later, Jennifer and her cousin Cathy arrived. The two were closer than most siblings and lived down the hall from one another at the apartment complex. Jennifer looked stunning in her black and white outfit, though a bit frazzled.

"I was starting to get worried about you," I told Jennifer, smiling broadly and holding her in a warm embrace.

"I fell asleep after getting home from work," Jennifer said. "I was so mentally exhausted. Thank God Cathy called when she did. Otherwise, I might've slept right through the whole thing."

Jennifer gave my father a hug and said, "It's so good to see you, Mr. Rob."

That was probably hard for her to say. She was still a little hurt by the magazine episode. During Jennifer's first visit to my father's house, he couldn't wait to show her the stack of free *News on Wheels* magazines he had accumulated. For some unknown reason, he thought she'd be impressed to see my bikini-clad ex-girlfriend on the cover of fifteen copies of the same issue. He had them fanned out like magazines in a hotel lobby in case she wanted to carry a few home. Jennifer believed he did it to intentionally hurt her feelings and, for a long time after, kept her guard up around him, despite my assurance he acted from pure stupidity not malice.

Inside, the justice of the peace said a few words, we replied "I do," signed a few documents, and, within minutes, we were married. Following the ceremony, we all celebrated at our favorite Italian restaurant with good food, good wine, and many laughs.

The dogs were thrilled when Jennifer returned, and they even seemed to miss little Cricket. With the emotional turmoil settled, we could focus on enjoying life again. Jennifer quit her job to manage the house and take care of me and the dogs. We spent our time bike riding, rollerblading, walking the dogs, or relaxing in the hammock together. We could be in the middle of chaos, yet still find time to laugh and be silly together. Even when we were doing nothing, we always seemed to make it fun. On pretty spring days, I took long lunch breaks and joined Jennifer for a home-cooked meal. I couldn't wait to hold her and kiss her sweet lips. No matter what I was doing, Jennifer was never far from my thoughts. Even short business trips became torture for me. I called her frequently, longing to feel her touch.

Five months after our wedding, in October 1998, Hurricane Georges rolled toward New Orleans. Jennifer and I drove to Lisa's ranch, a safe distance from the storm surge, heavy rain, and lightning of the storm, but close enough to experience the dramatic, billowing, gray clouds and strong gusty conditions—the awesome effects of such a massive storm system.

Unfortunately, the high winds knocked out the power shortly after our arrival. Without the aid of the air-conditioning system, the inside of the house was almost unbearable. At night, we crowded into the only room with a working window—the rest of the wood-frame windows jammed from years of decay.

The missing window screen ensured the local mosquitoes drank their fill of blood and, several times during the night, a mouse or some other small creature scurried across my body. Bonnie and Clyde were oblivious to the intruders. Clearly, they'd never make it as hunting dogs—sound asleep while the mice were having a party. On the other hand, two eighty-pound dogs barreling through Lisa's house in pursuit of rodents would've created utter chaos.

The stress of the evacuation revealed the first indications Lisa's marriage was in trouble. The arguments and ugly words exchanged were a stark contrast to the affection and kindness they shared early in their marriage. All that remained between them was bitter, cold hostility.

It made me realize how lucky I was to have someone like Jennifer.

Over the next two years, life fell into a comfortable pattern—perhaps too comfortable for me. Although I had lived most of my life in and around New Orleans, the city never felt like home. I enjoyed the lifestyle we had, but I was increasingly restless at work, feeling my contributions weren't being recognized. Once my attitude soured, it was only a matter of time before my performance followed.

"Jennifer, I talked to my boss today about a job in Houston," I said casually, peeling off my work clothes.

"What? Why did you do that without asking me?"

"I thought we talked about it last month. Remember, I told you how unhappy I was. You said I should do what I think is best."

"That didn't mean I wanted to be left out. I'm not ready to move now—we just got settled. And my family—Cathy is going to have her baby soon."

"Well, I don't have to take the job. I need to let my boss know by tomorrow if I want to put in for it. There's no guarantee I'll get it anyway."

"Are you sure this is what you want?"

"No, I just need a change. I'm starting to shut down at work, and my boss has noticed my attitude is getting negative."

"Why? I thought you loved your job."

"I did until a few of the guys on the team got promoted, and I didn't. You know what an impact I made for them. It chaps me I'm not getting the credit."

"You don't have to move because of it. Aren't there any other jobs you could do here?"

"I'm miserable. I just want something different. Look, it's only going to be an hour flight away. And, knowing your family, I'm sure they'll visit as much as you let them."

"Jason, I need you to really think about this and be sure you know what you're doing," Jennifer pleaded. "But I'll go if you really want to."

Although I had my own doubts about the wisdom of the move, I successfully deflected each of Jennifer's concerns. The move promised to upend our lives and force Jennifer to leave the only city she'd ever known. The new job was less prestigious and didn't appear to be very challenging or, for that matter, particularly interesting. I also doubted we could find the same freedom the lakefront offered, not to mention the great access to bike riding. Despite the glaring risks, I felt compelled to do something—anything, to escape the rut I imagined myself in.

CHAPTER FOUR

Gone to Texas

"Hello there! I wanted to come down and welcome y'all to the neighborhood. My name is Toni," the elderly woman said with a strong east Texas accent. The laces of her spotless white walking shoes were tied into perfect symmetrical bows. The shoes matched her patent leather belt, freshly ironed cotton capri pants, new dentures, and cotton sun visor. Beneath the hat, her silver hair was teased and sprayed into the shape it probably had held for the past thirty years.

Jennifer dropped the shovel she was using to create a curved garden bed and her flip-flops carried her to the woman. "Hi! I'm Jennifer—and this is my husband, Jason," she said. I said hello and then busied myself with the landscaping project to avoid being dragged into the conversation.

"I hope y'all will feel right at home here," Toni said, her eyes hidden behind dark, wraparound sunglasses.

"That's so sweet of you. We really love this place. It's so beautiful," Jennifer gushed.

"What are you going to plant in your new garden? Ernst and I have won the Garden of the Month award six times since we moved here."

"I was thinking of some azaleas up next to the house and some Indian hawthorn across the…" The words faded as I led Bonnie and Clyde to the backyard where they settled on their giant canvas dog beds and I relaxed on the chaise lounge. An hour later, Jennifer joined me.

"Sorry, I didn't have time to stay out there and talk," I said.

"Oh right, I'm sure you were busy. Don't worry; she said she's going to send her husband, Ernst, down to meet you."

"I can't wait," I said sarcastically. "What did you think of our new neighbor?"

"She's very nice, Jason. Let's be careful what we tell her, though."

"What do you mean?"

"She's a gossip. She couldn't wait to tell me about the previous owners. I told her I wasn't interested in their personal business."

"So what's the big scandal?" I asked disinterestedly.

"A preacher and his wife lived here, and one day she went crazy. She was forty-four years old and began having an affair with a twenty-eight-year-old guy. The husband didn't know anything was going on until she moved all her things out of the house—left him and her two kids without so much as a note."

"I guess we don't have to worry about that. You've already snagged a guy three years younger than yourself."

"You're thirty-seven in a couple months, that's only two years, Jason."

"But today it's…" I hesitated. "I was wondering why he was at the closing by himself."

"Are you going to come help me finish up?" Jennifer asked.

"Sure, as long as I don't have to talk to the old geezer. Maybe you should put on some shoes so you don't hurt yourself with the shovel."

"I've been gardening my whole life. I think I know what I'm doing."

"Jennifer, you could slip on the mud…"

"Jason, I said I'm fine! You're not even wearing gloves. You're one to talk."

"It's just that you could…"

"That's probably Ernst now," she said, spotting the gray-haired old man shuffling toward us.

"This is going to be torture. I wonder what stories he's going to have."

"Be nice, Jason. I want us to have friends here."

Jennifer said hello and then continued the game of chicken between her tenuously-covered feet and the muddy shovel. Ernst talked to me for what seemed like an eternity. He told me about his career with the electric company, his stint as a professional baseball player for some team I can't recall, and then on and on about each of his children and grandchildren. I don't think he paused to ask a question during the monologue, though it was just as well given my aversion to small talk.

The neighborhood was on the outskirts of Sugar Land, which was itself on the edge of the city of Houston. In most respects, our red brick, two-story home was a significant upgrade. It was thirty years newer and, at three thousand square feet, it nearly doubled the size of our home in Metairie. The large house, however, sliced the yard to one-quarter the size we enjoyed in Louisiana. It was clear our playtime would have to happen somewhere other than the tiny spit of land.

As the months rolled by, we settled into our environment. I was glad to have a fresh start, but my job as a business analyst proved less satisfying than I had anticipated. With little autonomy and no responsibility, I struggled with the transition from the dynamic, high-pressure role I held on the design team for a billion dollar development in the Gulf of Mexico. Jennifer landed a job as a convention services manager for a major hotel and soon gained recognition as one of their top producers. The long work hours, exacerbated by two hours of grueling rush-hour traffic, left Jennifer quite drained. Despite the demands of the job, including the occasional late night and weekend shift, Jennifer insisted on cleaning the house and preparing lavish home-cooked meals each day.

Apart from work, Jennifer and I missed the long walks along the lakefront and having a place for the dogs to run free. We were far removed from anything remotely resembling the shores of Lake Pontchartrain and the only natural body of water nearby, the Brazos River, served as a sanctuary to alligators and poisonous snakes. Despite the lack of natural settings, we found a pecan tree-filled park and large man-made pond a few blocks from our house. A short, wood-planked footbridge connected a tiny island, some ninety feet in diameter, to the larger park area. Upon the island stood five large oak trees encircling a white, wood-framed gazebo. Though lacking the aesthetics we were accustomed to, the little island appeared to be a safe place to let the dogs off their leashes.

At the island, Bonnie always played the retrieving game to win. When I threw the buoy, she sprinted to the ledge, soared a dozen feet, and then swam furiously toward the floating target. Clyde, in contrast, eased himself into the water and then moved out fast and smooth. On the times Clyde chased her to the buoy, she took into account the direction of his approach and turned to keep her body between Clyde and his goal, often moving the buoy from one side of her mouth to the other to get it even farther away. Clyde was continually frustrated because no matter how many times he adjusted his tactics, she was always one step ahead.

When she didn't go after the buoy, she crouched on the bank a few yards from the point Clyde planned to exit. As Clyde approached, she leaped and tried to wrestle the prize away as he sank momentarily beneath the surface. Despite the ferocity of the ambush, he rarely let her win.

Past the Bonnie gauntlet, Cricket waited for him, barking excitedly and pacing nervously at the water's edge. After a gentle handoff of the buoy, Cricket darted away, zigzagging, like he intercepted a pass, then ran under the gazebo just beyond Clyde's reach. In the safety of the narrow cave, he taunted Clyde, his intermittent growl reminding me of nervous laughter. Though Clyde barked relentlessly in frustration, he, without fail, gave Cricket the toy each time he came to the ledge.

As long as I felt like throwing, they felt like retrieving, and as far as I could throw was never too far for them. When we finished, Clyde carried the buoy the entire way home. No matter how much he was panting, the trophy remained planted firmly in his mouth.

Jennifer eventually trained Cricket to swim and retrieve a smaller toy. Sometimes, Clyde followed Cricket to the buoy and gently held a piece of it, Cricket swimming furiously to keep pace with his big brother. Once, after grabbing the buoy, Clyde turned unexpectedly and swam over the oncoming Cricket. The little dog disappeared momentarily, then slapped the water in a futile effort to stay afloat. Fearing the worst, I jumped in and swam quickly to him. Unaware of the severity of our situation, Clyde continued to shore, the buoy clutched proudly in his jaws.

I was making slow progress toward land, struggling against the weight and drag of my waterlogged shoes, when Bonnie, recognizing I was in trouble, decided to rescue me. She dove in and crawled atop my head, scratching my arms and back in a clumsy attempt to help. Despite the dunking I received, I somehow pushed Bonnie off while keeping Cricket afloat. I reached the shore exhausted and a bit angry that Jennifer continued to film the events rather than attempt to help me. In response to my assertion that I nearly drowned, she created a new song that included the lyrics "drowning in the sea of love." My anger turned to laughter as she sang the silly words in her signature dramatic fashion.

We had great times on the little man-made island. It was only ninety feet across with a few oak trees and a gazebo, yet the dogs were free to roam and the lake gave the feeling of wide-open space.

At the house, there seemed to be no end to the projects. Ironically, one of the reasons we bought a new home was to avoid the chaos and work we endured in Metairie. But there we were again, pulling up carpeting, putting in tile floors, landscaping the backyard, painting walls, and tackling other discretionary efforts. It didn't leave much time to rest on the weekends. The mornings were spent cycling and walking the dogs, and the afternoons were consumed by the latest project.

As part of the landscaping effort, I decided to plant bushes along the perimeter of the bare yard. Ideally, I'd have dug the holes twice the diameter of the root ball to foster the plant's growth, but the bone-dry clay soil necessitated making them barely big enough to cram each plant into. I was only a little way through the backbreaking project when Jennifer called.

"I bought us a whole new office—solid oak desk, table, filing cabinet, and bookcase. It's perfect for my new business! My inventory should be here in about a week," Jennifer said, referring to the latest chapter of her business career. Ironically, she decided to quit the hotel business after receiving a long-sought promotion to a sales manager position. The pay was better, the hours much improved, but the skills she had honed to perfection in the service side of the business didn't translate to the sales side. The endless cold calls, constant rejection, and intense pressure to meet sales goals became more than she could handle.

"Should I be afraid to ask what it cost?"

"Don't be silly. It's only a couple hundred dollars—when you see something good at Sam's you have to buy it, because it won't be there next time."

"Jennifer, that sounds like a lot of furniture. How are you going to get it all home?"

"I have four guys tying the boxes to the roof."

"Four guys? How do you expect me to unload it by myself?" I wasn't surprised by Jennifer's transport idea. She believed the roof of her green SUV had unlimited carrying capacity. The previous year, she had workers tie down a heavy, cast-iron gas grill, bowing the roof and creating quite a challenge for me to unload it.

"I know how strong you are, I'm sure you can handle it. Oh, wait—Brian's here." Our neighbor Brian was about five years my senior, though his full cheeks and quick smile gave him a youthful appearance. He, his wife, Patsy, and Jennifer, all hailing from New Orleans, could talk for hours about places and events that I, despite living in the city for twenty years, never heard of.

"Brian's sure the wind will blow the boxes off the roof. He said the guys were using the wrong kind of string."

"I think Brian's right. Can you wait till I get there before you do anything?"

"We're going to have the guys load the boxes into the back of his Tahoe. I'll see you in a little while. Get ready to build our new office!"

A few minutes later the large SUV scraped slightly as Brian pulled the heavily loaded vehicle into our driveway. I surveyed the project that promised to occupy me for quite a while.

"Jennifer," I said with a laugh, "you wouldn't have made it out of the parking lot. Man, these are heavy." The massive, seven-foot-long, three-foot-wide boxes each weighed close to fifty pounds.

"It's a good thing Jason works out," Jennifer remarked to Brian. "Y'all should be able to handle a couple of boxes."

"Brian, Jennifer called and told me what you did. Thanks for helping out," I said.

"It's no problem, I couldn't leave her there. I could see what was going to happen."

"Someone could've been killed if these went airborne," I said. "Should we try to grab either end of this one and slide it out?"

"I think we need to use a dolly. I'll be right back."

Over the next few weeks, the office was assembled and Jennifer's massive Mary Kay cosmetics inventory arrived. She soon discovered, after canvassing the neighborhood and her circle of friends for potential clients, that many other women had the same idea. Months later, with only a small dent made in the inventory and a larger dent made in some of her friendships, the dream of the pink Cadillac died.

In the summer of 2001, Jennifer and I set out to hike a series of fourteen thousand-foot peaks near Durango, Colorado. It had been almost a year since our last hiking trip and we were both looking forward to the challenge. On one morning, we left the hotel at sunrise to provide plenty of time for the long hike ahead.

"Keep an eye out for the trailhead parking area," I said. "There'll be a 'Four-Wheel Drive Only' sign."

"OK. I can't believe we are here. It is so beautiful!"

"Yeah, it is. The weather is going to be perfect for hiking. Do you think you'll be able to handle the climb?"

"I made it to the Keyhole, didn't I?" Jennifer asked, referring to her introduction to the sport of day-hiking— the grueling climb up Long's Peak, one of the fourteeners of the Rocky Mountains.

"You impressed the hell out of me last year. I can't believe you made it over the boulder field," I said, referring to the section of the hike where we scrambled over giant, smooth rocks the size of Volkswagens.

"There was no way I was going past the Keyhole. I know you were disappointed. You should've kept going—I would have waited for you." The trail from the Keyhole to the peak was a narrow ledge, really a series of ledges, marked roughly by painted circles on the face of the mountain. Many sections of the hike produced a strong sense of vertigo and, on the previous visit, I found myself leaning in toward the mountain on much of the trail.

"Honestly, I was glad you wanted to turn around. The hike was humbling—way harder than I remembered from the time with my friends."

"That's funny. I remember you bragging the whole way up how you and your cycling buddies jogged most of the trail and made it to the top with no problem."

"Well, apparently I let myself go. Anyway, I hope I'm in better shape this year. This trail doesn't have the boulders, but it has more elevation gain. Do you remember how silly we got on the way down from the Keyhole?"

"People looked at you like you were nuts. I couldn't stop laughing either."

"That's what exhaustion and thin air will do to you, I guess." As we continued up the dirt road in search of the trailhead, it narrowed to a heavily rutted ledge on the side of the mountain. "I'm glad you didn't quit after our hike in the Grand Canyon."

"What did you expect? I had surgery a week before."

"You're the one who wanted to go farther down the trail. Remember, I kept telling you it was going to be a bitch climbing out."

"It was so beautiful, I—you need to stop the car! Please stop the car!"

"Don't worry, there'll be a sign where the parking lot is."

We travelled another hundred yards and the rutted road began to scrape along the underside of the car.

Jennifer became panicky and demanded, "Stop the car and let me out! Right now! Stop!"

The road, only two feet wider than the car, lacked a guardrail to separate us from a pretty dramatic drop-off. The midsize car was no match for the giant ruts ahead. Jennifer followed on foot as I slowly backed down the narrow ledge to the parking area. There, at the edge of the road in tiny lettering, a small sign read "Four-Wheel Drive Only." By the time we got on the trail, our nerves were frayed. I really don't remember if we enjoyed the hike.

But I do remember my heart sank upon returning to the cabin. We learned a tropical storm named Allison had formed quickly and moved ashore near Houston, dumping torrential rains. The floodwater rose and soon reached the rooftops of houses in some parts of the city. My thoughts immediately focused on our dogs, fearing there might not have been enough time to evacuate the animals from the kennel. I imagined Bonnie, Clyde, and Cricket trapped in their cages, filled with terror as the water rose, and they struggled to survive. With the phone lines jammed, there was no way to know what had happened to them.

The next day, we made the four-hour drive to the Albuquerque airport and the three-hour flight to Houston. Even if the dogs were fine, I wanted the trip to be over. Thankfully, the flooding was ten miles east of the kennel, and the dogs were no worse for the wear.

Five months later, I watched the second plane hit the World Trade Center and realized the world had changed. The events pierced my sense of security, creating a deeper appreciation for the peace I felt at home. Travel, which for years had almost been an obsession, no longer beckoned.

Despite the exhilaration of the hikes, I grew more restless with each passing trip, feeling as though a piece of my heart was left behind with the dogs.

Long walks with Jennifer, time with the dogs, bike rides, and lazy afternoons in the hammock became my preferred way to spend vacation time. Jennifer still wanted to explore new places together, yet I had been all over the country before meeting her and found nothing that compared to the life we shared at home. The flights, rental cars, crowds, and budget accommodations had worn me out over the years.

CHAPTER FIVE

The Long Slide

Clyde crawled up and sat beside me on the black leather couch. Every twenty seconds, his muscular body began to shiver uncontrollably—as if waves of freezing air were passing over him. I held him and stroked his soft, dense fur until the shaking subsided. Later, I noticed Clyde stumble a few times as he navigated the couches and played in the yard.

"Did you see that? He tripped again," I said worriedly.

"I didn't notice anything different, Jason. Dogs do trip sometimes, you know," Jennifer replied. Something was definitely wrong. Jennifer probably didn't notice because she'd grown weary of me talking about Clyde's antics. *Look at Clyde! Did you see him leap over the back of the couch? Look at him swim! Look, he's hunting for mice...look how his brow is furrowed and his tail is trembling.* She had the well-earned impression I was obsessed with every move Clyde made. I couldn't understand the sudden clumsiness; he was only five years old, incredibly strong, with unstoppable endurance, and was far more agile than most expected for a ninety-pound dog.

The next day, I took Clyde to the vet.

"He keeps stumbling—there's something wrong with his coordination," I said.

"I don't see anything wrong with him. He looks good to me," replied Dr. Karelis.

"Did something go wrong with the procedure? Clyde didn't have these symptoms before."

"No, it was a routine teeth cleaning; he's probably a little groggy from the anesthesia."

"It's been over a day; he shouldn't still be having effects of the anesthesia, should he?"

"The dog is fine," he said, visibly irritated. "There's nothing wrong with him."

Before I could protest, he walked out of the exam room.

When his coordination failed to improve over the next few days, I took Clyde to another vet. After a battery of tests, he determined the thyroid gland wasn't functioning properly. Along with a prescription for a daily dose of thyroxin, we brought Clyde home and went about our lives. But Clyde didn't seem the same to me. He still played fetch on the island; he just wasn't as graceful as he had once been.

Months later, we kenneled the dogs while we took a short trip home to visit family. Upon our return, Cricket and Bonnie were in their usual state of near-panic, but Clyde was different from previous times. As I loaded him into our SUV, I noticed he was shaking and appeared to have lost at least ten pounds. I brought him home and wrapped him in blankets to try to warm him up. When he didn't show any signs of improvement over the next few hours, I called the vet.

"He's shaking quite a bit and stumbling worse than when we brought him in last time."

"Why don't you bring him by tomorrow? We'll check his thyroid level and adjust the dose if needed."

"How long will it take to figure this out?"

"We'll get the results in two or three days, and then we'll go from there."

"I don't think we have the time, he's getting worse by the minute."

"What's he saying? Ask him to send us to Gulf Coast," Jennifer said, referring to the specialty veterinary practice known for their ability to handle complex cases. Jennifer wrestled the phone from my grip and implored, "We need you to refer us to Gulf Coast. We don't have time to wait."

"No, I'm sorry. I can't refer you until I'm comfortable it's something we can't treat. It's for emergency cases only."

"I don't think so," Jennifer responded sharply. "Just have his records at the front desk. I'll be taking him to another vet. Good-bye."

"Why the hell did you do that?" I asked angrily. "Now we don't have anyone to help us with Clyde. You're always picking a fight with people when you don't need to."

"My friend told me about a doctor at the Rose-Rich Vet clinic. She said Dr. Moore goes out of her way to help. I know she'll be able to help us."

We loaded up Clyde and retrieved his records en route to our latest vet. Once in the reception area, Clyde began heaving up what little fluid was left in his stomach. The veterinary tech brought us to a room where Dr. Moore reviewed the records and examined my ailing dog.

"I don't know what's wrong with him," she sighed. "But he'll probably be dead in a few hours if we don't figure out what's causing this. He appears to be crashing."

"Can you refer us to a specialist?" Jennifer asked.

"That's the only hope. I'll call ahead at Gulf Coast so they'll be waiting for you," she said, following us to the front of the building. I loaded Clyde into the backseat next to Jennifer while the doctor described the quickest route to the hospital.

"Thanks, Jennifer," I said as we embarked on the forty-minute drive to the specialty clinic. "I'm sorry I yelled at you earlier. I thought you were alienating our only hope."

"It's real simple," she said. "I don't want to be friends with the doctor. I don't care if he likes me or not. I just want to make sure Clyde gets treated."

"Yeah, I don't know why the hell I'm always trying to be so damn polite."

"It's gonna be OK, big boy, Mommy's here," Jennifer said sweetly to Clyde, gently caressing his head. "He's shaking real bad, Jason—try to hurry!"

By the time we arrived at Gulf Coast, Clyde had weakened considerably and his trembling and vomiting intensified. The technicians rushed him to the back and started IV fluids while the doctors ran some tests. An hour later, the doctor met us in the exam room and laid Clyde's folder on the table.

"It looks like he has Addison's disease, though we're going to have to wait on some additional tests to be sure," he said.

"What's Addison's disease?" I asked.

"The dog's adrenal glands aren't making the normal mineral steroids and corticosteroids. Without supplementation, his muscles and organs won't function."

"What about his thyroid?"

"It looks fine, I'm sure it's not related to the thyroid. The dog doesn't really fit the profile—the disease is more common in young female dogs, not five-year-old males."

"What could've caused it?" Jennifer asked.

He listed a few things like chronic infection, steroid use, cancer, and—adverse reaction to anesthesia. The teeth cleaning procedure came rushing back into my thoughts—something must have gone wrong.

"You'll need to give him an injection of Percortin every twenty-eight to thirty-two days, depending on how it affects him," he said. "You'll have to supplement him with prednisone as needed. Stressful situations or anxiety will increase his need for steroids because his body is unable to produce any."

"When can we take him home?" I asked.

"He's going to have to stay for a few days until we can get his electrolytes in balance."

After four days of intravenous fluids, Clyde regained much of his weight and, more importantly, his coordination. The treatment plan was simple enough—an injection a month and some pills as needed. I soon realized "as needed" was not a very useful prescription. We needed to give him pills when he got upset or when he *might* get upset. Unfortunately, Clyde was high strung and nearly everything made him excited or nervous. With the least bit of anxiety, he'd start trembling and we'd have to pop a prednisone into his mouth.

We were relieved Clyde was back to normal and we could return to our long walks and island expeditions. Yet

Jennifer's good mood didn't last. Without the structure provided by a job, she found it difficult to fill the days and find meaning in her life at home. After a brief, unrewarding return to the hotel industry, she enrolled in a few classes at the community college, volunteered at a nearby animal shelter, and taught arts and crafts at a center for developmentally-disabled children. The calendar was filled and her friendships many, but the loss of connection to family stoked her sadness. Jennifer missed being a part of the frequent festivities that, between birthdays, holidays, and anniversaries of the extended family, brought twenty or thirty of them together every few weeks. Even though she spent a couple of hours each day on the phone catching up with her mom and siblings, the sense of loss remained. She ended each conversation with an open invitation to visit and stay as long as they wished. And, unsurprisingly, every month, one or more of her family members took her up on the offer.

"I'm so excited to see the kids again. I bought passes to Astroworld for Saturday—it's going to be a great time," Jennifer said, referring to the ninth visit in three years of her brother, Steve, and family. Steve was nice enough, though his wife, Beth, was hard to be around for any length of time—she frequently shouted at the kids and peppered her husband with a merciless barrage of insults. I could tell Steve's spirit was broken by the way he walked—eyes downcast and head hung low. Because I was his only refuge during the visits, he took every opportunity to get out of the house and run errands with me.

"It's been awhile since we've been to the park," I said to Jennifer. "It'll be fun. We're definitely going to ride the Texas Cyclone again. I've never seen you smile so much."

"I'm glad you bought the picture. We both look so funny with our eyes wide open."

"When's your brother getting here?"

"I think they'll be here in another hour—just in time for dinner."

"Good, I'm getting hungry. What are we having?"

"Steve wanted po' boys, so I bought five pounds of shrimp."

"I love your fried shrimp. I knew there was a reason for the giant tub of potato salad in the fridge."

"I hid some in a mayonnaise jar for you to take to work next week. I know how much you and Steve love it. If I didn't put some away, it would be gone in no time."

"He's a bit extreme about it. At least I don't make potato salad sandwiches for breakfast, lunch, and dinner—I have some self-control."

"I've seen your self-control. Three or four helpings of self-control," Jennifer laughed.

"By the way, can you make up an excuse to bathe Jack when they get here? Maybe tell him you're going to groom him."

"I'm not going to bother my brother right when he gets here," she replied sharply.

"But that's when we need to do it. Otherwise, they'll get in the carpet. The little dog is always covered in fleas. I had to treat all our dogs after the last time he was here."

"He gives him a bath before he comes."

"He washes him in Ivory dishwashing liquid. Who gave him the idea it works for fleas?"

"That's what we always used growing up."

"Well, it doesn't work. Listen, I really don't want to get fleas in the house. I lived through hell in college with an infested apartment. I sprayed and bombed the place a dozen times and the fleas kept coming back. I finally had to move out."

"If it's so important, grab the dog when he gets here and take him to the tub. I can't believe you are making such a big deal about a little dog."

"Damn it, I don't want fleas. I'm not asking much—just that your brother not bring a flea-infested dog to our house every time he visits."

"He's so good to you, and all you can think about is his little dog. He helped you with the ceiling fans last time he was here. I guess it doesn't buy him anything with you."

"I just want your family to show a little respect for our house. I already have to put up with the screaming between him and his wife—and they both constantly scream at the kids. I have a headache after the first day. I don't think I'm asking much, considering all I have to put up with."

"I don't want to talk about it anymore. You don't fight fair—you're always bringing up the past."

"I'm in the past because it keeps happening. How can I ignore we've talked about the damn dog so many times before?"

"Let's drop it. Steve and the kids will be here soon. You're ruining the weekend already."

"Fine. I'll drop it." Maybe it was the stress of dealing with Clyde's issues or maybe I was growing weary of treading the same ground, but I found myself increasingly frustrated with our minor conflicts.

The visit passed much like previous ones—a lot of great food, but accented with a couple of needless arguments. During his stay, Steve constructed a set of wind chimes, similar to the set he built for his mother's one-acre yard, comprised of six large aluminum tubes, varying in length from five to eight feet, and hung the contraption from the eave adjacent to our kitchen. Two flat, sharp-edged, dinner-plate-sized aluminum discs, designed to amplify the wind's ability to move the central glass disk, hung in series at the base. The device was attached ten feet off the ground, yet only a half foot of clearance remained beneath it. With the slightest breeze, the jarring noise could easily be heard inside the house.

Despite my protests, Jennifer wouldn't entertain the idea of trashing the thoughtful gift. Luckily, the proximity of the chimes to our neighbor's home precipitated a flood of complaints to the homeowner's association and, soon thereafter to my relief, the giant gong lay motionless in the garage.

A year after Clyde's diagnosis, Jennifer adopted a tiny Shih Tzu puppy. The flat-faced, fluffy creature, promised to fill the lapdog role Cricket eschewed. Sandy, like most puppies, engaged the resident dogs at every opportunity. Despite her friendliness, the established pack members, perhaps put off by her odd appearance, growled each time she approached.

Concerned for the welfare of the little pup, I reminded Jennifer of the issues Bonnie had with stuffed animals—the way she gnawed a hole in each, pulled out the squeaker and ripped off the button eyes. The procedure, completed in less than two minutes, left only a pile of stuffing surrounding an eyeless husk. The only exception was a softball-sized stuffed red spider that she, after plucking the eyes out, carried and protected for months.

"Honey, after this much time, they really should've worked things out," I remarked.

"They just need more time. Besides, you know how much I've always wanted a lapdog. Why are you trying to get rid of her?"

"The dog isn't very bright. She's been here over a month and is still peeing in the house. Bonnie and Clyde learned the inside-outside thing within a few days—even after being paper-trained. Besides, Clyde is shaking more with all the commotion."

"What am I supposed to do? I can't take her to the pound. I'm sure they'll work it out."

A few days later, I sat in the backyard and caressed the little puppy as she crawled on my lap and turned upside down. Bonnie approached and, before I could react, clamped her jaws on Sandy's head and squeezed. The puppy's agonizing scream coupled with a sharp blow from my hand, caused Bonnie to release her quickly. The right eye, bulging from its socket after the unprovoked attack, left the little puppy reeling in pain. Within minutes, we arrived at Rose-Rich Veterinary where Dr. Robinson put his thumb on her eyeball and gently pushed it back into the socket. The disoriented little dog stopped crying and, amazingly, appeared to be in pretty good shape.

Perhaps, the doctor thought, Bonnie was jealous of the attention given to the new dog or feared her position in the pack was at risk. I thought it more likely she sensed my frustration with the little pee-generating machine and decided to take care of the problem. Fortunately, my sister-in-law Shelly had an affinity for Shih Tzus and, the next day, I gladly drove six hours to New Orleans to add one more to her collection.

To help control Bonnie's aggression, Dr. Robinson prescribed the dog version of Prozac. Though she mellowed out some, it didn't change the growling and unpredictability. One time, she let loose on an old grumpy dog we were watching for a friend. Clyde pretty much ignored the ill-tempered forty-pound dog, but when he showed aggression toward Bonnie, she grabbed him by the shoulder and pinned him to the ground. Though she released the dog when it screamed, the skin had already been punctured.

Concerned the next target might be a child, we doubled up on the medication, somewhat improving her mood.

Unfortunately, the high doses of Prozac led to bouts of pancreatitis and diarrhea, causing us to scale back the medication and just keep her away from volatile situations. Not long after, a neighbor child startled her while she was resting, holding her neck and trying to kiss her. Bonnie turned quickly, reacting in defense not aggression, and dragged a tooth across his cheek. Other than a small scratch, the child was unhurt, but it added to the picture of a problem dog who couldn't be trusted.

Within another year, Clyde's shaking and coordination problems returned. Without additional doses of prednisone, Clyde had trouble just walking. He ballooned to a hundred eighteen pounds due to his steroid-amplified appetite and swelling. The medicine also elevated Clyde's body temperature, causing him to struggle in the summer heat. By the time I arrived home each day, he was flushed and panting heavily, requiring a few minutes of hosing down before his body temperature returned to normal. Despite their destructive track record, it was painfully obvious they needed access to the house while we were at work. The full-glass back door precluded a doggie door, so I stuck a sheet of foam board to the door frame with Velcro, punching a large opening in the bottom half to allow easy passage for the dogs. Later, after the dogs shattered a number of the makeshift doggie doors, I substituted plywood for the foam and reinforced the Velcro with bolts and wing nuts. After finding a host of flies, mosquitoes and, sometimes, wasps in our home, I dumped the plywood and hung large, plastic, industrial freezer door flaps, accenting the back of house with the look and feel of a warehouse entrance. Jennifer wasn't thrilled about the eyesore I had constructed, but couldn't resist Clyde's needs.

Shortly after the new entrance was operational, Jennifer became concerned someone might see the open door, hop the fence and rob the house—or worse. To address the problem, I replaced the full glass door with a half glass version and installed a doggie door. The doggie door, sized to accommodate Clyde's height as well as Cricket's bad legs and short stature, consumed almost the entire lower half of the door. As far as improving the safety situation, it was of minimal benefit—at over two hundred pounds, I could easily crawl through the opening. We'd be safe only if the would-be thief had a serious weight control problem. But, for the dogs, especially Clyde, it was a great improvement in their lives.

It was clear the current medicines weren't managing his condition properly, yet the only possible alternative was Florinef dosed with hydrocortisone. Though effective, the treatment was rarely used because dogs require high doses of the expensive medicine. The eight-hundred-dollar-per-month price tag, though initially shocking, was worth it to me. The change in medicine had an immediate, positive impact on his health, allowing him to regain his coordination and slim down quite a bit.

Upon returning to our long walks, another problem emerged. Clyde's front nails wore to the point of bleeding, casualties of an impaired stride that left him dragging his front paws slightly with each step. Knowing Clyde would be crushed if we took Bonnie for a walk and left him behind, we worked hard to come up with a solution. After several trial-and-error attempts, rubber screw coverings, each topped with the head of a thumb tack, were glued to his nails. Clyde had what looked and sounded like his very own tap shoes. Despite the small victory, we still couldn't understand why he was dragging his feet.

Near his eighth birthday, Clyde suddenly collapsed and was unable to stand without my assistance. At Gulf Coast, they found he had developed diabetes and worked the next several days to stabilize his blood sugar levels.

"You should really think about what to do with Clyde," the vet said.

"What do you mean?" I asked.

"With his other underlying problems, it will be very difficult to manage this new condition. The steroid will cause blood sugar elevation and increase the dog's appetite. The increased food consumption will also lead to higher blood sugar levels."

"I'll have to figure out a way to manage this—there has to be some way," I said hopefully.

"You need to understand he's likely going to go blind from this. It is only a matter of time—maybe in a couple of months."

Twice each day, I measured and plotted his glucose levels to determine the dosage of insulin, which changed based on the amount of stress, food consumption, and physical activity he experienced. Getting a drop of blood to measure was almost as difficult as determining the right amount of insulin. I could only find a few places, each one tender, where blood formed a droplet. Clyde was a good sport about the new protocol, despite the discomfort of the pin prick inside his cheek.

Clyde and I grew closer with each passing day. He needed and loved me and, of course, I loved him. He was always with me when I was home—never more than a few inches away. This was just another challenge we had to face, and hopefully overcome, together.

Despite Clyde's mounting health problems, we took road trips whenever possible. Bonnie and Clyde were good sports about the long drives, patiently watching the miles go by while Cricket hyperventilated, nervously pacing between the console and Jennifer's lap. Sometimes we'd visit Jennifer's mom at her small, rustic home on the Alabama coast. Her one-acre, heavily wooded lot, teeming with mice and squirrels, was a favorite destination for Bonnie and Clyde. Other times, we travelled to north Texas or Arkansas to hike the forested, rolling hills. Whether we were wandering through the dense woods, scrambling up the rocky trails, or just relaxing by the lakeside, Clyde was always up for the next adventure.

CHAPTER SIX

The Flood

In August 2005, two years after Clyde developed diabetes, Hurricane Katrina slammed into the New Orleans area. In the days that followed, many of our family members, their homes rendered uninhabitable by standing water or lack of power, evacuated to our home. Cathy and Claude, their son, Dillon, three dogs and a cat, were the first guests. A few hours later, Steve and Beth, their two children, and their shaggy, flea-bitten dog, arrived. The next day, Jennifer's aunt, Trish, and grandmother, Marie, joined the group, followed soon thereafter by my father.

"Hey, here comes the Red Cross," my father observed.

"Mr. Rob, they're from my church, it's not charity," Jennifer remarked sharply.

"I'm glad the Red Cross showed up. I was getting hungry," my father replied, oblivious to the awkward moment he was creating.

"Dad, will you give it a rest—they don't think you're funny," Rob interjected. Rob lived a few miles away and had a knack for showing up right around dinner time.

"What? We're just having a little banter with the Red Cross folks."

"Look, yesterday you said they were from Meals on Wheels. Jennifer doesn't think it's funny," Rob said.

"All I said was I'm glad they showed up. What's so wrong about that?" my father asked.

"No, you said they were from the Red Cross, that's what the problem is," Rob replied, his frustration and voice both rising.

"All I said was I'm glad they showed up."

"Hey, can you guys drop this crap?" I asked. "I can hear you in the next room. Everyone's on edge as it is."

"Look, it's little Jason, the house diplomat," Rob mocked. "While you're in here, I want to talk to you about Dad." Rob closed the glass double doors separating my father's makeshift bedroom from the rest of the house.

"What is it?"

"Dad's not getting enough vegetables," Rob observed. "You need to get him on a better diet."

"Hey, I've kinda got my hands full here. The 'Red Cross' brings what they bring. I'm not going to complain. If you want him to have more vegetables, get in your damn car and go get them. Better yet, why don't you two go off and eat dinner somewhere else? Last I checked, all the grocery stores and restaurants are open in Houston."

"Because he's not going to pay for a meal when he can eat here for free," Rob said, motioning at the white-haired, old man sitting at the edge of the daybed.

"Well then stop bitching about everything. If you want something different, take care of it."

"I don't know what you have against vegetables."

"Let's drop it, Rob. Hey, somebody needs to go check on Lisa," I said, turning my attention to the old man. "It's been days since you left her house and nobody's heard from her." Lisa lived in a small town near Hammond about twenty miles west of Mandeville. Following the breakup of her marriage, Lisa bought a tiny, run-down house on three acres to accommodate her favorite horses, Black Beauty and Schnapps.

"She didn't want to leave her animals," my father said and then shared the hardships he endured during his stay there—no running water for showers or toilets, dwindling food rations, and Lisa's increasingly surly attitude.

"I know, you already told us the story," I said.

Rob interjected, "I thought your buddy Claude was going to check on his way back today."

"I'm not counting on it. He's made the trip to Mandeville four times and hasn't done it yet."

"I'm not driving seven hours to check on her if he's going right by her house," Rob said.

"Well if he doesn't stop, it doesn't do us much good, does it? Do you really want Lisa living in those conditions? She's probably losing her mind already."

I heard the familiar sound of Claude's diesel engine idling in front of the house. "Looks like Claude's here, let me go check and see if he stopped by Lisa's." I walked to the driver's door of the hulking vehicle and raised my voice to compensate for the loud, rumbling exhaust. "Hey, Claude, how was the drive?" I asked, feigning interest.

"There weren't any cars on the road. Made it in four and half hours."

"You must have been doing eighty the whole time," I calculated.

"Yeah," he replied, not feeling the need to expand.

"Did you get a chance to check on Lisa?"

"No, they had a tree across the road at her exit. Couldn't get by. I'm heading back as soon as Cathy comes out. Maybe we'll pass by tonight."

"I'd appreciate it; she doesn't have any running water. Where's Dillon?" I asked Cathy as she approached carrying only her suitcase.

"Oh, Jennifer asked to let him stay with y'all for a while," Cathy said.

"What? When are you coming back?"

"We'll be back in two weeks. Dillon is so excited to stay with Aunt Jennifer."

"Two weeks? You know there's a lot of commotion in the house and, with Grandma, Jennifer's going to be distracted. We've got chemicals under the sink, sharp edges everywhere. The house isn't childproof and you know how easily she gets distracted."

"Dillon's going to be just fine. Steve's going to help Jennifer keep an eye on him. See you later," Cathy remarked as the powerful engine dragged the truck forward. I walked back inside, frustrated beyond words.

"Jennifer, can you come in the bedroom for a sec?" I asked.

"Sure, what do you need?"

"What's the deal with Dillon? Cathy said you asked for him to stay with us."

"I didn't ask her. She said she needed to focus on building back their business—and she has a conference she needs to go to."

"How the hell can we take care of him? We've got ten people and eight dogs here as it is. How are you going to keep an eye on him—he's always breaking shit."

"I'll watch him, hon. Don't worry; everything will be fine."

"For Christ's sake, he's still crapping his pants—he thinks it's funny."

"They really needed me to do it."

"Hell, that asshole husband of hers can't even be bothered to check on Lisa. Drives right by her exit every time. She could be rotting there for all he cares."

"He said the road wasn't passable," Jennifer remembered.

"Funny, how'd my old man drive his crappy, little car out of there? Claude's four-wheel drive truck can't get down the same roads? He's full of shit."

"Jason, keep it down, my family can hear you through the door."

"I don't care. And another thing, Steve asked me how the local schools were earlier today. What's that about?"

"He wants to enroll his kids so they don't fall behind. The schools are all closed in Mandeville and his job is starting back in two weeks. He asked if they could stay with us when he heads home."

"You've got to be kidding! What the hell are we running here, a damn day care facility? Damn it, Jennifer, your family treats you like a doormat—like your time isn't worth anything because you don't have kids."

"Leave my family alone! They've always been so good to me—and they're always there for me," Jennifer defended.

"I don't care. Call your sister and tell her to make other arrangements and do the same with your brother."

When Claude failed to check on Lisa, Rob reluctantly agreed to make the long drive. He returned nearly twenty-four hours later, Lisa's green convertible following him into the driveway. As Lisa began to unpack her vehicle, Walliford and Tango stretched, marked the new territory and headed toward the house. Bonnie and Clyde barked aggressively at the window, anticipating a renewed test of wills. I brought the dogs to the backyard to let them get reacquainted. Clyde, far less fit than he was at their last meeting, refused to yield to the interlopers. He stood his ground, followed Walliford from bush to bush, and marked on top of his scent. After ten minutes, the introductions were complete and the dogs began to play together. I headed to the front to welcome my sister.

"You got water all over my car! The ice chest leaked all over my car!" Lisa exclaimed.

"I didn't know it was leaking," Rob said meekly, worn out from sixteen hours of driving in the last twenty-four. "An ice chest isn't supposed to leak."

"My Jaguar is ruined!" Lisa yelled.

"Hey, will you guys cut this crap out? You're in my front yard making a scene," I snapped.

"I'll shout anywhere I want," Lisa replied. "I didn't ask to come here, Rob made me."

"Your toilets were overflowing and you had no running water," Rob replied. "You couldn't stay there."

"I was fine. Why did you have to put the ice chest in my car?"

"I didn't have room in mine," Rob replied.

"Shut up, both of you," I said. "Get this stuff unloaded and stop the griping."

"He ruined my car…"

"That's it," I said, grabbing the large ice chest from my brother's hands, interrupting his meticulous search for the leak. I repeatedly slammed the offensive item into the trunk of the nearby oak tree, leaving a pile of food and foam debris at its base. "Now, we won't have to worry about the damned ice chest," I said.

"Are you insane? That was a perfectly good ice chest!" Rob believed.

"Then what was all the bitching about? Lisa, Rob made a long drive to go get you—cut him some slack," I said.

"I didn't ask to come here."

"Well, you're here now—why don't you try to make the most of it?"

"Jason," Steve interrupted, "Jennifer needs you." Leaving the lunacy behind, I followed him inside, finding Jennifer in tears.

"What's wrong?"

She held her hand over the receiver and whispered, "It's Aunt Helen. She said Eric was heading to Arkansas and didn't have enough room for her and Flo. He told her to head our way. I can't take anymore."

"Let me talk to her," I said, grabbing the cell phone from her hand.

"Helen, I'm sorry. You're going to have figure something else out. We've got twelve people already here, and we can't take on any more. If you come, you'll be sleeping in your car."

"We don't have anywhere else to go," Helen pleaded.

"I'm real sorry, you'll have to talk to your nephew about that. I hope you can work it out, take care," I said, disconnecting the call.

"Why'd you have to be so mean?" Jennifer demanded.

"I took care of it for you, didn't I? Next time, don't involve me if you don't want me to handle things. Your cousin can't be bothered and somehow it's our problem. He's heading up to the big palace his in-laws have, and they can't make room? He just doesn't want to deal with the old ladies."

"I know we can't take them here. I just hope she doesn't tell my mom. She won't understand."

"Luckily for us, the interstate's washed out between here and your mom's. Otherwise, they would've been here days ago—along with their four dogs."

"You're right," she laughed. "Let's take the buds to the lake. I need to get out of here for a while." Minutes later, the dogs were loaded into my SUV and the argument forgotten. The outings to the island were important for all of us, especially Clyde. The commotion in the house overwhelmed him, increasing the frequency of his shaking episodes. The need to protect his territory against numerous dogs, including the dominant duo, Tango and Wally, and the continual screaming of the kids created a high level of daily stress for him.

After three weeks, the infrastructure around New Orleans recovered enough to enable all our guests, except Marie, to return home. Grandma Marie's home, untouched by the floods, remained under evacuation orders due to widespread looting and violent crime.

"Jennifer, when are you going to take me home?" she asked repeatedly.

"Grandma, your house is flooded, I can't take you back right now. You're going to stay with Jason and me until your house is safe."

"Take me to the trolley. I can take the trolley to my house."

"You're in Sugar Land, Texas. We can't take a trolley to your house," Jennifer replied, casting a concerned look my way. Each day, Jennifer's grandmother drifted further from reality—sometimes believing she was being held prisoner. Often, she'd slip out of the house and wander the neighborhood, asking anyone and everyone where she could catch the trolley to the Ninth Ward.

She only appeared to have command of her faculties while she was in the kitchen. At her age, it was amazing she could still walk, let alone prepare a meal for us. Each evening, she commandeered the kitchen, moving with purpose between the stove and the sink. Clyde, of course, sprawled his massive body right in the path.

"Clyde, get up boy—move," I said, tapping him on the hindquarters.

He lazily rose, walked around the bar and laid down a few feet from his initial position. Concerned his large body and the slippery tile floors might be too much for Marie to navigate, I encouraged him to move again and, of course, he returned near the same spot, wondering why I interrupted his rest to move a few feet.

"Jennifer, the dog looks like a cow!" Marie said. "He's so big."

A week later, Hurricane Rita formed in the Gulf of Mexico and quickly grew in strength to a category five storm. When the early projections showed Sugar Land in the possible path, I convinced Jennifer to take her grandmother and Cricket to Cathy's house in Mandeville. Within a day of their departure, the evacuation routes became jammed with panic-stricken residents fearing a powerful sequel to Katrina. The conditions on the road quickly deteriorated—gas stations depleted of fuel, cars abandoned on the side of the road, and several animals dead from heat exhaustion. After hearing reports of the chaos, I was content to stay behind with Bonnie and Clyde and, perhaps foolishly, brave the storm. Fortunately, the massive system made landfall far to the east, providing Sugar Land with only a gentle, dry breeze as evidence of its passing.

While in Mandeville, Jennifer was able to arrange for Marie to stay with family. I felt an incredible sense of relief when Jennifer pulled into the driveway with Cricket her only passenger. Our lives could return to normal—trips to the island, long walks, and peaceful afternoons in the backyard. Without the continual stress and distractions, we had the time and space to enjoy each other's company once again.

Yet we didn't return to the old days. Months after the crowd departed, our lighthearted, carefree times, so frequent before the storm, were few and far between. While the troubles of those in New Orleans occupied few of my thoughts, Jennifer dwelt upon their struggles continually. The guilt of living comfortably in Texas while her family worked to rebuild their lives weighed heavily upon her. I couldn't understand what she was going through—what it meant to lose connection with the life she once knew. The childhood memories, the hangouts she and her friends enjoyed as teenagers, the neighborhood she grew up in— all of it was changed forever.

It wasn't just the loss of a city or even of memories; it was the loss of her identity.

CHAPTER SEVEN

Slipping Away

"He looks good this time. Do you notice he's doing better now with the thyroxin?" Dr. Moore asked. Every month or so, we brought Clyde in for exams and special lab tests to ensure his Addison's was being managed properly. During one visit, she identified a problem with his thyroid and placed him on supplements.

"He sure is. We don't even need his tap shoes anymore. He's walking normal again," Jennifer replied.

"I'm so glad it's helping. Clyde is such a sweet boy." Dr. Moore had bonded quickly with Clyde. In fact, once she understood how anxious Clyde became in the waiting room, she sometimes examined and treated him in the back of my SUV. "By the way, do y'all want an old yellow dog?"

"Why?" Jennifer asked as we followed Dr. Moore to the kennels.

"A man dropped off six dogs and told us to euthanize them all. Said his wife left and he couldn't handle them anymore. We only found homes for two before we needed the space for our patients. Three had to be euthanized and this old girl is the only one left. She's been in the cage three months and we're out of space again."

"She's a beautiful dog," Jennifer said. Haley, the furry prisoner, was six years old, about three-quarters the size of Bonnie with longer, thicker fur. The color was a little darker than Clyde's and her narrow face gave her more of a wolf-like appearance.

"She's really sweet," Dr. Moore added. "I took her home to stay with my animals, but she kept digging out to follow me. It breaks my heart."

"Honey, let's take her. Clyde really likes her." Jennifer pleaded.

"What do you mean Clyde likes her? He doesn't like other dogs."

"He was sniffing her through the kennel fence and wagging his tail when we first came in. Didn't you notice?"

"He doesn't look all that interested now."

"C'mon hon, she needs us."

"I guess since she'll be euthanized if we don't, there's really nothing to lose."

"Miss Haley, you're coming home with us," Jennifer said happily, gently stroking the dog's soft coat.

I soon realized Clyde's "friendliness" at the kennel was more curiosity than anything else. Once in the car, Clyde ignored the new addition and growled if she got too close. "Yeah, I can see how much Clyde likes her."

Jennifer smiled. She knew I didn't have the heart to take the dog back.

The next day after work, I returned home to a warm greeting from Bonnie, Clyde, and Cricket. The new arrival, however, was gone, leaving behind only a small hole, burrowed under the fence through the hard clay soil. Searching the surrounding streets for Haley, I happened upon a neighbor who had not only seen the dog, but had followed her for several miles before losing her in a field of tall grass dangerously close to the interstate. I searched the area for hours and, as night fell, accepted she was probably hit by a car. I called Jennifer, who had flown to New Orleans that morning, and told her the unfortunate news.

The following day, surprisingly, Haley was back in the house. I filled the hole, placing a cement block on top to deter her escape attempts. Within a few hours, I received a call from another neighbor who saw Haley heading, again, for the interstate. I hurried home from work and scoured the area without success. Disappointed and frustrated, I called Jennifer to let her know Haley was probably gone for good this time.

Later in the evening, I heard a noise upstairs and found Haley hiding behind the guest bed. Somehow, the sixty pound dog had snuck in without being detected. When Jennifer returned the next day, Haley realized she had found her permanent home and stopped digging.

Haley spent most of her time on the stairwell landing or upstairs in the guest bedroom, afraid to interact with the resident canines. Not even food could entice her to join the festivities downstairs—preferring to go hungry if we didn't bring her bowl to a "safe" area upstairs. Jennifer and Haley took long walks daily, usually covering four or five miles. Haley wasn't interested in pulling, she was content to trot or walk right by Jennifer's side.

Even though Clyde's lack of strength and shaky coordination prevented us from walking long distances, we made it to the lake each day. At first, Clyde could make it into the SUV under his own power on a ramp I built for him. When he began to stumble more frequently, I built a platform for him. When he could no longer navigate the platform, I lifted him in and out. The drive to the lake, covering only a few blocks, provided enough time for him to get completely wound up. The incessant barking began a few blocks from our destination and my ears were ringing by the time we parked.

Once at the lake, Bonnie jumped out while Clyde waited impatiently to be lowered to the ground. He ran as fast as he could, managing only a slow jog, moving as though he carried a fifty-pound vest. Once in the water, he retrieved for a long time. At first, he could make it in and out of the water on his own. As time went by, I had to help him with the one-foot ledge. Though Clyde's life was limited by his physical abilities, he never lost his spirit for living or his love for us. With each new problem he developed, we compensated. *Can't walk, I'll drive you. Can't get in the truck, I'll lift you. Can't make it out of the water, I'll reach in and get you.*

While Clyde's physical strength may have waned, his emotional range certainly expanded. Each day, he became more loving and sensitive, yearning to be held and caressed. If I was near him, he dolphin-nosed my hand or tugged at my arm with his paw. After Jennifer and I fell asleep each night, he wormed his way into our bed. Despite his lack of coordination, he was stealthy when attempting to join us. Once safely between us, he leaned his back against Jennifer and extended his arms and legs toward me. I often awoke after sliding, inch by inch, to the edge of the bed. On the few occasions I tried to move his one-hundred-ten-pound frame, he moaned as if he was being tortured, prompting Jennifer to warn me to cease and desist. Clyde quickly learned his routine led me to surrender my space and sleep on the couch. After a few weeks of insomnia, I purchased a daybed and positioned it next to my side. While the bedroom setup appeared strange to our friends, it allowed me to get a good night's sleep, and my buddy could be comforted by the people he loved more than anything in the world.

After nearly three years of twice-daily blood sugar measurements, Clyde began to resist the jabs in his mouth. The skin had deteriorated from the hundreds, maybe thousands, of punctures, making the blood more difficult to measure. Instead of forming a droplet, the blood smeared into the many creases of the damaged skin. A few weeks after switching to pee strips to reduce his discomfort, they consistently indicated high blood sugar. The levels spiked incredibly high and I had a heck of a time getting Clyde back in balance as higher doses of insulin led to higher blood sugar readings—the exact opposite of what was supposed to happen. Through frustrating trial and error, I worked his blood sugar back to normal over the next few days. As time went on, his diabetes became more and more difficult to manage.

A few months later, near his eleventh birthday, Clyde was retrieving the buoy at the lake as usual. This time, however, he couldn't locate it consistently. On a few throws, he swam past the buoy and then turned frantically until he spotted it. When I fished him out of the water, I noticed one of his eyes was a shiny, silver-gray color. Clyde needed help again, but the earliest appointment available with an eye specialist was almost two weeks away.

Within days, Clyde lost vision in his other eye, leaving him completely blind. Despite the impairment, he was still able to enjoy visits to the tall grass where the mice lived. He stood very still, his tail raised and quivering, his brow wrinkled, listening intently for the sounds of mice. Every few minutes, he lunged at the sound, sending a frightened mouse scurrying across the walkway into another clump of grass.

At home it was a different story. He bumped into walls and furniture, unable to orient himself to the new darkness. Because the floors downstairs were completely covered with tile, his paws were of little use in determining his location. Sometimes, he lost his balance, ending up spread-eagle on the slippery floor, lacking the coordination and strength to right himself. Once in the yard, he had a heck of a time finding his way back into the house.

To compensate, I became his seeing-eye human, providing guidance or a lift when needed.

Excited and anxious, after the two-week delay, we made the hour-long drive to the vet. Clyde, always nervous on road trips, was especially upset this time because he couldn't see.

The vet looked Clyde over and said "His vision can be fixed with a relatively simple surgery to replace the cataracts with synthetic lenses. It will cost about $1,200 per eye."

"That's great news! When can we schedule him?"

"I don't know if I want to do the surgery. The dog's in such poor health. It'll be difficult to manage the surgery and recovery with his underlying conditions."

"He usually has a lot more energy. He's just a little groggy from the tranquilizer I gave him. He gets nervous when we drive places."

"No, I don't think he'll make it through the surgery."

"Please, he doesn't have any other chance. I'm going to have to euthanize him if we don't get his eyesight back. He can't manage around the house, he can't figure out where he is."

"Well, I'll call your veterinarian and we'll decide if and how we can proceed."

Heartened by the slight shift in his attitude, we made the first available appointment for surgery—in three weeks. A week later, they deferred the surgery a month because the vet decided to take vacation early. I cancelled the appointment and set up the surgery at Texas A&M vet school in College Station, Texas, nearly three hours away. We still had to wait until after Christmas, but I could rest easy, knowing it was going to happen.

The days passed and we made the best of it, going on walks every day and to the tall grass when we could. Clyde quickly learned the basic commands needed to get around without his sight. Though frustrated at times, his spirit never wavered. One time at the park, I set him down and, before I could leash him, he took off for the tall grass fifty yards away. I jogged alongside, giving verbal commands, to keep him from running into the trees. It was great to see such enthusiasm, yet I hooked him up each time after that.

Every day brought us one day closer to Clyde getting his sight back. I looked forward to it like a child looks forward to Christmas. When the day finally arrived, Clyde was relaxed and took everything in stride. The surgery, though successful, left him weaker than hoped for in recovery. Each day, they insisted another was needed to stabilize him and run tests. After four days, the five-thousand-dollar-bill was quickly forgotten when Clyde came through the door, wagging his tail furiously and straining against the leash. Clyde must have been thinking how great it was someone finally turned on the lights.

The following weeks entailed a bit of discomfort but also a lot of joy for Clyde. His need for eye drops every four hours, necessitated coming home at lunch and waking in the middle of the night, but I didn't mind—Clyde was healthy and happy once again.

Moving slow but steady, Clyde returned to retrieving the buoy at the lake and hunting for squirrels and mice. A few weeks after surgery, Clyde was also strong enough to go on walks around our block. One day, he hesitated at a forty-foot-wide, half-mile-long meadow, filled with tall grass and weeds. I unhooked his leash to let him enjoy a bit of freedom. He jogged through the field, excited by the new scents and enjoying the feel of the soft grass under his paws. He slowed for a few steps, sniffed the ground, and then bounded off again. We probably covered a little less than a mile, but it was the most active I'd seen him in a long time.

And it was the most fun he'd had in a long time.

CHAPTER EIGHT

A Little More Time

The day after his long run, Clyde stretched his arms skyward and felt the warm sunlight wash over his body. He lay comfortably on his favorite piece of furniture with his toes and nose almost touching each end of the leather sofa. He felt a little weak and his muscles a bit tender from the exertion, but content to be in the company of his mates. Suddenly, Bonnie squealed, leaped off the adjacent couch, punched through the doggie door, and sprinted to the back fence with Haley and Cricket in hot pursuit. Clyde rolled off his couch and, moving as fast as he could, lumbered behind them. He soon joined Bonnie in frenzied barking directed at the last known position of the squirrel. Haley sat quietly, staring into the upper branches of the oak tree, patiently waiting for the creature to reappear.

Startled by the intense pain in his chest, Clyde fell silent and, a few moments later, stumbled to the ground. His rapid, shallow breathing did little to relieve the burning sensation in his lungs. Clyde couldn't understand what was wrong. All he could do was wait, endure, and hope Mom would come home soon.

He heard Bonnie and Cricket cry for help as Jennifer pulled into the driveway. He struggled to his feet and managed a few steps *before collapsing again. Dizzy and weakened, he tried to bark, but was unable to draw enough breath.*

Jennifer knew something was wrong—Clyde always waited for her at the gate. She rushed inside the house, shouting his name repeatedly. As she stepped back into the yard, Clyde appeared from behind the garage. As she ran toward him, he collapsed in the garden.

"Hon, I need you to come home, something is wrong with Clyde! He can't stand up and I can't pick him up. He's breathing real hard!"

"He's probably dehydrated," I said distractedly. "Once we get some IV's in him, he'll be fine."

"Maybe you're right. Maybe we should wait a little while, and see if I can get him to drink some water. I don't want you to have to leave work."

"OK, but give me a call and let me know how he's doing," I said. A few seconds after hanging up the phone, I called Jennifer back.

"I'll be there in fifteen minutes."

When I arrived, Clyde lay motionless in the garden, save the heaving of his chest, with his head on Jennifer's lap, muscles rigid, paws clenched in pain. He tried to rise as I approached, managing only a slight wag of his tail. I carried him to my SUV and laid him in the back next to Jennifer. We called Dr. Robinson on the way to Rose-Rich and described his symptoms.

"It sounds serious. Maybe you should take him to Gulf Coast. I can call in a referral for you," he said.

"I'm pretty sure Clyde is just dehydrated and needs to get some IV fluids quickly," I said. "I don't think he'll make it thirty minutes to Gulf Coast."

Minutes later, I carried Clyde to the back operating room and the vet started to get the IV set up. He moved the stethoscope around Clyde's chest and said, "I can't

help him. I'm pretty sure it's congestive heart failure."
Once fitted with an oxygen mask, Clyde's breathing slowed
and he looked calmer, yet his paws remained clenched in
pain. The vet gave Clyde a shot of painkiller and, within
moments, he appeared more comfortable. "I don't hear
any heartbeat on the right side. We don't have the capabil-
ity here to do anything with him. The only thing you can
do is bring him to Gulf Coast. We can send you with a bottle of oxygen to keep him breathing normally for the trip."

"Will we be able to be with him?" Jennifer asked.

"No, I don't think so. They'll likely take him to an oxygen tent and try to find some combination of medications
to help his heart. I don't think the odds are very high."

He said it would be tough to find a combination of
drugs that could keep his salt levels in the right range—low
enough to manage the heart condition, yet high enough
to control the Addison's disease. It could be several days
before we knew if he had a chance or had to be euthanized.
It hit both of us hard—the thought of Clyde lying there
alone and scared in what might be his final hours. He had
beaten the odds at every turn and now we were faced with
another setback. Though there was little hope of finding
an effective treatment, we decided to try for another miracle. Jennifer sat in the backseat as I laid Clyde and his oxygen bottle next to her.

A few seconds into the drive, Jennifer broke down and
cried, "Hon, why are we putting Clyde through this? He's
already been through so much. I don't want him to die
alone in a cage at Gulf Coast. I can tell he's dying." The
tears streamed down her cheeks.

I pulled into the gas station and filled the tank, trying
to collect my thoughts. My heart hurt for him—we'd been
through so many ups and downs together. Every other time
we found a way to bring Clyde back from the edge, and he

rallied for months, sometimes years. I grasped for answers, yet only confusion reigned. Clyde was in pain and his breathing was becoming labored again. His only hope was forty minutes away, but it was a long shot and he'd likely die alone in a cage. Since getting sick years earlier, Clyde had only been apart from us during the times he was hospitalized to save his life. He was so afraid we'd leave him, he panicked each time we headed for the vet.

I thought about the remote possibility they could save him—find the right combination, walk the fine line between the diseases. Even then, Clyde would be much weaker than before, limiting his life to the house. No more walks, no more swimming—just there for us. It wasn't fair to him—we had to let Clyde go. After all we'd been through; it was a horrible way for it to end.

Clyde didn't resist when I loaded him onto the gurney. They took us to the back room, laid Clyde on the exam table and gave us a few minutes. We talked softly to Clyde and told him how much we loved him. We caressed his head and body and continued to reassure him. I wanted to change our decision, I wanted to run out of there with Clyde and try for the miracle. He looked so helpless, so trusting—and I was about to end his life.

We called Dr. Robinson in and he injected the chemicals, stopping Clyde's heart within seconds. I stayed with Clyde and talked to his lifeless body for at least a half hour. All the emotion that was bottled up over the years poured out. I was sorry for all the mistakes I made managing his disease. His problems were so difficult and interrelated. Along the way, so many unnecessary challenges were created for Clyde.

We were silent for the drive home. The shock and grief overwhelmed both of us. It all happened so fast. Bonnie was near panic when she met us at the gate. She ran to the vehicle looking for Clyde. She could smell his scent saturating it. It was a routine she'd repeat each time I came home for the rest of her life. On each of the three days following Clyde's death, Cricket went to the corner of the yard and barked for twenty minutes, his head held skyward. Haley was affected in a different way. She no longer hid upstairs; she was no longer afraid of Clyde.

The weeks following Clyde's death were filled with the most intense grief I had known in years. Several times a day, I looked at the stack of Clyde's pictures I kept in my desk. I sometimes felt him lying by my side, his paws stretched skyward. I couldn't stop replaying the events in my head, often closing the door to my office and breaking down, wondering why I had given up on Clyde that day.

Clyde burrowed his way into the deepest recesses of my heart. I had been cold for so long I wasn't prepared to have such intense feelings over the loss of a dog. Twenty-five years earlier, the loss of a dog was just an unfortunate part of life. Now, it was a good friend who had died.

It was a good friend who loved and trusted me—and I let down.

Part Two

ENDLESS FIELDS

CHAPTER NINE

Awakening

Despite the strong wind, it was a great day for riding—seventy degrees, clear skies, quiet roads. The blistering pace normally pushed by the collection of former racers and weekend warriors was only marginally affected by the relentless buffeting. We spent most of the morning in an echelon, snaking along narrow roads like brightly colored birds in a tight, rotating V formation. For experienced riders, the echelon is a beautiful, fluid machine, rivaling the efficiency of the birds it attempts to emulate. The cyclists instantly adapt to every change in course direction and wind intensity, quickly locating the small cave of minimum wind resistance. Riders pull through steadily, maintaining the rhythm of the group, spending only a few moments at the tip before rotating off, gliding quickly to the rear and diving once again into the comfort of the slipstream.

One critical skill, beyond bike handling, is the ability to spot a rider who's about to get dropped—his bike surges, his breathing becomes rapid and shallow, his eyes lock on the wheel directly ahead. It's incredibly hard to bridge even a few yards at twenty-five miles an hour as the wall of wind quickly saps your strength.

Years of competitive racing in and around Louisiana provided plenty of experience with this type of riding, yet the endurance and strength I once enjoyed had long since faded. Dead tired and thirty minutes behind schedule, I returned to the parking lot. After only sixty miles, I felt like I'd just completed a particularly challenging century ride.

Maybe it was the bike. The fifteen-year-old, handmade Italian steel bike was probably twice the weight of the newer aluminum or carbon fiber framesets. The heavy, inefficient wheels, worn bearings, and wide, Kevlar-reinforced tires added greatly to the rolling resistance. The top tube, mismatched from the half dozen times I stripped, sanded, and painted it, didn't help the aesthetics. Sentimentality kept the old junker going long beyond its useful life; however, declining fitness and tired legs cried out for a more efficient machine.

Bonnie met me at the iron fence and wagged her tail hopefully. I slowly pushed the gate open and rolled the bike carefully past her. She lingered at the gate while I hung the bike in the garage, retrieved her canvass dog bed and laid it in a shady spot next to the table. There she joined me as I reclined on a cushioned lounge chair under the umbrella. Cricket pushed through the doggie door and climbed upon the bed with Bonnie.

"How was your ride?" Jennifer asked as she joined the family in the back yard. Haley trotted past me and began investigating the holly bushes.

"It was beautiful out there, but it was hard. The wind was unbelievable."

"You look very relaxed. Are you going to get cleaned up so we can go to lunch?"

"I was hoping we could take the dogs to the lake," I replied. "It's such a nice day." I stroked Bonnie's head as her tail thumped gently against the bed.

"I'm already dressed. Let's go out to a nice lunch instead," she replied hopefully.

"How about the hammock? Or, we could lay out a blanket and play Scrabble," I said, referring to our highly competitive tournaments that often came down to the final turn or two, unless the dogs scattered the tiles out of curiosity or carelessness.

"Come on, Jason, we never go anywhere."

"Alright, where do you want to go?" Haley lunged toward a branch of one of the bushes, bit and then chewed as if she'd eaten a spicy jalapeno pepper. Another bee had met its end.

"Maybe Café Japon off Kirby. They have the best sushi."

"That sounds fine, I'll get the tempura. Can we take the dogs to the park after?"

"Maybe. I want to finish working on my crochet. I wish we had some shade out here. I'd love to work on our patio," Jennifer remarked, revisiting a familiar topic.

"There's plenty of shade under the sycamore. I can set the table there for you."

"No, I want to be on my patio. I don't want to sit in the yard. It's ridiculous I can't even use my patio."

"What's wrong with the umbrella? It's like fifteen feet across," I said, pointing to the giant structure above my head.

"I'd rather have an awning."

"An awning will make it look like we live in a trailer."

"I don't know why you're so stubborn."

"Jennifer, I enjoy the sun. If we cover this area, I'll feel like I'm living in a cave when we're in the living room."

"It's always so bright in the house." Haley moved to another bush, stood motionless for a short while, then snapped her jaws shut. One less bee to worry about.

"OK, let's go to lunch," I relented. "Give me a couple minutes to get showered and I'll be ready."

"Anne and Jeff asked about you again," Jennifer said, following me into the house.

"What did you tell them?"

"I said you wanted to go, but something came up. It's embarrassing I'm always there alone."

"You know I can't get my ride done by nine. Sunday's the only day I can meet the group and clear my head. Why can't we go to a church with an afternoon service?"

"Because it's the church where all our friends go. I don't want to go anywhere else."

"What's the big deal? You didn't even go to church when we met. We might've gone twice the whole time we were in Metairie."

"I was raised in the church. I miss going."

"Look, I'm trapped in an office all week. I need to get on my bike when the weekend comes."

"You can make time for an hour, can't you?"

"It's not the hour; it's when the hour is," I explained.

"We're getting left out of things because you aren't in the church. I want us to have more friends."

"Alright. I'll try to make the eleven service."

"Come on, hon. Our friends all go to nine-thirty."

"Sorry, that's as far as I'll go. I promise to go a couple weekends a month, and on the others you can go to your nine-thirty."

"How about this coming weekend?"

"No, I need to go riding. It's the only thing that helps me get my mind off what happened to Clyde. Maybe the following."

"Jason, why don't you pray to Jesus to help you?"

"Because it won't help."

"What do you mean?"

"I mean there's no point to it. Let's leave it alone. I don't want to talk about it."

"Talk about what?"

"Please let it go."

"No, I need you to tell me. What's going on?" Jennifer demanded.

"Look, I don't believe in God, all right? I've been trying for years because it's so important to you—it's just not happening."

"How can you not believe in God? You took communion a couple of months ago."

"I took communion because everyone was walking forward. I didn't want to embarrass you by staying behind."

"Don't you realize you're only supposed to take it if you believe? That's why I bought your beautiful gold cross. I thought you loved Jesus."

"I didn't think it was a big deal," I said, my mind drifting momentarily to the heavy, solid-gold cross hanging from the braided, gold chain around my neck. Other than my wedding ring, it was the only piece of jewelry I'd ever worn. Even though I didn't believe, the cross was special to me.

"How can you not believe in God?"

"I just don't. We almost never went to church when I was a kid. My mom was the only one in the family who believed in God—and look what happened to her."

"God doesn't promise to keep bad things from happening; he only promises to help you through it. Do you really think all of this just happened by chance?"

"All I know is that I don't want to spend my Sundays inside. And, while we're at it, I'm getting a little tired of the constant pressure from you—and the ridiculous television station you always have on."

"I like those shows."

"It's nonstop: the TV, the music, your prayer group—it's like being married to the 'church lady' from *Saturday Night Live*. We never go on bike rides together anymore because you're always tied up at the church and, on the times I do go to church with you, you sing and cry with your arms raised the whole time."

"Don't you dare make fun of how I praise God!"

"I'm sorry—I didn't mean to say that. Let's just drop it."

"What about how much you enjoyed the Chris Rice concert? And all the Jars of Clay music?"

"Yeah, I like it—it still doesn't get me past all the doubts. I can't believe in something just because I want to."

"Don't give up, hon. Please think about coming with me next week."

In the following weeks, I thought about her question a lot—did I really think this was all random? Sure, didn't every intelligent person? Weren't people who believed in God weak, gullible, simple-minded, or all of the above?

Despite my bitterness and doubts, I truly wanted to have the hope and confidence our friends claimed to have—that they could count on God to help them cope with the challenges in their lives. I wanted to believe in heaven—a place where Clyde was restored to health and running free in endless fields of tall grass.

Yet, each time I thought about the concept of God, my brain worked overtime to point out the inconsistencies. *If the universe was created for us, why is our planet on the fringe of a small galaxy in a sea of galaxies? How does time pass in heaven— how can our hyper-stimulated minds cope with eternity when we get bored on a three-hour plane flight? Where did God come from? Where is heaven? If you leave behind your loved ones, how can you be at peace in heaven?* But the key question I came back to was *why did God let my mom suffer and die so horribly?*

Besides, the big bang theory and evolution explained the whole thing, didn't they? The infinitely dense point in space exploded and, over ten or so billion years, formed the galaxies and planets. Then a few billion years later, lightning struck a warm sea filled with the right mixture of chemicals, and life began. Throw in another couple of hundred million years of evolution and that one random mutation morphed into pine trees, mosquitoes, eagles, salmon, snakes, and, of course, humans.

Curiously, I blindly accepted the science-based belief system while demanding proof of God's existence. Once I began to scrutinize the foundation of my beliefs, I realized I was also on shaky ground. *Where did the matter come from to initiate the big bang? What is our universe expanding into? If life was the result of random events, why wouldn't life just appear at discreet points in time, live out its life, and then die? How could the ability to reproduce spontaneously occur? Why didn't the process of natural selection improve the organism's ability to feed and multiply and eventually lead to depletion of food and starvation of the colony?* Somehow, there had to be the random creation of a predator to keep the population in control, or at least another species to convert the waste material back into usable food.

Why are there so many separate and distinct species? Incredible genetic variation has occurred in dogs over the centuries, yielding some no bigger than my hand, others close the size of a horse, and everything in between. Different coat textures, colors, fur length, body shape, snout appearance, tail length, and on and on. *How do dogs always know it's another dog? With all the genetic variation foisted upon dogs through the ages, why hasn't one line diverged far enough to create confusion, much less a new species? So how can a completely different species arise out of natural selection? Why aren't new species being created today? Why don't we see the random creation of life that had to have occurred so frequently in the past?*

Another issue was fur—or, more accurately, the lack of fur on our bodies. *Why did we lose the fur and hard feet of our supposed ape ancestors?* Wouldn't it make more sense from an natural selection standpoint to not have to worry about freezing to death or finding the right shoes? My dogs can handle temperatures from the single digits to above a hundred without a wardrobe change. They can dive into an icy pond without a wetsuit. They can run on asphalt, snow, concrete, or rocks without a change of shoes. Seems like fur and hard feet would provide great advantages without any apparent disadvantages.

The more I looked at it, the more I saw a leap of faith was required for both belief systems. And, with that perspective, it was just as reasonable, perhaps more reasonable, to believe in God. Though I hadn't prayed in over twenty years, the pain of losing Clyde helped me put my bitterness aside and reach out to Him.

"God, please heal my mind and heart," I begged several times a day. "Hold Clyde in your arms, restore his health, and let him run in endless fields." It felt unnatural and, after all I had said and done, a little self-serving to pray out of desperation, yet I continued to ask for his help. I wanted to believe Clyde was safe and we'd one day be together again.

One evening at church, I prayed the painful memories of Clyde's last day, constantly looping through my mind, would soon fade. After a few minutes, I imagined Clyde lying upside down on the living room carpet, his right arm extended skyward, his left bent at the elbow and the wrist—his head back, eyes closed, jowls relaxed exposing a few teeth.

I held the vision in my mind and savored it—he looked so peaceful and content. The beautiful image helped me smile sometimes when I thought of Clyde.

CHAPTER TEN

Sunrise

In the last few years of Clyde's life, I let him off leash during our morning walks. If he found anything of interest, I had confidence I could run him down before he got into trouble. Clyde loved the freedom—trotting through gardens and in and out of driveways, occasionally startling someone on their way to the newspaper. With Clyde gone, I was able to let Bonnie off leash during our predawn expeditions. Without fail, she walked the same paths her brother had taken, nose working overtime, hoping to catch his scent. Although Bonnie was in decent spirits afterward, she wasn't the same dog. Something inside had begun to burn out.

On the physical side, Bonnie was changing as well. Her silky fur had become rough and wiry from her shoulders to her tail with heavy dandruff enmeshed in the brittle fibers. She weakened noticeably, our walks becoming shorter, and simple tasks like getting on the couch appearing more difficult. The vet chalked it up to aging, but I was surprised at how quickly she was deteriorating. I didn't have the mental energy to devote to the problem. I accepted the vet's prognosis and moved on.

Before Clyde died, I didn't have time to notice, much less solve, Bonnie's problems. Time wasn't an issue now—the hours I had spent each day tending to Clyde were now mine again. I was finally free of all the stress, but it wasn't what I wanted. I wanted Clyde. All the hassles, all the frustration—I would have gladly accepted for more time with him.

A few months after Clyde's death, Jennifer handed me an article regarding an adoption event at the Citizens for Animal Protection shelter. The story of a lonely, black Lab-mix puppy—the spitting image of Bonnie, tugged at my heart. I was almost certain I didn't want another dog. None could possibly measure up to the incredible friend I once had. Even if it was a decent dog, I'd never let it get close. I didn't want to feel the intense grief again.

An hour later, I walked through a maze of volunteers, visitors, and dogs at the shelter. The dog featured in the article had been adopted, leaving dozens of less-famous animals still looking for a home. I wandered through a sea of dogs, hoping for a connection and finding none.

Realizing I wasn't ready to move on, I walked back to my vehicle and reflected on Clyde. I opened the console and pulled out the picture I so often looked at—Clyde lying on the carpet, his head on my shoulder, his body by my side, peacefully sleeping. The image brought the familiar rush of emotions—love, longing, despair.

I glanced up and noticed a "Hound Rescue" banner draped on the side of a large bus. My eyes were immediately drawn to a window, against which a dog with cream-colored fur—the same shade as Clyde's, leaned. As I approached the bus, the dog turned, revealing a small, white patch of fur on the crown of her head and light cream-colored patches on her shoulder blades—just like Clyde! Of the dozen dogs inside the bus, she was the only one waiting at the front of her cage as I walked through. She licked my fingers through the small openings in the steel mesh, wagging her tail wildly as I read the card attached to her cage: Angel—Doberman/Lab mix, four months old, twenty-five pounds, reason for adoption—needs too much attention, very active.

"Are you guys connected to the shelter here?" I asked.

"No, we're from Tyler. We're just here for the day."

"How long have you had this one?"

"We got this one and her sister yesterday."

The sister was a beautiful puppy, appearing less anxious and excitable than her cage-mate sibling. The little girl's only flaw was she looked nothing like Clyde.

"Can I take this one out for a walk?" I asked, pointing at the thin, cream-colored, miniature Clyde.

"Sure, let me get you a leash."

We walked for a while and then sat together on a small patch of grass adjacent to the parking lot. As I caressed her soft fur, she laid her paws on my shoulders and began licking my face. With my free hand, I dialed Jennifer's number.

"You won't believe it. There's a puppy here that looks like Clyde. I want to adopt her. What do you think?" I asked, already knowing the answer.

"You need to get her! Bring her home!"

"Thanks, hon, you won't believe how sweet she is."

Two days later, after spaying, she slept peacefully on the drive to her new home. Once the groggy new addition arrived, Haley, Bonnie, and Cricket took turns carefully inspecting her. With introductions complete, she climbed onto the couch, curled up on my chest and fell quickly asleep. Soon thereafter, feeling completely at peace with my decision, I joined her.

Angel was certainly a name reflecting her beauty and affection. For whatever reason, she didn't respond to it and neither did I. I wanted to name her in honor of a good animal, like I had done for Clyde, to set her life on the right track. Kelly, a big, pretty lab we often shared the island with, was the first name to come to mind. Most days, she was already retrieving when Bonnie and Clyde arrived and still retrieving when we left. There were a few dustups between her and Clyde, both animals being the dominant members of their packs, but they usually got along pretty well. Even after she developed bone cancer, she continued to walk several miles each day and relentlessly retrieve until she collapsed and died. Strong, courageous, loyal, sweet, dominant—Angel's new name was Kelli.

Once Kelli recovered from the surgery, we went on our first long walk together. Kelli immediately pegged the dial past one-hundred percent, pulling the leash taut, muscles straining to accelerate the large human tethered to her neck. She was completely unfazed by the discomfort, but the choking and struggling quickly depressed me. Once she was outfitted with a chest harness, we both enjoyed the walks more.

Despite her small size, the tenacious creature generated sled-dog power. With no desire to sniff and mark, she pulled relentlessly; legs crouched slightly, moving in a steady, determined rhythm. Often, I broke into a jog, attempting to satisfy her needs, yet the pressure on the leash never waned.

Because we were clearly at two different levels of fitness, I searched for safe places to let her run free. One of the first destinations was a small reservoir ten miles north of our house. The pond was part of a large wilderness area that served as natural drainage for heavy rainfall in the city. Separated from the main road by a wide canal and tall levee, it was surrounded by thousands of acres of swampland and dense woods. Each visit, Jennifer and I threw the buoy dozens of times, yet the puppy never seemed to tire. Bonnie fatigued after a few throws and watched most of the proceedings from the shore. Haley had no interest in the water, content to hunt along its banks and patiently wait for the walk that always followed Kelli's swim time.

On one of the first visits, Kelli, unaware of proper pond etiquette, retrieved another dog's buoy. The giant dog pursued Kelli who, startled and fearing for her life, ran to me for protection. It was the only time Kelli ever backed down from another canine at the pond. It didn't matter how big the other was; Kelli was the dominant animal in every encounter she had. I was always a little concerned she might come across an ill-tempered creature and end up on the losing side of the standoff.

Kelli's affection and playfulness quickly lifted the gloom from our home. When I noticed characteristics similar to those of my old companion—tugging at my arm for more caresses, leaning against me, pressing her hips against my side, sleeping upside down with arms stretched skyward, or impatiently waiting for time in the hammock—I was able to relive the joy of Clyde's early years.

Cricket responded to the new puppy's relentless thirst for play. It had been years since I had seen Cricket in such carefree, silly spirits. Bonnie showed great affection for the new arrival, reveling in the opportunity to mentor the puppy along the banks of the canal near our home. Kelli followed the expert hunter and watched intently, learning the proper way to flush mice and launch surprise attacks on water fowl.

Haley was initially indifferent to the new addition, but, as Bonnie's health continued to deteriorate, she assumed both the pack leader and mother roles. Until then, she had been almost invisible in the house and in our lives, yet now she was in the middle of everything. If Haley and Kelli weren't exploring, they were wrestling or playing tug of war. Their sessions, filled with growling, lunging, and biting, hardly looked innocent—sometimes appearing as though Haley was trying to seriously hurt Kelli. After breaking them up on a number of occasions, I realized I was just getting in the way of their fun. Haley was simply teaching Kelli the skills she might one day need to defend herself.

CHAPTER ELEVEN

Kodi!

"Hon, I found a dog in the parking lot at my office," Jennifer said. "She's all beat up and pitiful."

"Don't bring her home—take her straight to the pound. Bonnie's not doing well."

"I'm already pulling in our driveway. You'll have to take her in when you get home from work."

"We already have four…" I stammered as the call disconnected.

I headed home that day in October, anticipating a battle over the stray dog's future. We'd been in violation of the three-pet deed restriction since Kelli joined us six months earlier. We couldn't take the chance of adding a fifth dog, especially one off the streets.

I pulled to the back gate and studied the new arrival. About the same size as Kelli, she appeared, beneath the grime, to be painted with an inverted color template of Kelli's—black traded for cream and brown replacing white. Based on her white, sharp teeth, I guessed her age at less than a year, though the cuts on her head and large raw patches on her chest gave her the appearance of an old junkyard dog.

I watched as Kelli and the stray rolled and wrestled in the yard, acting as though they'd known each other all their lives. The dog backed off a bit and clacked her jaws as a bear does while attempting to intimidate its opponent. Every few minutes, she grabbed one of Kelli's legs, tripped her, and quickly pinned her to the ground. Then, she rolled on her back as Kelli locked her jaws around her neck or tugged on her legs.

"Maybe the poor thing was a bait dog," I said. "She had to be around aggressive animals to learn how to clack her jaws like that. And it explains the cuts on her head."

"She's so beat up—and kind of mean looking. No one is going to want this thing." Jennifer was right. She not only looked mean, she looked downright homely sitting next to Kelli. The odds were against anyone adopting such an unappealing creature. She'd probably end up in the cage for a long time—or worse. More importantly, Kelli, who'd never shown an interest in dogs outside our pack, appeared to love the little thing.

"I don't have the heart to take her in," I said, eliciting a big smile from Jennifer. "And, from the way they're behaving, it looks they might've been separated at birth."

After a badly needed flea bath, the new family member met Bonnie, Cricket, and Haley. In the middle of introductions, Kelli mounted a sneak attack, initiating a new round of running and wrestling. This time, Haley joined in—grabbing her neck while Kelli locked onto one of her back legs. As they tugged at her, she popped up and zigzagged through the yard at top speed, fell to the ground, and let them do it to her again. She had so much energy—and personality.

"How about we name her Kodi?" I asked. "It can be short for Kodiak, like the bears in Alaska, you know, the ones who clack their jaws."

"That's kind of an odd name, don't you think?"

"Well, her formal name will be Kodiferus Jones. I think that better fits her unique looks, don't you?"

"You come up with the craziest stuff sometimes. I'll just call her Kodi," Jennifer said, smiling warmly at the newly-named family member.

Strangely, within days of Kodi's arrival, all of the leashes hung on the fence were severed in half—each nylon strap cut cleanly, as if a knife had been used. After a round of replacements met the same fate, I began locking the leashes in the garage to keep them safe from the leash vandals that, for some reason, were targeting our home.

Until Kodi's wounds healed, I leashed her neck collar, making it difficult to walk the spirited animals together while connected at different points. A pretty, blue harness, bought to match to Kelli's and make the walks easier, wasn't embraced as a welcome change by the little puppy. Actually, she feared the new harness, often hiding when I began to hook up Kelli.

The deep brush burns under her arms, the cuts and nicks on her face, the limp in her right leg, the fact she adored small children and hid when teenagers visited, all pointed to a sad conclusion. She must have been beaten by teens or attacked by dogs while confined by a harness and probably escaped by severing the connecting rope. Trust would need to be built slowly with the traumatized creature.

A few weeks after rescuing Kodi, we took her to our new vet at Stanford Pines. Their on-site lab promised to help manage Bonnie's failing health, and visits to the old practice dredged up too many painful memories. Along with the normal shots, the vet recommended we have Kodi spayed. My inclination, based on Bonnie's erratic behavior, was to wait until after the first heat so she could mature properly. The vet assured us the spay had no effect on the dog's personality, while waiting had its own set of risks—a pregnancy or, something I hadn't considered, she might dig out in search of a mate.

The day of surgery, the vet called and said he couldn't find her uterus, even after extending the incision. He brought in other doctors to consult and each thought it strange. Sadly, the vet and his associates didn't have the sense to realize Kodi had already been fixed.

We were home only a few minutes when the sutures began to unravel, allowing part of the six-inch incision to pull open. I rushed her to Lexington Animal Hospital.

"We're going to have to use staples to hold this together," Dr. Stanley said, examining the fresh wound.

"I don't know why they tried to close such a long incision with stitches," I replied.

"Sometimes sutures are fine as long as you use several layers. Oh, look here," she said, pointing to bumps surrounding the incision. "She's got a bacterial infection covering most of her abdomen."

"How could they have missed that?" I asked, my frustration rising.

"I don't know. It's definitely a bacterial infection."

"Can you give her a local for the staples? I don't want her to go under anesthesia again. She's still groggy from the surgery. I think my last dog developed Addison's from getting too much." I then recounted an abbreviated version of some of the trials and tribulations of Clyde's life.

"Unfortunately, we'll have to put her under. There's no other way. Don't worry, we've got a very experienced staff, and I personally supervise the anesthesia."

Following the procedure, Kodi was outfitted with a head cone to keep her from chewing at the staples. Catching it on just about everything as she walked through the house, she scratched continuously in a futile attempt to dislodge the irritating device. When I left for work the next day, I kenneled Kodi to keep her from getting into trouble. That evening, after finding her in a complete panic, hurling herself against the walls of the kennel, I removed the offensive cone and hoped for the best. She gently licked at the incision site and, fortunately, didn't try to rip the staples out. Once the wound healed, I used wire cutters and tweezers to carefully remove the staples, figuring the less contact with a vet, even a good vet, the better.

Once Kodi was strong enough, we returned to our long walks. Kelli and Kodi were fairly easy to manage at a walking pace, but rarely did they let me walk for long. They pulled relentlessly, increasing our pace until I was on the verge of falling over. Often, my mind drifted back a dozen years to the long, predawn walks with Bonnie and Clyde that I, for so long, had missed. We also visited Kelli's favorite natural oasis, the pond several miles north of our house. The weekend trips, filled with hours of running and retrieving, had been scuttled with all the activity surrounding Kodi's arrival.

At the top of the tall levee separating the pond from the main road, I unhooked Kodi and Kelli, allowing them to sprint the quarter mile to the lake. Kodi loved the water, despite a swimming technique that barely kept her afloat. Kelli always reached the buoy long before her, quickly snuffing Kodi's competitive instincts. Instead, she sprinted through the shallow sections, sending showers of water flying. She charged out to attack Kelli and then retreated to a defensive position in the water. Kelli gave chase and they wrestled and played for hours.

A few weeks later, as they sprinted toward the lake, Kelli turned abruptly and headed into the dense woods with Kodi following closely behind. I ran to the edge of the thicket and screamed for them to return, stunned they disappeared so quickly and so completely. If they didn't return, it would be nearly impossible to track them down. *What if they come back while I'm wandering aimlessly in the woods?* My chest tightened as I heard a dog yelp far in the distance.

Fifteen minutes later, Kodi, panting heavily and highly excited, emerged. I hooked her up, said "Go get Kelli!" and followed her into the woods. The swampy terrain, densely covered by thorny bushes atop mucky soil, slowed our progress considerably. "Go get Kelli!" I reminded Kodi every few steps. I trudged on, calling Kelli's name, fearing a run-in with some wild creature caused Kelli to cry out. The silence compounded my anxiety, thinking she'd bark if she was still alive.

After twenty minutes, we happened upon Kelli—shivering with fear and covered with abrasions. "Kellibells! Thank God you're safe! Calm down, girl, everything's going to be OK," I said, hugging her wiggling body and caressing her face while she licked me and danced with joy. "Good girl, Kodi!" I said, giving a warm embrace to the day's hero and providing her with a share of the caresses. Though our route appeared aimless at times, Kodi knew exactly where she was going.

Relieved we escaped disaster and sad we'd never return, I drove my puppies home.

At the house, the two youngsters spent most of their time in the yard with Haley. Kodi, the primary target of Kelli and Haley's aggression, wasn't just a good sport about it, she encouraged it. Like the day she arrived, she initiated contact and had them chase her. Then, she fell to the ground as they grabbed at her neck and limbs. Just like the combat prior to Kodi's arrival, it always looked serious.

Haley also began teaching her new charges the art of squirrel surveillance. Haley's technique was different from the wild barking and jumping once exhibited by Bonnie and Clyde. Instead, she sat motionless, mesmerized by the halting movements of the tiny creature, patiently waiting for the squirrel to approach before launching an attack. Kodi adopted the sit, stare, and wait technique and was able to keep her composure until Kelli's frenzied leaping and barking took their toll. Kelli's thighs, heavily muscled from hours of pulling a two-hundred-pound human, allowed her to easily soar above the fence top, kicking off slightly as half her body floated momentarily above the barrier. Kodi, lacking Kelli's graceful vertical leap, charged at the fence and grappled her arms atop the splintery, wood boards. She held on, muscles straining, head scanning from side to side, frantically searching for the intruder.

Haley believed nothing, not even a six-foot wood fence, should get in the way of squirrel pursuits. If she couldn't dig under, she chewed off the bottom of the fence board. When I blocked the bottom with steel mesh, she found a weak board, broke it and pulled the plank off. On one occasion, with adrenaline surging through her body, she scrambled over the top and found herself trapped in the neighbor's yard until I came home.

I guess the neighbor dogs share some of the blame for the fence destruction. Bailey, a huge, somewhat chubby, black lab, and Tiger, a brindle, tiger-striped boxer mix, desperately wanted to play with our dogs, though you'd never know it by the way they "talked" to each other through the fence. Despite their apparent hostility when separated, I often came home to find Tiger and Bailey engaged in a high-energy wrestling match with my canines. The fence boards had either been pulled off, chewed through or, sometimes, snapped in half from brute force. After quick repairs, I'd leash the escapees and walk the long block to repatriate them to their own territory.

"Did they get out again?" Mike asked as Tiger and Bailey wagged their tails.

"This time they pulled two boards from your side." I didn't know Mike very well despite the close proximity of our homes. Mike was an ex-pro football player—easily six-four, two-hundred-fifty pounds. He was an intimidating presence, yet had a kindness and warmth that belied his tough exterior. "I think you have some nails exposed," I added.

"Thanks, I'll get Ben out here to cut some planks and nail them up. I'm real sorry the dogs keep harassing you."

"It's not a problem at all. I really enjoy watching them play. It's a shame they have to work so hard to get together. Hey, what do you think about me setting up a gate between our yards? They're bound and determined anyway—might as well make it easier on all of us."

"You know how to do that?"

"Sure, I'll take off two boards and hang one in the middle of the gap. I'll set it up with wing nuts so I can take it off easily."

"That sounds like a great idea. Bailey and Tiger sure get lonely sometimes." Mike appeared impressed by my quick solution to the problem, not realizing I had been thinking about it for weeks and waiting for an opportunity to pitch the innovation.

"I'll ask you before I take the board off each time. I don't want you to feel like we're commandeering your yard."

"Jason, anytime you want to let the dogs play, just open 'er up. I promise it won't bother me a bit."

"Thanks, Mike. I'm pretty sure it'll put an end to the destruction. I'll have the new setup done by the weekend."

With the new gate operational, the first of many running battles was initiated—five dogs racing through the gap, sprinting, wrestling and tumbling end over end into the large expanse of Mike's yard. Sated by their daily interaction, the destruction of the fence, as predicted, ceased. The only exceptions occurred when we vacationed with the dogs. The disappearance of their friends caused sufficient anxiety for Bailey and Tiger to tear down a section of fence in their desperate search. One time, we forgot to close the doggie door and found the two happy dogs lounging in our house. No damage was done and it was nice to return to such an enthusiastic welcoming committee.

While life was filled with adventure and excitement for the new arrivals, Bonnie's time, only nine months after Clyde died, had come. She lost her sight a few weeks after Kodi arrived, a result of veterinary mistakes and failures on my part. Blindness, weak muscles, and bad hips impaired her balance, causing her to fall frequently. Her nasal passages became swollen and caused her to work for each breath.

On several occasions, I made an appointment to have Bonnie euthanized, only to cancel and hope the next day she'd improve. I finally went through with it, feeling it had to be done, yet knowing she wasn't ready to give up. The painful images of her last day, seared into my memory, continue to haunt me as I write these words. At least with Clyde I knew, despite the mistakes I made, I tried everything I could think of to help him.

CHAPTER TWELVE

Exploration

After our harrowing experience, I began searching for a safer venue to let the energetic pups run free. The local dog parks were tested and quickly abandoned, as the small, confined spaces, feces-laden grounds, and the stench of filthy ponds left me quite depressed. Kelli's dominant, sometimes hostile, reaction to the other canine visitors, made trips to the park nerve-racking as well.

A combination of safety and aesthetics was the goal—long, quiet trails snaking through dense, green foliage, shaded beneath towering pine trees, leading to a picturesque lake or cool stream where the dogs could run free without the risk of getting hurt or lost. In and around the heavily developed, flatland known as Houston, a place possessing any of those attributes, much less all, was a tall order.

Twenty miles south of our home stood Brazos Bend State Park—a beautiful nature preserve with tall trees, colorful birds and ducks, deer, feral hogs, poisonous snakes and, the most popular attraction of the park, alligators. A walking path encircled hundreds of acres of swamp, its waters obscuring all but the heads of alligators silently drifting by, its banks supporting the immense reptiles bathing in the warm sunlight, their massive jaws held open. The wide dirt trail was shaded by a canopy of Spanish moss-laden oak trees whose branches were strung together by a patchwork of giant spider webs, some seven or eight feet in diameter, each hosting a brightly-colored, hummingbird-sized, poisonous banana spider, motionless in its center, waiting patiently for its next meal.

On our visits, we avoided, as much as possible, the routes with the highest probability of encountering an alligator. According to the park rangers, there had never been an attack, though I doubted the creatures, possessing the speed, agility, and strength to take down wild pigs, would hesitate to snatch one of my dogs if given the chance. Instead, we jogged the less-popular, narrow horse trails near the rear of the park, enjoying the quiet solitude far removed from the domain of the ancient reptiles.

During one early morning run, a rhinoceros-sized pig emerged from the woods fifteen yards ahead, bringing us to a dead stop. Surprised by our approach, he hesitated, turning his massive, hairy head toward us. Kelli and Kodi barked wildly, straining against their leashes and lunging toward the giant creature. The beast stood motionless, glaring at the wild dogs. Each scenario I imagined ended poorly—if he charged us, I'd have to drop the leashes, run like hell, and hope the puppies had enough sense to follow me. Hope of a peaceful outcome faded as eight Cricket-sized piglets exited the woods and, one after the other, crossed the trail behind the giant pig, sending the puppies into a frenzy. The hog stood defensively but, thankfully, followed the last piglet into the woods.

We finished our run and returned from time to time, yet my anxiety increased with each visit. Jogging the narrow trails through dense underbrush, I not only worried we'd run across a more aggressive hog, I feared we might startle a poisonous snake.

Only twenty minutes from our house, the park was a beautiful, unspoiled, wild retreat. Unfortunately, it was a bit too wild for us.

Huntsville State Park, about an hour north of our house, offered miles of single-track mountain bike trails, towering pines, lush foliage and, beyond the reach of Houston's smog, each breath drew clean, crisp air. Both in prime physical condition, Kelli and Kodi had no trouble with the seven-mile, heavily rutted trail. Stopping only to answer nature's call, we ran from the moment we left the parking area, occasionally dodging oncoming mountain bikes and passing those struggling on the hills. The relatively short, steep inclines, almost effortless with the two powerful dogs pulling me, became the highlight of the dogs' visit. Their excitement was palpable as they approached each hill, knowing they were about to run full out and pull for all they were worth. On the flats, they learned to dial their effort back to keep me upright and, on the descents, they learned to cut their speed even more. Even with their best efforts to accommodate my pace, I occasionally twisted an ankle or knee as one of thousands of steps failed to properly account for the bumpy, leaf and root-covered ground.

We returned to the park as often as the oppressive south Texas heat and humidity allowed. Jennifer and Haley occasionally joined us, following at a leisurely pace, as we ran the trails ahead.

As the months passed, Jennifer and Haley joined us less and less, as the long drive home, heavy traffic, and blighted views of Houston's roadways quickly eroded the pleasant memories of the hike. I didn't care for the drive either, but realized the unpleasant journey was the main reason we could enjoy solitude on the trails.

Galveston Island, a popular beach destination ninety minutes southeast of our home, paled in comparison to my memories of Florida's clear, blue water and miles of white, sandy beaches lined with swaying sea oats. The Galveston beach was little more than a narrow spit of rock and sand between a four-lane highway and the murky, brownish-hued, foamy ocean.

A dozen miles south of the main stretch, the seawall ended and the road veered west a few hundred yards, exposing a broad beach dotted with small cottages and large hotels. At the state park near Jamaica Beach, we explored the Texas version of coastal paradise.

After acclimating to the sight of broken beer bottles and the smell of rotting seaweed, I began to notice the positives—the sound of crashing waves, the songs of gulls flying overhead, small birds tracking the water's edge, scurrying inches from the rapidly moving tongue of water, searching for small periwinkles and other crustaceans. Confident the dogs had sufficient distractions, we let them run free. They sprinted ahead, flushing the small birds and gulls flocking at the water's edge.

Kodi crouched slightly a few yards offshore, hiding most of her body in the shallow water, and waited for Kelli to retrieve her. Always more interested in moving forward, Kelli ignored or didn't understand the new game. Kodi lunged from her semi-invisible position, sprinted to the shore and slammed into Kelli, knocking her to the ground. Quickly on her feet, Kelli gave chase and they wrestled playfully in the surf. Every quarter mile or so, Kodi began the game anew and, after a few direct hits, Kelli began to look over her shoulder more often.

For the next few months, we returned to the small beach refuge at least once a week. On one visit, the wind was blowing offshore, calming the normal wave action. Without the distractions of the heavy surf, and with new scents in the air, Kelli sampled the breeze more frequently than normal. A few hundred yards down the beach, she raised her head skyward, sniffed furiously, and sprinted from the water's edge with Kodi locked on her heels. Within moments, they crossed the sand dunes and, despite my frantic pleas, accelerated across a small road. I ran after them, my steps slowed greatly in the soft sand, watching as they headed toward the divided highway a half mile away. They sprinted across the heavily traveled road, completing a large arc beyond. They raced back toward me, crossing the road once more, their joyous celebration replaced by confusion as I spanked their hindquarters so hard my hand hurt.

Dodging another bullet, we ended our Galveston expeditions.

Quite a step down from the beauty and freedom of the weekend excursions, the dogs still enjoyed their walks through the neighborhood. One morning, we were startled when, with only a grunt as a warning, the six-foot brick wall adjacent to the walking path shook as the resident dog slammed into it. I nearly jumped out of my skin when his massive head, barking and biting furiously, and half his hundred-pound Labrador body reached over the wall. Not wanting Kelli and Kodi to respond to the provocation, I pulled them away before they could get into trouble.

Kelli and Kodi became obsessed with the mysterious, massive, barking head floating atop the wall. On subsequent walks, they strained against their leashes within a block of the house and tried to scale the wall, responding to their tormentor. Each time, I pulled them back—causing Kodi to do the occasional backflip when she hit the end of the leash too hard.

To avoid the commotion, I crossed the road and walked the grass-covered levee until we passed the aggressive canine. After testing the new route a few times, Kodi tumbled over directly across from the Lab's home. She laid on her side, panting heavily, eyes darting rapidly. Responding to my request to get moving, she took a few steps toward the wall, strained against the leash, and then fell over again. I slid her gently along the grass by her chest harness until she popped to her feet and, once again, pulled toward the wall and dropped to the ground.

"You want to go see your friend?" I asked Kodi playfully. In response to my question, Kodi's tail beat furiously against the ground and she quickly stood and pulled against the leash. As we approached the wall, the massive dog shook the brick structure and locked his arms at the top. Kelli and Kodi leaped and nipped at him while he barked and bit. It was all in good fun—I think—Kelli and Kodi didn't show any signs of aggression. I can't speak to the feelings of the Lab, but each day he was waiting for our arrival.

One morning, a few moments after visiting the Lab's house, Kodi fell to her side. The same routine had begun, only this time her target was the levee. Knowing I'd eventually lose the test of willpower, I acquiesced and followed her across the road. At the levee, we turned left and passed behind the water treatment plant. A hundred yards beyond, the path atop the levee disappeared under thick weeds, and the east edge widened to include a vast expanse of tall flowering plants and dense grasses. The nearest road lay a mile north across a wide, deep canal, the nearest house a half mile south across the rough, grassy terrain.

Once off leash, they showed enthusiasm I'd never seen before. And with Kelli and Kodi, that was really saying something. Kodi sprinted out thirty yards and then charged straight at Kelli, ramming her chest at full speed. They tumbled end over end down the levee, chased each other into the grassy area, over hills densely covered with tall weeds, and sprinted along the wood fences looking for squirrels. They ran and ran, sprinting back to me every few minutes to ensure I was alright. Each time they returned, I praised their thoughtfulness and smiled as they quickly returned to their fun.

The place was ideally suited to Kelli's abilities and desires. She ran large sweeping loops a quarter mile through the wild flowers, easily topping speeds of thirty miles an hour. Kelli's long, lean body moved like a thoroughbred race horse—pure poetry in motion. Kodi, sporting the same weight, lacking an inch in stature, gaining an inch in width, appeared bullish as she barreled after her. She could keep pace with Kelli and cut sharper corners, though it always appeared she was moving slower than her elegant friend.

What Kodi lacked in grace, she more than made up for in personality. After a few visits to our new spot, Kodi revisited the game of hide-and-seek she developed in Galveston. After running with Kelli for a while, she fell behind and drifted off into the tall grass. While Kelli looked ahead, she quickly dropped to her belly and lay motionless. Kelli, noticing her friend was missing, ran to me and scanned the horizon for signs of Kodi. I walked to a point on the levee about thirty yards in front of Kodi's hiding spot.

"Go get Kodi! Kelli, go get Kodi!" I shouted. Kelli's ears perked up and she bounced her front legs, hopping along the levee top, searching for Kodi. "Go get Kodi!" I repeated. Kelli sprinted into the grass, unsure of her destination, making tighter and tighter circles, eventually coming within a few feet of the crouched canine. Kodi then sprang from hiding to chase Kelli back to me. A little farther down the levee, Kodi dropped back and hid, beginning the game anew. Though Kelli lost interest after four or five episodes, Kodi never tired of the game. I had to keep track of Kodi's location, because she was nearly invisible in the dense cover and wouldn't budge until someone retrieved her. After heavy rains, Kodi's repertoire included an aquatic version of the game. With only her head exposed, she resembled a small, furry hippo, wallowing in the muddy, shallow puddles.

Despite our proximity to houses and surrounding roads, there was a sense of wildness. After a period of unusually heavy rains, a pond, more than one hundred feet in diameter and a foot deep, formed adjacent to the levee. The pond persisted for months, attracting species of ducks and birds normally found twenty miles south in Brazos Bend Park. Each visit, Kodi sprinted a quarter mile to the water's edge, lunged in, scattering the birds. She jumped and swam through the shallow water and then commenced her hippo routine. She dunked her head under, searching for aquatic inhabitants, then chased any ducks that were bold enough to return. Kelli eventually retrieved her, initiating the high-energy bouts of wrestling and chase.

Every now and then I saw what looked like wild dogs or coyotes moving in the distance. Though they were hemmed in by major highways and fences, they seemed to thrive in the relatively tiny oasis. The tall grasses provided a steady diet of mice and the canal, even in dry conditions, was a good source of water. During the spring, when the wind was just right, I could hear the faint sound of pups crying, apparently coming from an old broken-down, tin shack about a quarter mile from the levee.

A little after dawn one day, Kelli, making her normal rounds through the grass, stopped, lifted her head, and immediately ran toward the tin shack. "Kelli! Come!" I shouted. Ignoring my command, she advanced within ten feet of a coyote, then stood motionless. After twenty seconds, they simultaneously turned and went their separate ways. I don't know what was said, but, from then on, when the coyotes saw us coming, they dropped down and hid. When we approached downwind, Kelli and Kodi sometimes got close enough to see them and give chase. The coyotes had no interest in playing; they just wanted to be left alone, disappearing quickly into the grass or, if they were near the canal, into one of the drainage pipes.

The levee was our favorite destination for many months until heavy equipment moved in and new housing construction began, causing us to walk farther along the levee before off-leash play could begin. When a road at the far end of the levee opened, we had to shorten the walk by a quarter mile. As the development progressed, they filled the pond where Kodi once played and built roads where the tall wildflowers had been. The coyotes disappeared shortly after the grass was cut and the mice that once provided sustenance were quickly dispatched by hawks.

With the increased construction came another unwanted byproduct—human waste. Kodi was the first to find a pile and, before I could intervene, happily ate it. Kelli wasn't interested in consumption; she had bigger plans. I watched her stop in the distance, sniff, then smear both sides of her face against the ground, then roll onto her back and wiggle. She sprinted back to me, wagging her tail, wearing what looked like a brown sweater. On the long hike home, she held her head high and pranced as if leading a parade. Kodi trotted alongside, sniffing her from time to time, gazing at her with great admiration. It was during those times I was reminded they were dogs.

So, it was back to the leashes and back to the sidewalks. The only respite for Kelli was at the park where she found a few targets interesting enough to captivate her attention. I unleashed the pups at the canal, allowing them to sprint a hundred yards to a fence behind which several rabbits and small dogs resided. They raced along the fence line, barking at the inhabitants until I caught up to them. It wasn't much—barely enough to let them stretch their muscles a bit.

Their favorite targets were the many squirrels found attending to pecans both on the ground and in the trees. When we saw one, I made the dogs sit, yelled the word "Squirrel!" and unhooked their leashes. They sprinted to the tree and Kelli leaped seven or eight feet off the ground, often missing the squirrel by only a few inches. Kodi, always giving it her best shot, was too heavy to get any real air—barely reaching six feet on a good day.

Kelli's long, powerful legs covered a lot of ground quickly, often creating a fleeting sense of panic, until she turned and headed back toward me. She loved to run—no, she lived to run. And I loved to watch her.

Kelli's life was complete freedom and pure joy.

CHAPTER THIRTEEN

Destruction

"Who did this?" I demanded with a stern voice. Kodi's tail wagged nervously, thumping against the frame of the small kitchen table, as she lowered her head and tucked her ears. Kelli quickly disappeared into the dining room, hiding quietly under the mahogany buffet.

"Who did this?" I repeated in a softer voice, pointing to the shredded pillow. From the safety of her hiding place, Kodi's tail increased its tempo and her body began wiggling.

"It's OK, girl. I know you can't help it," I said, crouching to meet her eyes. She immediately dove toward me, her body convulsing with delight at having been pardoned so easily. Kelli sprinted to join us and their dancing revved into high gear. After a few moments, they both pressed against me, demanding full body rubs as further proof they were forgiven.

The dogs could sense my mood by the tone of my voice, and I could predict the amount of damage they did by observing their behavior upon my return. On days when something was shredded, they skipped their normal euphoric gate-side greeting and hid inside the house. They knew their behavior was unacceptable, yet couldn't control themselves when "in the moment."

With Kodi onboard, destruction became commonplace. Anything left out in our absence was likely to be ripped to shreds. Often, I came home to find their giant dog beds pulled outside through the doggie door, and, on a good number of occasions, the stuffing covered the backyard like a polyester snowfall. Jennifer soon lost patience with the continual mess and thought the dogs should be relegated to the yard while we were away. Not wanting my puppies to lose their house privileges, I often hid the damage, hustling home to destroy evidence of canine wrongdoing prior to Jennifer's arrival.

The puppies didn't make it easy on me—a new, previously unrecognized, target appeared almost weekly. Our oversized, green couch, adorned with giant soft fabric cushions and large throw pillows, became the first victim of their destructive instincts. One by one, the pillows were torn apart, often leaving the den covered in a blanket of down feathers. Because the couch was Jennifer's favorite place to spend time, the dwindling pillow count was certain to be noticed—and the dogs were destined to live the tough life in the yard.

As a stopgap measure, I moved all but two pillows to the closet. The large store of replacement pillows would hopefully provide enough time to change the dogs' behavior. The pillow count steadily dropped in the closet, the loss of each increasing the odds the dogs would be sent outside. I continued to clean up after them, correct them, and hope for the best.

One day, they stripped the skirting off the couch, exposing a two-foot section of the white base fabric. Luckily for the pups, I had saved a few undamaged sections of the pillow cases, planning one day to have them repaired, and was able to cut them to fit the torn section. The replacement pieces, bearing the identical color but different texture than the skirting, appeared a reasonable match—as long as viewed from a distance.

Surprisingly, the dogs ceased the couch dismemberment after the stockpile dwindled to the final two pillows. Each day that passed without discovery, I felt I had won a small victory for the dogs. I resolved to tell Jennifer about it once the dogs were past their puppy stage. When we were finally caught two months later, all Jennifer could do was laugh about the lengths I went to protect Kelli and Kodi and that, despite sitting on the couch every day, she hadn't noticed it.

Other household items were routinely destroyed, necessitating a thorough walk-through prior to leaving for any length of time. If shoes or, better yet, pillows were forgotten, they were dragged outside and torn to bits. No matter how vigilant, there were always oversights—such as the day I returned to find ten dry-cleaned shirts, normally hung on the outside of the iron fence, ripped to pieces in the yard. The dogs, noticing the foreign objects on the edge of their domain, pulled the offending items through the bars and initiated a furious game of tug of war.

Haley and the puppies weren't satisfied with destroying items exclusive to our house. I began to notice unfamiliar, partially eaten shoes and toys in our backyard. At first, I suspected kids might be throwing items over the fence to tease the dogs. I discovered instead, when the dogs were reported wandering the neighborhood one day, that the foreign objects were the product of canine raiding missions. By the time I arrived to retrieve my charges, a neighbor had corralled Kelli and Kodi, but was unable to track down Haley. I found Haley resting comfortably in our backyard, with no escape route visible in the six-foot fence bounding the street. Walking the perimeter of the fence, I spotted a small tunnel burrowed into a neighbor's yard—the likely source of the shoes and toys. Once in their yard, the four-foot fence separating the dogs from freedom was no match for the athletic trio. To deter future missions, I filled the hole and lined the fence with concrete blocks.

The tiny backyard, poorly suited to the antics of three, very active, large dogs, became a casualty of their destructive pursuits. Before Kodi arrived, I added a layer of sod to cover the muddy mess created by the paws of Kelli and

Haley who routinely sprinted to bark at the neighbor dogs beyond the fence or chase a squirrel on its ridge. What began as a narrow, muddy fairway, relentlessly expanded to cover the entirety of the yard. With Kodi's addition, the intensity and frequency of yard-play increased dramatically. Once in chase mode, sharp, hard turns, each uprooting another tuft of grass, were the norm in the confined backyard. By spring, there wasn't a single blade of grass remaining—not one.

Once covered with yet another layer of sod, the yard returned to its lush, green color. By the fall, however, I was adding sod by the truckload to replace torn up areas. The sod, grown on a clay base, took on the consistency of cream cheese when wet. The canine paws, coated with the sticky material, effectively transferred the contents of the yard, ounce by ounce, into the house. With each new layer of sod, the yard rose ever higher, eventually creating a natural barrier against that patio that allowed a large, muddy pool of water to form following a rain shower or operation of the sprinkler system.

On wet days, the dogs tracked the filth into the house, plastering it on the downstairs furniture, and grinding it into the fibers of the upstairs carpet. I cleaned the house nearly every day, soaking a large towel and scrubbing until the leather couches returned to their original color, mopping the paw-print patterned floors, and vacuuming the dirty carpeting.

I finally reached my breaking point when the lack of drainage led to the sod rotting in place. I took up much of the last layer and replaced it with sheets of plywood and large, flattened, corrugated cardboard boxes. And, to prevent the formation of the small pond, I built up the patio with stepping stones.

As a last resort, I shut off the sprinkler stations in the backyard to help alleviate the mud problem. The jets of water didn't send the dogs inside; they loved to play in the middle of them. Kelli stood to the side of the rotating sprinkler and tried to eat the stream of water as it jetted across the yard. Kodi stood directly in front of the jet, enjoying the sensation of the spray against her body. Excited by the sprinklers, they usually initiated one of their wrestling matches.

Due to an abnormally hot and dry summer, the forty-foot-tall sycamore tree, our only refuge from the sun, began to die. Without the aid of the sprinkler system, what little rain we received couldn't make it through the impermeable layers of sod. Despite a renewed watering campaign to salvage the tree, most of the water stubbornly rested on the surface and evaporated.

Over the next few weeks, I often thought about the dying tree. It was only a five-foot stick when I planted it a few years earlier—a Valentine's Day gift for Jennifer. As it spread its large leafy branches, it became our favorite place to sit in the yard. The majestic tree that once grew so quickly, continued to wither and die—seemingly from the inside out.

I couldn't help feeling the tree was somehow symbolic of what was happening in our marriage. After Katrina and the deaths of Bonnie and Clyde, the relationship never regained its footing. The relationship that had once been effortless increasingly required hard work and patience just to get along. No matter how hopeful our weekends began, they often ended in senseless arguments. The kind words and actions that followed, too few and far between, couldn't penetrate the thick layers of defensiveness and resentment.

We were in a dysfunctional loop—fighting, ignoring, and making do, with neither able to figure a way out. I knew there had to be a better way.

Never mind, I'll worry about it tomorrow—the puppies want to go for a walk.

CHAPTER FOURTEEN

Transitions

"Why is she bringing the dog here?" I asked angrily. "There's no way in hell we're taking on someone else's problem—we have enough on our hands."

"Don't worry, Anne only needs help getting him cleaned up," Jennifer assured.

"Why doesn't she take the dog to a groomer or to the shelter—why here?"

"Anne already took the dog to the vet for a checkup and shots. They gave him a bath there."

I was a bit guarded when Anne arrived, fearing I wasn't getting the whole story. The five-pound animal was in really rough shape. If I didn't know it was a dog, I might have had a tough time guessing. The hair, matted completely to his body, made the skin feel thick, hard and lumpy, as if a braided wool coat had been fused to his skin. The hair around his face was mixed with dirt, grime, and eye discharge, tacking one ear down and covering one eye.

As Jennifer carefully cut the hair away from his underbelly, the smell of stale urine almost made me puke. While trimming his legs, I found his rear dew claws had grown in a semicircle and lodged deeply in the swollen skin. Jennifer struggled to hold him as I clipped the nails and pulled a quarter inch from each leg.

"Anne, how the hell did a vet examine this dog and not notice all this?" I asked.

"Dr. Karelis said he was fine," she replied.

Now it was starting to make sense—the same vet who performed the teeth cleaning on Clyde all those years ago. Anne took him there because her teenage daughter was a part-time receptionist at the clinic.

We did all we could with scissors, but most of his body required a shaver to remove the knotted hair from his skin. The little guy struggled mightily, yelping each time skin was accidentally taken off with the hair.

"Jeff won't let me keep the dog—and I don't want to bring him to the shelter," Anne admitted.

"Don't worry, we'll take him," Jennifer quickly interjected. "He's so pitiful and sad," she said, referring to the goofy-looking thing sporting an overbite large enough to accommodate my finger in the gap between his upper and lower teeth.

I was angry she dumped this on us—that the vet had let this dog go untreated—that our dog situation was about to become complicated again.

As she was leaving, Anne said, "Cindy enjoys working there because he lets her and the other office girls assist with the procedures."

"What do you mean by assist?" I asked.

"They get to watch the surgeries and sometimes he lets them help with the anesthesia."

It finally confirmed what I had assumed all along—something did happen with Clyde's anesthesia. I thought I'd feel better if I ever found the truth, but it did nothing to undo the suffering Clyde endured, or the loss I felt.

We named the little dog Buster, in honor of Jennifer's father. It took a while for him to trust and bond with us after the shaving ordeal, but he quickly assimilated into the pack. Though Cricket tried to discourage a friendship, Buster kept after him—attacking at every opportunity, trying to drag Cricket down by grabbing the back of his neck and hurling his body at him. Because Cricket was a small dog, Buster just assumed he was another puppy. Eventually, Cricket warmed to him and began to play.

Jennifer babied the little guy from the moment he arrived. His favorite way to travel was wrapped in her robe with his head popped out the top. It was commonplace to come to the kitchen table for breakfast and see Jennifer cooking eggs with Buster monitoring the progress. He never tired of being treated like a baby—and she never tired of treating him like one.

Buster was incredibly tough (or not very smart) when it came to the big dogs. He always wanted to be a part of the action. During the many backyard battles, Buster persistently tried get in a shot on one of the big dogs. He barked from the perimeter and then lunged in, grabbed a leg, and darted off, nearly getting squashed a number of times. He had very quick reflexes and seemingly anticipated the movements of the other dogs.

Because of his size, there were any number of ways Buster could get into trouble. He could easily fit between the slats of the iron fence leading to the driveway and could get under the fence to Tiger and Bailey's yard. Upstairs, he lunged at Kelli, hanging from her jowls or ripping at her legs when she walked by. They played so roughly and moved so quickly we became concerned Buster might fall through the slats lining the upstairs den. His tiny stature necessitated several modifications to miniature dog-proof the yard and house.

At night, Buster curled up next to Jennifer's neck and slept soundly until any of the dogs tried to sneak into bed. Then, he immediately lunged at them, his high-pitched, small-dog bark jolting me awake.

It was amazing Buster survived the high-intensity beginning of his stay with us. There were so many ways he could've been injured—not to mention he was small enough to be carried off by one of the many hawks patrolling the skies. When you're that tiny, it doesn't take much for things to end badly.

A few months after Buster joined our family, Hurricane Ike headed for Houston. We decided to ride out the storm, partly because of our experience with previous evacuations and partly because of the logistical difficulty of transporting and sheltering five dogs.

The house rattled, the windows shook—the noise was unnerving for us and terrifying for the dogs. Haley, never before venturing onto the bed, curled up by my head and shook uncontrollably. Kelli laid sideways and wiggled herself under the bed, repeating the exercise each time I dragged her out. While Kodi and the other dogs showed little sign of stress, Kelli and Haley grew more anxious as the night wore on.

We came through the storm relatively unscathed with only one small tree snapped and few branches broken on the larger trees. The main legacy of the storm was the loss of power for about a week. Though miserable with the heat and high humidity, we made the most of it, using flashlights to take showers and find our way around the house.

I enjoyed the lack of television and internet, their absence allowing me to truly relax. We took long walks with the dogs, reinitiated our Scrabble tournaments and, for the first time in some cases, actually talked to our neighbors. Brian and Patsy's refrigerator, powered by the generator they procured prior to the storm, served as the refuge for our food stores. Each morning, Jennifer visited for a cup of freshly brewed coffee and, in the evenings, I fired up the grill and shared our dwindling stock of deer meat. Once the power returned, everyone resumed to their old routines, and the camaraderie quickly faded.

Kelli, unfortunately, had lingering effects from the storm. If there was a loud noise in the house, she ran outside and hid in the bushes next to the garage, refusing to move until I dragged her in. During thunderstorms, she wedged herself back under the bed. Over time, the fear lessened but never completely dissipated.

Shortly after the storm, Haley developed small lumps on her back and sides. The diagnosis from Dr. Stanley was devastating—malignant mast cell tumors. A year before, she had a bleeding, grape-sized lump removed from her chest. The initial surgery, which also removed a few inches of surrounding flesh as a precautionary measure, was thought to be successful. Dr. Stanley offered the option of chemotherapy as insurance, but it was thought to be only minimally effective against mast cell tumors and Jennifer didn't want to put Haley through months of nausea, weakness, and discomfort.

This time, surgery wasn't an option because of the sheer number of tumors and the likelihood more would soon emerge. We'd just have to make her as comfortable as possible. With an arsenal of pain medication, steroids, and antihistamines, we tried to manage as best we could.

We took her to the park most nights to let her chase the squirrels. She thoroughly enjoyed herself, unwilling to let her declining health slow her down. And, despite her worsening condition, she continued the rough play in the backyard with Kelli and Kodi.

I wasn't very close to Haley at the time she fell ill, intentionally keeping my emotional distance to avoid the pain I felt after losing Bonnie and Clyde. She was Jennifer's dog—I had enough on my hands. The effort to remain detached was short-lived as our time spent together at the park and her intense suffering melted my defenses. I became loving toward her and caressed her at every opportunity. In the past, she often ignored me, but, in her pain, she often came to me, stood between my legs and dropped her head submissively, asking to be caressed.

With each passing week, more tumors appeared and the existing tumors grew larger and bled frequently. I doubled the pain pills and still found her whimpering within a few hours of every dose. I called Jennifer, who had taken a trip to visit family, and told her she needed to return immediately if she wanted to see Haley alive. When she arrived the next morning, Haley collapsed and began breathing heavily, grunting and convulsing with each shallow exhale, lying in the garden only inches from where Clyde had fallen two years earlier.

At the emergency vet clinic, they dosed her with tranquilizers and pain medication to calm the panicked breathing. She relaxed and appeared comfortable as we spent our last moments together. Her body, covered with bloody tumors, left only the top of her head available for caresses. We talked to her for ten minutes, told her we loved her, and said good-bye.

In the weeks that followed, I felt sadness, frustration, and loss, though not as intensely as I had with Bonnie and

Clyde. Mostly, I thought about the courage she displayed, adapting and making the best of her situation, not wallowing in sadness and lamenting her misfortune. Haley's last days, though spiked with pain, were spent in the company of the dogs she loved, watching squirrels and birds, and feeling the caress of her friends.

Shortly after we lost Haley, Marie died, leaving Jennifer grief-stricken and, unfortunately, burdened with guilt. Before we moved to Texas, Jennifer visited Marie frequently, taking her to the grocery and helping out around the house. Since moving away, Jennifer had only seen her a dozen times. "She was so good to me," she'd say tearfully. I couldn't do anything to make it better; after all, I was the one who convinced her to leave Louisiana.

Against this backdrop, the stock market collapsed, taking with it half our savings. The magnitude of the loss and the speed with which it disappeared created a heightened sense of insecurity for Jennifer. She wanted something tangible, something that couldn't evaporate with the next financial crisis—something made of bricks close to her family in Mandeville.

"Cathy said he'll design the home and get us everything at cost. He'll only charge us fifteen thousand dollars to manage the project," Jennifer said, referring to Claude's generous offer. "And I get to choose the tile, granite, cabinets, lighting—everything."

"We've never built a house before, what do you know about picking out this stuff?"

"Cathy does it all the time for people, they have a budget for each category and you go to the store and look at the selection."

"Jennifer, we don't live in Mandeville. I'm not going to make a bunch of trips to pick out towel racks and faucets. You'll be doing this pretty much on your own. Don't you think we should buy an existing house? There's eleven thousand on the market right now—it's a huge buyer's market."

"Hon, Claude hasn't signed a contract in over a year and a half. He could really use the work—it'll be good for him. I'm sure he'll sell us the lot real cheap. They need to get rid of some of their inventory."

"It's a mistake to get into a business deal with family. It never works out, and then there are always hurt feelings."

"Maybe in your family. Mine's different—we always look out for each other."

"Yeah, maybe so," I said with resignation.

We bought a small, corner lot lined with hundred-foot-tall oaks, situated across the street from a heavily wooded area, giving our property the feel of a country estate. Fontainebleau State Park, a wild preserve similar to Brazos Bend, bordered our neighborhood a few blocks to the east. A nearby bike path, snaking twenty miles through dense pines, provided the opportunity for a great workout or chance to relax and clear my head.

As an added benefit, Lisa lived only twenty miles from our new home, making it much easier to visit her and, hopefully, rebuild our relationship. From time to time, I loaded up Kelli and Kodi and drove to her small house in the country, finding Tango and Walliford always waiting for us at the gate. It was ironic that Tango, despite several near-death experiences, freezing cold nights, sweltering hot days, mosquitoes, and cheap dog food, had already outlived Bonnie and Clyde by a couple of years. Of course, Walliford, at fifteen or sixteen years of age, had lived long beyond the normal span for a large-breed dog. Each time I played with Tango, I couldn't help but think of Clyde. He had so many of the same mannerisms—especially the way he'd dolphin-nose my hand if I dared to stop petting him for a moment.

As soon as the hatch of the SUV opened, Kodi sprinted to the horse pen and leaped over the four and a half foot steel fence, chasing the horses until they began kicking and stomping in vain at the attacking ninja dog. I ran in and retrieved her, but it was only minutes before she jumped the fence and took after them again. Kelli could have easily cleared the fence, but she had no desire to tangle with the large creatures. After a few visits, I realized it would be best to leave the pups at home. It was only a matter of time before Kodi found herself in the wrong place at the wrong time.

During our frequent visits to Mandeville to select light fixtures, paint colors, or whatever, we drove to the construction site at dawn and walked the dogs along quiet, tree-lined streets, reaching the lakefront in less than twenty minutes. Kelli and Kodi weaved back and forth, straining against their leashes, overwhelmed by the multitude of squirrels along the route. At the lake, pelicans roosted yards from the bank, and colorful sailboats tacked into the gentle breeze. The two-mile walk along the seawall reminded me of the outings with Bonnie and Clyde on the Metairie lakefront.

Unfortunately, each trip also uncovered some major problem at the house, usually attributed to a miscommunication, but always resulting in more expense. I found it interesting, though not surprising, the misunderstandings were, without fail, our fault. It was hard to keep track of all the issues—the bathroom wall set a foot shorter than the tub, the giant, watermelon-sized, four-hundred-watt front door lamp set at chest level, the cabinets built two feet shorter than planned, the discolored, loose, and uneven tiles, the spliced, mismatched granite countertop—the list seemed endless. Worst of all, when the project was completed, the square brick house with narrow rectangular windows, oversized garage door, flat roof line, costing thirty percent more than planned, looked, well, like a barn—one big, expensive, ugly, gray barn.

One afternoon, while I was excavating clay and sugar sand from the base of one of our giant oak trees, Claude stopped by.

"What are you doing?" he asked.

"I've got to get the roots uncovered before the tree dies," I said. "We had an arborist come out because the leaves are thinning near the top. He said about a foot of the sod and fill had to come out or the trees would eventually die."

"I don't think we filled it that much."

"Check this out," I said, pointing to the decaying grass exposed beneath eighteen inches of densely-packed mud and sugar sand. "Looks like the old ground is way under."

"Well, I've never had any complaints about trees dying before."

"Hey Claude!" Jennifer said, joining us in the front yard. "Do y'all want a beer?"

"Sure," he said.

"I need one," I replied, semi-dehydrated from shoveling and carting heavy wheelbarrows full of mud to the adjacent wooded area. Despite hours of effort, only a fraction of the first of four tree bases had been completed.

"What do you think? Looks great, doesn't it?" he said to Jennifer, pointing to the house and beaming with pride.

"We just love it," Jennifer gushed. "It's beautiful."

I glanced at Jennifer in disbelief. "Claude, there's a few problems we need to get taken care of though," I interjected. Jennifer's smile faded and she excused herself to retrieve the beer.

"Like what?"

"Well, I can't even see the bricks in a lot of places," I said, motioning toward the red brick façade obscured behind a layer of grey mortar. "And the extra grout makes the joints look too wide."

"That's the way Jennifer wanted it. It's tumbled brick—it's not supposed to fit tightly together," he replied defensively. "Jennifer wanted the 'washed' look. That's why the mortar is on there. It looks good the way it is."

"Look, I'll pay to have someone come out here and power wash or acid wash that stuff off the house. I don't want a grey house with giant grey lines. It looks like a child did this."

"Alright, but you'll be ruining the look."

I certainly hope so. "Claude, they put the awning a foot above the door—it looks awkward."

"That's the way it's supposed to be."

"Look at the house next to us; the awning is a foot lower—and all the houses on this street are the same. You can see the white underside from the street. It looks ridiculous."

"Jennifer was here when we put it up; she knew where it was being placed."

"Claude, I'm not trying to be difficult. I can see why they put it there; the iron crossbar couldn't lay flat against the soldiered brick above the door, so they just laid it on top. Maybe Jennifer was here, but she can't be expected to notice everything. She doesn't know anything about building a house." *That's your damn job.*

"If it's that important to you, I'll get the crew to come out and move it," he said angrily.

"I appreciate it. While we're at it, can you do something about these lights?" I asked, pointing toward the four motion-sensing, ninety-watt bulbs set half-way up either side of the front of the house. "They'd be fine if I was trying to land on an aircraft carrier, but it's a little much for the front of a residence."

"That's exactly what Jennifer wanted; she wanted to be safe getting in the house."

"The lights don't do anything for the side of the house where our yard and entrance to the garage are. If anything, they should have been set on the corners where you could angle one toward the front and one toward the side. We don't have any power outlets on the side of the house— there's no way to set up lights—we're going to be in the dark on the patio."

And on it went—negotiating each problem until I got satisfaction or decided it wasn't worth the fight.

"How did it go?" Jennifer asked, bringing the long-promised beer to the front yard after Claude left.

"He wasn't happy about it."

"I hope you were nice to him," she said.

"He didn't make it easy. I had to beg and dance for each one. It was like I was dealing with my old man."

"Please try to get along. You know how much my family means to me."

"Yeah, I do." *Unfortunately, I do.*

Despite the benefits of the new house, I focused mostly on the negatives—the frustration of dealing with Claude, the exorbitant cost, the poor planning and workmanship, and so on. I usually arrived with a good attitude, only to have some new problem set me off on an angry tirade. The house became a recurring wedge issue, with me continually pointing out the flaws and Jennifer defending her family—even when she knew they were wrong. Though we eventually got past each new conflict, the damage was done. Word by word, deed by deed, it piled on like thick layers of clay sod.

Kelli and Kodi were my source of happiness through it all. No matter what was happening between Jennifer and me, it was forgotten when I came home to their love and affection. Watching them live life with total abandon helped me put aside the frustration I felt.

CHAPTER FIFTEEN

Buddy

"Are you ready?" Jennifer asked. "The park opens in a few minutes—I told Sharon we'd meet her there." A few months after finishing the Mandeville house, a volunteer from Sugar Land Animal Control invited Jennifer to the opening of the new Sugar Land dog park.

"I'm almost ready," I replied. "I don't know why you want to go back to a dog park. Remember when we went to Millie Bush Park? The place was small, the ponds were dirty, the ground was mostly mud, and you couldn't take a step without landing in a pile of crap."

"I promised my friend we'd meet her. We're only going for a few hours. If it's not good, we don't have to go back."

Unaware of the poor aesthetics of the two-acre enclosure, Kelli and Kodi ran and wrestled joyfully, relishing the chance to play in the wide-open space. I walked behind, ready to intervene if a dog made the mistake of challenging Kelli, while Jennifer searched for her friend.

Ten minutes after arriving, Jennifer called my cell, "Hon, meet me at the concessions. There's a dog I need you to see—he looks like Clyde!"

"You know the last thing we need is another dog." Kelli and Kodi had only recently ended their campaign of pillow shredding and dog bed destruction.

"I know—please come and see."

I hooked up the two pups and walked out to meet the alleged Clyde-like dog.

"Jason, this is Sonny. Doesn't he look like Clyde? Isn't he adorable?"

Look like Clyde? Adorable? The dog had short, stubby legs, his eyes were wide-set across a pink nose and his tail curled like a—*pig—he looked like a bear-pig!* The same height as Kodi, an inch wider and ten pounds heavier, he sported fur the exact color of Kelli along with the small, diamond-shaped, white patches on the shoulder blades. His large, square head gave the Shar-Pei-Lab mix a Pit Bull appearance and his odd combination of features made him more unsettling than Walliford in his prime.

"Well, adorable isn't the word that comes to mind. I'm not seeing the resemblance to Clyde at all. Don't you think he's a bit odd looking?"

Kelli and Kodi sniffed the dog while we talked to the people from the animal shelter. Kelli wagged her tail and assumed dog pose position, her arms stretched forward, back quarters arched, clearly wanting to play. Sonny, who still had his testicles, became interested in playing a different kind of game. When his calm demeanor escalated to frenzy, Kelli snapped at him, putting an end to his unwelcome advances.

"We also have a big, pretty Lab named Buck. He's been with us six months like Sonny," Sharon said. "I don't think he has as good a chance of being adopted because he's so spirited and big—he's a hundred and twenty pounds."

"Jason, we need to get a big dog. I'm not comfortable in the house alone all day," Jennifer said, her fear reinforced by a spate of recent home invasions in our area. Sonny immediately dropped a few notches, being only slightly larger than our existing crew. Buck sounded more like what we needed—if we needed anything. A good security system—or a gun was probably a better idea.

Sharon warned, "Unfortunately, both might have to be euthanized soon if we can't find them homes. There's limited space at the shelter and we've kept them longer than normal because they're such sweet animals."

On the drive to the shelter, I remarked, "You know, I won't be able to walk the dog with Kelli and Kodi. It'll be impossible for me to handle a third dog, especially a big one, on our runs. Any new dog we get will be yours to walk."

"That's what I want. I don't feel safe walking Buster during the day. There's a lot of sections where I'm all alone."

"You don't think Buster could handle the situation—the way he flings his body at Kelli's jowls, and then hangs onto her with his goofy overbite?"

"You know what I mean. Besides, I really miss the long walks with Haley. Buster can't go very far."

When we arrived at the shelter, they brought Buck, very excited and eyes looking a bit wild, to the grassy area behind the facility. He did look like Clyde, wearing the same colored fur atop a similar-sized frame and sporting Clyde's hound face.

"Jennifer, let me walk him first—he looks pretty powerful," I offered.

"No, I need to get used to it if I'm going to walk him," Jennifer countered, reminding me I was attempting to be too helpful.

She connected her hundred-fifteen-pound body to the hundred-twenty-pound Lab and walked toward the field. When he spotted a Doberman, Buck ripped the leash from Jennifer's hand, nearly pulling her to the ground. He grabbed the dog by its neck, took it to the ground, and then released it.

I ran to the site of the altercation and, restraining the dog, shouted to Jennifer, "This isn't going to work—you're gonna get pulled into traffic or break a hip." I walked the big guy around the field, thinking it might be the last time he got out for a while.

Undeterred, Jennifer retrieved Kodi, hoping the playful puppy might calm the big male down. Kodi could get along with any dog—no matter their size, shape, or disposition. Despite Kodi's warm greeting, the Lab growled her off, quickly ending the experiment.

As we neared the entrance, a thirty-pound dog, out for a test walk with potential adoptive parents, broke free and charged toward us, lunging and biting at the massive lab. Luckily for the insane little dog, Buck didn't retaliate. I felt bad for the big guy—he was too large, too powerful, too energetic and, from months in captivity, too unstable. If we didn't accept him with our high tolerance for chaos, no one would. And, in fact, no one did. Months later, they euthanized him.

That night, I kept thinking about Sonny. The big, sweet, playful animal had been stuck in a small cage for the last six months—about half of his life. If we didn't take him, he'd be in a cage the rest of his life. No one could get past his high energy and his menacing looks. Only one couple looked at him in the six months he was there, returning him after only one night.

I knew there were thousands of animals in the same situation and hund\reds being euthanized each month. Though we wouldn't be making the slightest dent in the problem, I could see his face, I could imagine his frustration and anxiety building, day after day, until he became cage-crazy like Buck. I couldn't let him end that way, we'd try to make room for one more.

The next day, Jennifer took Buster to see if he and Sonny could get along. While Kelli and Kodi tolerated Buster lunging his five-pound body toward their jowls, an aggressive animal could easily misinterpret his behavior. If she were alive when Buster joined the pack, Bonnie would've taken him out within a few days. Sonny, appearing far more powerful than Bonnie, could end five-pound Buster's life with one quick bite.

After a few days, Jennifer was satisfied the new dog was right for our pack. Once the big guy was fixed, Jennifer brought him to meet Kelli and Kodi on neutral turf at the dog park. The dogs played together for an hour before we loaded up the vehicles and took our new dog, affectionately named Buddy the Bear-Pig, home.

Once in the yard, Kelli immediately took Buddy to the ground and dominated him. Kelli knew every dog move in the book and could easily take him down before he knew what hit him. Buddy's only strategy, lacking the skills to adequately defend himself, was to throw his heavy body on her and hope for the best.

Shortly after Kodi engaged Buddy in mock combat for the first time, she shrieked, ran inside, and hid. Buddy, confused by Kodi's change in demeanor, followed her.

"What's wrong, girl?" I asked the shaking, cowering creature. "He reminds you of the old days, huh? Don't worry, he doesn't mean any harm. He can't help the way he looks." I stroked her soft fur, and, though not understanding my words, she calmed down.

"Look, he's really a big marshmallow. Come on outside, let's try it again." Kodi followed the bear-pig through the doggy door and soon reengaged in their mock battle. Seconds later, Kodi returned with a shriek to the safety of her hiding place. It took a few more days until she realized the truth of my words; there wasn't a mean bone in his body.

I jogged with Kelli and Buddy before work each morning, leaving Jennifer to walk Kodi and Buster later. Kodi didn't mind being left out. In fact, she didn't even leave the bed when I rattled the leashes and called her to join us. At first,

Buddy had trouble walking the mile and a half loop, his fitness eroded in the small confines of the shelter. His spirit, however, remained strong, allowing him to push farther each day, becoming more excited every time I picked up the leash.

Within a month, he could run the entire route without stopping. Even though Buddy and I were exerting ourselves, Kelli always appeared to be trotting. Actually, it was more like gliding—effortless and smooth, a machine perfectly designed for running.

Buddy's strength, excitement, and energy level made his presence in our house nerve-racking. With ears back, eyes wide open, and tongue hanging out, he routinely sprinted around the yard, punched through the doggie door, flew up the staircase, looped the upstairs game room, and charged back outside, five-pound Buster barking, lunging, and biting at his legs.

Buddy also reignited the destructive instincts of Kelli and Kodi, causing damage so frequent and widespread, that the dogs were relegated to the yard when we were away. Their expulsion occurred the day Buddy noticed a tray of chicken breasts cooling at the back of the counter. We arrived home from a quick trip to the grocery to find the six chicken breasts missing and dozens of sharp Corningware fragments, meticulously stripped of chicken drippings, on the floor. Despite finding a number of small blood stains nearby, none of the dogs appeared injured. And, fortunately, Cricket and Buster weren't beneath the counter when the dish crashed to the ground.

The levee, rendered almost unrecognizable by continued development, once again became a favorite destination for us. Buddy enjoyed running with Kelli and Kodi, despite his inability to keep up with his fleet-footed mates. With every ounce of energy applied, his short legs, thick body, and clumsy stride failed to put a dent in the gap unless they stopped or returned for him.

Unable to compete with the thoroughbreds in a foot-race, Buddy focused instead on the game of hide-and-seek. The first time I gave Buddy the command "go get Kodi," he immediately turned toward Kodi's position and charged up to her, flushing her long before she expected. The prospect of being located so easily by the slow-moving, but quick-witted, dog, took some of the fun out of the game for Kodi, though not enough to make her want to stop.

We enjoyed the oasis for months until, like the last time with Kelli and Kodi, they located a fresh stash of poop. When the dogs disappeared behind a hill and didn't come out the other side, I knew what they were into. By the time I arrived, Kodi and Buddy both had sampled some, and Kelli was wearing her latest fashion statement. It was back to the sidewalks again.

On our first trip to Mandeville, Buddy assumed protection of the yard was his responsibility and frequently patrolled the fence line. As if trying to provoke our guard dog, two dominant males from down the street stopped by from time to time and lifted their legs on the fence. Buddy, caught in the overspray while barking and lunging, wasn't the least bit amused by their behavior. Buster was always with him during these events, throwing his little body toward the mesh-covered iron fence.

In the mornings, I walked the three big dogs to the lake-front while Jennifer walked Buster. The distractions were endless with squirrels scurrying from tree to tree, dogs weaving around each other, and lunging in the direction of the latest sighting. Throughout the walk, I was constantly adjusting and untangling the leashes. By the time we covered the relatively short distance to the lake, I was already a bit fatigued.

Once at the lake, Kodi often walked on the ledge of the seawall next to the path. As many times as I pulled her off, she jumped back up, enjoying the vantage point of a much larger dog. Kelli and Buddy, jealous of Kodi's superior position, hopped up from time to time, creating quite a challenge to control the animals. One time, Kelli got a bit distracted and simply walked off the ledge, plunging six feet to the shallow water below. By the time I jumped in after her, she had already made five panicked leaps, sometimes landing on sharp rocks and slicing her skin.

A few hundred yards down the way, Buddy hopped up and, just like Kelli, fell off. Uncertain I could lift the seventy-pound dog over my head, I ran to the next staircase and called him to me. Fortunately, he didn't panic and slowly paddled his way to us.

In one wide section of the lakefront, bounded by a quiet two-lane road and shaded by a half dozen towering, squirrel-laden oaks, we often noticed dogs playing off leash early in the morning. After observing the group for a few weeks, we felt it was safe enough to let our dogs join in the fun.

Kodi often charged through the group, initiating a chase in which she became the prey. Once caught, she spun around like a ninja warrior, clacking her jaws at whoever dared approach. Buddy, the sweet, clumsy giant, made friends with every dog he met, never wasting a moment of playtime. Seeing Buddy play with such abandon made the effort required to manage him seem worthwhile. Kelli, having violated my trust so many times before, could only join in when she let me know she was completely focused by barking incessantly at the participants of the nearby wrestling match. Once free, she immediately and relentlessly attacked Kodi, much to her mate's delight. When her interest waned even slightly, I called her to me and hooked her up.

In February, we traveled to Mandeville to enjoy a few Mardi Gras parades with Jennifer's family. A few days into the visit, I noticed something was different from previous trips—no kids screaming in the house. We had the place to ourselves for once. I told Jennifer it was nice we had a little privacy.

"Cathy won't let me see the boys anymore. There's too many hard feelings about how we treated them."

"What do you mean how we treated them?"

"About the house."

"What? We were the ones who had to pay for all the screw-ups—it didn't cost them a nickel. Now their feelings are hurt? I've heard it all now."

"We shouldn't have been so critical. I love those little boys. My heart is broken she won't let me see them."

"Critical? Do you hear that whistling noise?" I said, pointing to the air-conditioning intake vent. "That's because he put in a ten by fourteen air return—ten by fourteen! There's no way that's to code."

"How do you know it's not?"

"Listen to the damn thing. If you try to put anything better than a spun fiberglass filter it bows up, and the unit struggles. And there's a twenty-five by twenty-five opening for the upstairs unit with five times the area as this little piece of crap. Why'd they cut such a big hole upstairs if it wasn't needed?"

"I don't want any more problems with them. Please don't make a deal out of this," Jennifer begged.

"Damn it, Jennifer. We've been screwed so many times on this house. I don't think I can stuff it down much more."

"I need you to apologize to them. That's the only way I'll ever get to see my boys again."

"Are you kidding? Apologize to them? No way in hell. They should be over here trying to make things right. Claude should give back his contracting fee. Everything cost us retail anyway. I could've called out the subs for what good he did us—most of the contractors he used were his friends. Who knows what kinds of surprises are hidden in the walls of this thing."

As I was going on and on, I glanced at Jennifer. Broken by all of the conflict, she sobbed quietly, holding little Buster.

"OK, I'll call Claude."

After accepting my apology, Claude invited me to come with him and his boys to their cabin in the country the following day. Hoping it might help mend fences, I reluctantly agreed to make the arduous drive. That morning, I woke early to take the dogs on a short walk and mentally prepared myself for the long day ahead. Once at the cabin, the minutes passed like hours as Claude, Dillon and Josh explored the property. I returned home ten hours later, completely exhausted.

"Can Dillon stay the night?" Jennifer asked hopefully.

"Hon, we need to get up early tomorrow," I interjected forcefully.

"Sure, Cathy will come by in the morning to pick him up," Claude said, heading to the door with Josh.

After the door closed, I asked, "Jennifer, when are we going to walk the dogs tomorrow? Please make sure Cathy gets over here at breakfast. I've got to start on the retaining wall sometime." The retaining wall was yet another by-product of the house ordeal. The sloping lot coupled with a thick foundation led to a dramatic drop-off as you exited the back door. Standing on the patio, my thighs were even with the top of the six-foot fence that was of little use in visually separating the yards. And, because sugar sand was used as fill instead of clay, the rain washed the grass away in a few weeks, leaving a series of muddy canyons plunging toward the half-buried fence. The project would entail digging out the eroded mud, setting huge posts in concrete and then attaching wood planks to counter the effects of rain and gravity.

Later, Dillon came into our bedroom crying, wanting to sleep with Aunt Jennifer. He poked at Kelli and hugged her neck. Startled, Kelli snapped at him, missing his face by a hair. Without thinking, I slapped her on the snout and yelled at her, causing her to drop her head and tuck her tail—terrified by my sudden aggression. She followed to my side of the bed and lay on the floor, afraid to join us.

At breakfast, I learned Cathy wasn't planning to pick up Dillon until after lunch. I toyed with the idea of waiting for Jennifer to go on our walk—maybe take a run to the store and pick up the lumber and concrete. But the walk on the lake was never the same late in the day. It was too crowded, there was too much commotion, and the dogs had too many distractions.

No, I might as well take the dogs myself.

CHAPTER SIXTEEN

Sunset

Kodi and Buddy wrestled playfully, disengaging occasionally to chase one of their new friends. Kelli waited, yearning to move again, while I spoke to one of the lakefront regulars.

"It's pretty cold out here, isn't it?" I asked knowingly, the gusty, frigid wind penetrating my fleece jacket and wool coat.

From her position near the water's edge, Kelli scanned the nearby oak trees, quickly spotting a squirrel twenty yards away. Kelly shifted her weight on her haunches, trembling as the squirrel flicked its tail and moved slowly, haltingly, down the large oak tree.

"It was much colder yesterday," John said. "We missed you out here, did you just get in?" John's large poodle,

Duncan, was now fully engaged in the wrestling match with Buddy and Kodi.

"No, I had to travel up to the country yesterday—it was a long day."

Kelli shifted anxiously—eyes transfixed on the squirrel as it reached the grass and scurried toward an oak tree ten yards away. Squirrel! She had heard it shouted many times in the park in Sugar Land. No one shouted it; they didn't have to. Kelli's instinct and conditioning gave the command when the squirrel moved onto open ground. She punched it, feeling a slight jerk as the six-foot leash reached its maximum length, peeling back the fingers attached to the other end.

"Kelli, no!" Within a few strides she was moving fast, her powerful thighs accelerating her body toward the target. "Kelli, no!" She heard her name and the command she knew so well, unable to comply even if she wanted to. "Kelli, come!" The squirrel ran for cover as Kelli closed within ten yards. It took a step back toward the oak, hesitated, and then darted across the street. Kelli closed the gap to a few yards when the squirrel ran between the bars of a short wrought iron fence and scurried up the adjacent tree.

"Damn it!" I turned, grabbed Kodi and Buddy, and quickly hooked the leashes to their harnesses.

Kelli leaped. Her shoulders soared nearly six feet vertically and her snout reached more than a foot beyond. Still, the squirrel slipped away. She pushed her legs forward, like she'd done so many times against the wood fence in the backyard. This time there was nothing but air...

"John, hold these two—I don't want them to follow across the street."

I heard Kelli scream. I turned to see her struggling atop the short fence, legs flailing, trying to find a foothold. She quickly wriggled off, ran back across the street and sat down. By the time I reached her, she was sitting quietly, her eyes transfixed on the tree providing sanctuary for the squirrel.

"What's wrong girl?" I asked, scanning for injuries but finding none. "Come on, let's go," I said in a soft voice. I wasn't mad at her for running off, just thankful she hadn't been hit by a car. She walked slowly at my side, her graceful stride replaced by a bow-legged gait.

"I don't know what happened," I shouted to John. "She's walking a little funny. She must have pulled something."

As we slowly made our way back, John said, "Hey, she looks like she's bleeding." Unable to see anything from my angle, I dropped to the ground.

"Oh God, she's been stabbed!" I cried. Kelli sat calmly as I held my hand tightly over the small hole. She didn't appear to be in pain—just confused. I quickly dialed my cell phone.

"Hello!" Jennifer answered playfully.

"Hon, I need help! Kelli's hurt!"

The phone disconnected. I hit redial.

"Hello?" Jennifer said.

"Kelli's been stabbed! She's dying!" The phone disconnected.

"I can't get a signal—I need to get her to the vet!" I shouted to John. "I don't know where to go—I can't remember where the vet's office is!"

"There's an emergency vet right down the road—I'll drive you," John said. "Do you want to take my car? It's kind of small and I need to bring Duncan."

"No, let's take my truck. We can fit all the dogs in there."

I carried Kelli, her chest pressed against mine, her snout on my shoulder, half jogging toward the vehicle. I sat in the passenger seat with Kelli leaned back against my chest, keeping her breast high and pressing my hand over the wound. John started the truck and slowly accelerated, unaccustomed to driving a large vehicle.

"Please hurry up, John—she's in bad shape," I urged, panic rising in my voice. The more distressed I became, the more overwhelmed John became. At each intersection, he hesitated for a few moments and accelerated slowly. When we reached the main road, Kelli moaned. I began to feel her slipping away.

"Please hurry up," I begged. "She's going to die!"

A few moments later, we reached the clinic. I carried Kelli to the front door that, for some reason, was locked. Moments after I began kicking the door and yelling, a member of the staff opened it.

"My dog's been stabbed, she's bleeding to death! I need help! She's dying!"

I followed the nurse to the back where another one reached for Kelli.

"We'll take it from here," the nurse calmly told me.

"You need to keep pressure on the wound. She's bleeding badly," I said, my voice shaking.

"We're going to get her prepped for surgery. You can wait out front."

A doctor met me in the waiting area. "We're going to have to do exploratory surgery and it could cost…"

"Just do it! I'll pay whatever it costs. Please just get her treated!" I insisted.

The clerk requested my signature on a financial obligation form, and charged $2200 to my credit card as a deposit. Minutes later, I signed a form approving CPR.

A tech came from the back and asked, "So, the dog was in a fight and was bitten?"

"What? No! She's been stabbed in the chest!"

She disappeared quickly behind the door. A few minutes later the doctor appeared.

"Her heart stopped beating and we've begun CPR. Even if we're successful getting her heart going again, she's been without oxygen long enough to do serious brain and organ damage. We've shocked the heart a number of times—she's not responding."

"If she's in surgery—isn't she on a ventilator?"

"The dog hasn't made it into surgery yet. She was being prepped when her heart stopped."

"Please keep trying," I said weakly. *How could she be slipping away?* I checked my cell phone call to Jennifer and the time on the bill. It had taken less than fifteen minutes from the time she was injured to the time we reached the exam room. Kelli was the most athletic dog I had ever seen. She was lean and muscular and could run three miles without getting the least bit winded. If any dog could make it, Kelli could.

An hour later, Cathy brought Jennifer to the veterinary clinic. "John told me what happened, hon. I'm so sorry about Kelli," Jennifer said.

"I can't believe..."

"Oh, hon, I wish I had been there with you," Jennifer said, holding me as I tried to regain my composure.

"I kept calling you. I thought you had the car. I couldn't remember..."

"It's OK, hon. It's going to be all right."

Another hour passed as I prayed for Kelli's life.

"Everything we've tried has been unsuccessful," the vet said. "We opened a section of her chest and the pericardial sac to manually pump the heart. We shocked her heart and gave drugs to stimulate it. We're out of ideas at this point. I need your permission to stop working on her." The surgeon entered the room and agreed it was futile. He didn't understand why she didn't respond—she hadn't lost much blood. I was too devastated and confused to understand the other things he mentioned.

"You can stop working on her," I said, letting go of the last shred of hope.

"I'll close the incision and get her cleaned up so you can see her again," the surgeon said.

Later, they led us back to the table where she lay. Her skin was warm, her fur soft and silky as always. She looked so alive, so healthy.

We returned to the truck and waited, caressing and reassuring Kodi and Buddy. On the way over, they repeatedly tried to join Kelli in the front seat, sensing she was in real trouble. The three hours spent alone, waiting for their friend to return, amplified their confusion and fear.

Kelli wipes her right eye with her paw when I pull the leashes out. There's nothing wrong, no injuries, just memories of Bonnie. Each time Bonnie wipes her paw across the cloudy eye, Kelli gently licks the area to help clean it and comfort her friend. Bonnie is completely at peace. She doesn't try to get up or growl Kelli off, like she would any other dog.

Two technicians brought Kelli out in a flimsy, cardboard box and set her in the back. I opened the lid, allowing Kodi and Buddy a chance to see her. They examined the body for a few minutes, then moved as far away as possible.

At the house, I laid her under the Satsuma tree, giving the dogs time to understand she was dead and not coming back. "I need to leave," I said. "I've got to go over some things. I'll be back in a while."

I returned to the lakefront and parked in the same spot I had that morning. I crossed the street to the four-foot-tall fence, feeling each of the half-inch-diameter, eight-inch-long, pointed spears jutting from the top rail, looking for any sign of blood. Nothing. I checked the sidewalk next to the fence, the path she took across the street, the place she sat as she watched the squirrel. Still nothing.

Ten yards closer to the lake, I found a few drops of blood splattered on some dead oak leaves. I picked up each sticky, crimson-coated leaf and put it in my pocket. With each step closer to the lake, the number of droplets increased, leading to a two-inch stain where I tried to call Jennifer. Overwhelmed with regret, I sat staring at the bloody area, unable to move, wondering how much time I let slip away that morning.

I returned to the truck, moving as I had earlier, covering the thirty or so yards in less than a minute. I drove to the vet as John had, stopping at each sign, cautiously accelerating, covering the eight blocks in less than three minutes. I headed back to the house, my mind flooded with thoughts of the horrible ordeal, replaying every step, analyzing every wasted moment, trying to understand how it could have happened so quickly.

I returned to find Jennifer and the dogs seated on a blanket next to Kelli. Sobbing, she caressed the lifeless body that appeared only to be sleeping. The dogs barely noticed as I entered the yard and joined them. I looked at Jennifer and broke down, overwhelmed with grief. I glanced at my swollen, bruised right index finger. I wished I had more to show for it—some evidence I had put up a heroic struggle. I sat motionless, thinking mostly about the horrible events, but also how much she meant to me.

As I approach the gate, Kelli and Kodi wiggle uncontrollably, their tails slicing the air. I enter and they do all they can to keep from jumping on me, unless it's muddy. Once inside the house, they leap over the back of the black leather sofa, turn around, put their paws at the top of the couch and wiggle joyfully. I rub their heads as they jockey for position.

I began to dig her grave. At moments during the day's ordeal, things didn't seem real. Once I started to dig, there was no longer any confusion. I conditioned her for the very thing that led to her death. The leap I had so often praised had now taken her life.

Kelli shrieks, tucks her tail and runs to me as she realizes a Great Dane is chasing her from the pond. The big dog wants to play, but Kelli doesn't understand.

I kept digging. I couldn't help feeling Buddy had been a mistake. Before Buddy came along, I could run Kelli and Kodi without the need for unstructured, off-leash play. Kelli didn't want to just hang out—we were on a mission. A minute or two of sniffing and wrestling was all she needed.

With the three dogs, the destination was the only enjoyable part of a walk. The journey to and from was often an unpleasant ordeal of being pulled mercilessly by the powerful, excited dogs. I constantly reshuffled the three leashes, each a different color to ensure I didn't accidentally let go of the wrong one. To facilitate the untangling, I held the straps with a clenched fist rather than looping the wrist and laying it across the palm.

If only Kodi was off leash, I wouldn't have been as distracted. If Buddy weren't with us, we wouldn't have driven to the lake, or stopped to play. I took him in, I thought I could manage it, but I wasn't up to the challenge when it counted. I felt like I had traded Kelli's life for his.

Kelli gently reaches her paw out to hold little Buster while he gnaws on her jowls in mock battle. She softly moans, enjoying the attention of her small friend.

After another hour, I finished digging Kelli's grave. I sat and felt her body, now stiff and cold. I went inside and asked Jennifer to help me bury her. We cried as I wrapped her in her favorite blanket and lowered her into the grave. We said a prayer and, shovel by shovel, I buried the dog I so deeply loved. I placed several pieces of sod over the mound and sat by the grave. I felt hopeless.

Kelli balances catlike on the small console area, leaning her body as we come into and out of turns. She curls up on the tiny platform and lays her head on my right arm, resting peacefully.

During the afternoon, Kodi sometimes laid on top of the grave and Buddy occasionally pawed away a few strokes of dirt. They knew she was there. They had seen her and smelled her. Buddy watched as I dug the holes for the retaining wall on the other side of the yard. He looked in each when I finished, appearing as though he hoped to find Kelli.

The next morning, the dogs didn't pull on our walk to the lakefront. They walked by our sides, frightened by the sudden disappearance of their friend. At the spot where Kelli was injured, the dogs sniffed the blood-stained ground vigorously while I described the horrible events to Jennifer. We collected a few more oak leaves, allowing the dogs time to take in her scent.

We happened across John and Duncan on the way back.

"I'm sorry about Kelli," John said.

"Thanks for trying to help," I replied.

"It was such a freak accident; there was nothing you could do."

"I don't know why they didn't get her into the operating room sooner. Maybe the surgeon didn't know what happened," I said.

"No, he knew. I was talking to him while you were inside."

"When? Where did you see him?"

"He was out front smoking a cigarette, and he struck up a conversation with me about my Red Sox hat."

"He was taking a smoke break?"

"Yeah, we talked for a while. He told me he was doing the surgery and I told him how she had gotten hung up on the fence and was bleeding. He said he knew and was waiting for them to get the dog ready for surgery."

"I still don't understand how it all happened so quickly. There wasn't much blood."

The walk home was quiet, neither of us having much to say. I wondered why she wasn't blaming me. If the roles had been reversed, I'm sure I would've let her have it.

Kelli wrestles playfully with Buddy, allowing him to gnaw on her neck and dominate her, slowly ceding the alpha role to him. She feels a sense of peace, knowing Buddy will do anything to protect the pack.

The days passed and a few family members called or came by to let me talk about it. Some just listened and I appreciated it. Others tried to help me make sense of what happened. The dogs slowly began to pick up their spirits. They looked in the Yukon each time we passed and seemed hopeful Kelli might appear during our walks.

It was time to head back to Texas. We stayed a few extra days to help the dogs understand Kelli wasn't coming back. We loaded the Yukon and the dogs dutifully jumped in. Usually, the dogs settled in quickly and slept most of the seven-hour ride. This time, Kodi and Buddy looked out the windows and paced nervously in the back.

Buddy kept trying to move his huge frame onto Kelli's preferred traveling position between the front seats. We let Buddy up for a short section of the drive because we knew the dogs were confused and upset. After a few slips, it became clear his larger size and clumsy nature made it a really bad idea.

I knew they were trying to figure out why Kelli wasn't there. Their anxiety amplified my own guilt and sadness. Jennifer and I tried to find things to talk about to pass the time, but nothing seemed to matter.

CHAPTER SEVENTEEN

The Trail Ahead

Aweek after returning to Sugar Land, Kodi, Buddy, and Tiger wrestled and chased each other, though without the normal intensity. Kodi often stopped and looked around, knowing things were different, but not yet accepting Kelli was gone. For nearly three years, they'd been together, forming a bond closer than most littermates. Without Kelli, part of Kodi's life was missing.

Like a fox leaping on snow-covered ground to punch into a rodent's burrow, Kelli lunges at Kodi. She takes her to the ground and gnaws on Kodi's neck. Sometimes, not wanting to be ignored, yet not feeling the need to participate, she barks relentlessly from the perimeter of the ongoing chaos.

Not surprisingly, after spending only a few months together, Buddy appeared to be mostly over the loss. During his life at the kennel, many dogs came and went. Kelli was just the latest.

Cricket went to the center of the yard and, for ten minutes, barked longingly into the air. He repeated the strange ritual three days in a row, just like he did following Clyde's death. It couldn't have been a coincidence.

Kelli springs into the air, lands like a feather on my lap, and leans back against my chest. Her balance is perfect and weight equally distributed. It's not like being pounced; it's more like a hug.

The next day at work, I glanced at the picture on the wall next to my desk. The image of all of us sleeping peacefully in the hammock—Buster curled on my chest, Kelli and Kodi by my side—made me smile, even when I was having a tough day. Then I realized Kelli had her eyes closed and was lying in the exact position I buried her. I took it down, knowing I'd never be able to look at the picture the same way.

Since returning from Mandeville, I was filled with a sense of dread each time I came within a few miles of home. The contrast was striking when I arrived at the house. No jumping. A few seconds of tail wagging and petting, and then Kodi and Buddy laid down. I didn't realize how much energy Kelli brought into the house.

Excited? I'll show you excited!

The change in Buddy was noticeable. He was maturing very quickly and becoming more serious. Because Kelli was the alpha, the other dogs were free to run wild without concern. They knew Kelli had their backs. Buddy came on board with no discipline and no boundaries. Though he was still playful, he quickly assumed Kelli's alpha role. He no longer tried to worm his way into our bed at night. Instead, he camped out on a leather chair so he could simultaneously monitor the front and back doors.

Kelli jumps in the hammock at the same moment I sit down. Maintaining perfect balance, she waits until I recline, then slides her curled body between my legs. She lays contentedly as long as I stay, desiring nothing more than to be with me.

The first weekend at home without Kelli, Jennifer and I took the dogs to Monument Park. Kelli, Kodi, and I had visited the heavily wooded park dozens of times. It was a far cry from the near-perfect conditions at Huntsville, with shorter and flatter trails and more people, bikes, and obstacles to avoid. The dogs didn't seem to mind the scaled-down amenities, and I was happy with the shorter drive.

In the old days, I let Kodi off leash for a while on the wide trails and, when Kelli was sufficiently tired, I sometimes let her enjoy a little freedom as well. Running as fast as I could go, she effortlessly put a large gap between us.

Strangely, neither Kodi nor Buddy pulled at all, wandering with more curiosity than enjoyment. It was a striking contrast to previous visits, where Kelli and Kodi were ready to run from the moment we pulled into the parking area. Even Haley, as a seven-year old dog, was more excited when she came to the park. One time she even leaped out the back window of the SUV when I reached in for the leashes.

Once on the trails, Buddy realized it was about the best place a dog could be—dense foliage, lots of scents and new things around every bend. I jogged comfortably with Buddy, moving as fast as his short, stubby legs could carry him. Kodi was happy at any pace. Fast or slow, Kodi knew how to enjoy herself. Buddy, whose looks belied his impressive endurance, never slowed down. He'd come a long way since leaving the pound four months earlier.

We sat on a bench overlooking the creek for twenty minutes. It was beautiful, and I felt a sense of peace, as everyone, myself included, found a way to enjoy the day despite our heavy hearts. Kodi sat with her hips pressed against me, and Buddy intently surveyed the surroundings. With Kelli, we wouldn't have stopped. The trails were meant to run—not sit around and contemplate the meaning of life. Once home, we let Tiger come over for a while. We spent the rest of the day working in the yard and laying in the hammock. Bittersweet. I had lots of good memories of Kelli and thought about how lucky Kodi was to have Buddy's companionship.

Kelli sees a cat in the yard adjacent to the rabbits. Instead of barking in frustration, she and Kodi run three houses down, turn the corner, sprint to the third driveway, and race into the backyard. Kelli and Kodi, surprised by the hostile reception of the twenty-pound black cat, hurry back to me, fearing for their lives.

The following morning, Jennifer asked, "Are you coming with me?"

"No, I need to be at the park with the dogs," I replied. "I don't see any point in going to church. The only place I have any peace is on the trails."

Kelli pushes the tennis ball back and forth, moving it forward like a soccer player. She takes the ball in her mouth, sets it on the table, knocks it off and catches it. She entertains herself for a while, then brings me the ball to play catch in the backyard. Kodi excels at the game, always positioned a few feet behind Kelli, getting the jump to ensure victory. Kelli wrestles the ball from her mouth, brings it to me, and drops it. The next throw, she carries it to Kodi, sets it on her back, and playfully chews the ball on the living table. I misdirect Kodi and hurl the ball where only Kelli can retrieve it.

A short time after we arrived at the park, we ran into our friends, Susie and Rani, and their dogs, Bandit and Raj. On previous visits, Kodi and Bandit wrestled playfully while Kelli scanned the surroundings for squirrels, waiting impatiently for us to resume our run. Kodi and Bandit picked up where they left off, and this time Buddy joined in.

Susie asked, "Where's Kelli?"

"She died a few weeks ago in Mandeville."

"Oh no—what happened?"

I recounted the story about the squirrel, stopping frequently as the emotion choked my voice.

"How horrible. I'm so sorry, Jason," Susie said. "Things happen so fast. That's how I lost my little guy, Charlie."

"Charlie?"

"I had him before I adopted Bandit. We were at a park near some railroad tracks, when a train spooked him. Before I could react, he darted into the woods. He ran all the way back to the parking lot and tried to cross the street. He was dead when I got there."

"I'm sorry to hear that," I said. "I'm really struggling with all the what-ifs. If we hadn't stopped to let Kodi and Buddy play, if I had worn them out by walking to the lake instead of driving, if I had a better grip on the leash, if I wasn't looking the wrong way."

"I was haunted by those things, too—why did I go to the park late that day? Why didn't I anticipate Charlie might be spooked by the train? Why didn't I hook him up when I heard the train?"

"Something similar happened to me," Rani said. "I pushed my father into having elective surgery and, when he almost died, I felt terrible. He was adamant I shouldn't feel guilty, because death not only takes away life, it can curse the living by making you relentlessly focus on the things you did wrong or could've done differently. Look, Jason, you loved your animals, you had the best of intentions. You have to accept this and move on."

The rest of the conversation was pleasant, and they wished me well as we continued on our way. Buddy and Kodi ran a few yards ahead of me along several miles of trails. Each time we encountered mountain bikes or people, I called and they dutifully returned. I felt good, and they had a great time.

Jennifer often spoke of God incidents—odd coincidences that she attributed to the works of God. I always assumed it was silly, wishful thinking, but maybe this was one of those coincidences—two women crossing my path with a comforting message when I was in deep despair.

After Bonnie and Clyde, I thought it a strange coincidence that Kelli and Kodi looked and acted like miniature versions of them, full of life and joy. One day, I watched as they ran and wrestled and tumbled end over end on the levee. I imagined it was a glimpse of heaven—Clyde's and Bonnie's broken bodies were restored and they effortlessly ran and played in endless fields of tall grass. We hadn't sought out Kodi; she came to us. There was no plan to replace Bonnie and Clyde; it just happened.

After another week in Sugar Land, I thought of taking Kodi and Buddy to Huntsville. I felt the same sense of dread as

I did on our first trip to Monument Park. Kelli had such an infectious excitement about her. You couldn't help but want to move when she was in the harness, pulling from beginning to end, as if she was made to be a sled dog. Buddy liked to run, but I sensed he was doing it just to be with me. Kodi was happy to be along for the ride—if we were running she was happy, if we were walking she was fine, and if she could sleep late, even better. There was never any doubt with Kelli. She ran because she enjoyed it, she hungered for it, she lived for it.

We made the long drive to Huntsville, arriving early on a cold, crisp morning. We walked the trail from the parking lot with Buddy straining against the leash. Once deep into the trails, I unhooked them and let them run. Both dogs could be trusted, especially Kodi. Though she chased Kelli on every mission, she never ventured more than twenty yards away from me after that sad day.

Buddy was very obedient—I called and he returned to me, asked him to sit and he sat. We ran a lot more than I expected or was prepared for. With something new around every corner, Buddy didn't want slow down, much less stop and rest. I couldn't believe how much energy he had and how well his stubby legs held up. Every time I closed within ten yards, he looked back and accelerated. Kodi's mood brightened after a while, and they ran together for much of the time.

Several hours later, we returned to the parking area, and I loaded up the exhausted dogs. Or at least I tried to. Despite the seven-mile run, Buddy wanted to go again. We made it about a half mile in, before Kodi stopped and turned back. Buddy also turned around. Once the adrenaline wore off, they realized the roomy Yukon was a great place to take a nap. It wasn't the same without Kelli, but it was still enjoyable. It was nice to see Buddy experience such freedom.

In the months following Kelli's death, Kodi grew closer to me. She often laid with her head on my lap as I sat on the couch, pushing down if I tried to get up too soon. At night, she snuck into bed and snuggled between us, her presence unnoticed until morning. The stress of living on the streets, losing Halcy, and especially losing her best friend, Kelli, had taken a toll on her. Her snout began to turn gray the week Kelli died, and continued unabated, leaving her looking much older than her three years. Still playful with short bursts of energy, she was enjoying sleep even more.

Buddy also connected with me and became a good companion. He often brought me a sock or stuffed animal to play tug of war, or sometimes a bone too small for his big paws to tightly grip. I watched television while he gnawed the fragment poking from my hand.

During one early morning walk, I feared something was wrong when Kodi fell over in the grass, refusing to move. I checked her and, finding nothing wrong, tugged at the leash until she resumed the walk. She continued a half block, then tumbled over again. Suddenly, she popped up and started chasing Buddy. She was back to the old routine she had with Kelli—falling over for the hell of it and playing possum until it was time for a sneak attack.

From time to time, I spiraled down as I reflected on the day I lost Kelli. I missed her a great deal each morning when I took Buddy and Kodi for a walk, when I watched the dogs run and play in the backyard and, most of all, when I returned from work.

Kelli burned brightly in the thousand short days of her life. She squeezed happiness and joy into every moment of the three years she was alive. She left behind so many wonderful memories—the image of her standing against the back of the couch and waiting impatiently for me to touch her, her body almost going into convulsions every time I came home, her courting and playing with Buddy, wrestling with Haley as a puppy, hunting with Bonnie on the banks of the canal, and running on the levee with her best friend, Kodi.

She was always ready and willing for a walk or some new adventure, always wanting to go faster than I could ever hope to go. She helped me feel the kind of love only a dog can give—unconditional and absolute adoration.

I'll always miss the constant pull of her leash, the excitement she brought to the house, and the love she brought into my life.

Part Three

SILVER LININGS

CHAPTER EIGHTEEN

Lost

Heading east on Highway 190, he tried to think of a better solution to the problem. Maybe she'd be adopted or—he didn't want to think about it. *And what if Emily found out?* The young child was comforted by the description of Sadie's new home—large grassy fields, horses to chase, dogs to play with, and young children to love. A shallow wave of guilt dissipated when he remembered the damage—torn

up carpeting, chewed corners of cabinets, ripped uphol-
stery, gnawed windowsills and, of course, accidents. He
regained his composure—*it was a stupid, destructive dog.* It
was just something that had to be done. At the exit for the
shelter, he decided to keep heading east.

Fifteen miles from home, it occurred to him someone
would surely pick up the dog at the state park. There had
to be plenty of food—leftovers from picnics, squirrels,
mice. She'd be fine, he assured himself. And, he reasoned,
it would be better than taking her to the pound.

He turned and drove two miles to the area near the lake,
looped the deserted picnic area and aimed the car toward
the exit. He released the excited puppy from her cage and
set her on the ground. She pranced and hopped through
the tall grass lining the parking lot, her tail wagging with
excitement. He reached into the car for one of her favorite
squeaky toys. He squeezed it several times, then threw it as
far as he could. By the time she found the toy and turned
around, the car was already moving up the road. She ran
as fast as her legs would carry her, yet the car soon disappeared around the bend.

She continued along the quiet road until her legs and
lungs, weakened by the long hours spent in her kennel
each day, burned from the effort. With the unfamiliar scen-
ery and scents, she didn't know what direction to head. She
reached Highway 190 and anxiously paced on the shoulder, peering into the windows of the fast-moving vehicles.
A blaring horn terrified her, sending her sprinting back
into the woods. There, she hid in the thick brush, shaking
with fear.

Hours later, she was on the move again, her black coat
baking in the intense South Louisiana heat. Several miles
down a narrow, dirt trail, she found a small, muddy puddle
and drank greedily. At dusk, she felt the first hunger pangs
as her evening meal failed to arrive. When fatigue finally

overcame her, she hid in a patch of tall grass and drifted to sleep. She woke often, startled by the unfamiliar sounds in the woods.

Each new day passed like the previous one—walking in the searing heat, scrounging for food scraps, searching for water. Sometimes, her spirits rose as the sound of an approaching car rekindled hope her family might come for her. Hunger gnawed at her constantly. Her pads were scraped and worn by the hundred-plus-degree asphalt. A cloud of mosquitoes floated above and fed off her weakened body. What little food she found ran through her due to parasites and diarrhea. As time passed, she began to walk less and sleep more.

It had been more than a week since the morning she spent with her family. She missed Emily's touch and wondered where she was. She curled up in the ditch along the paved bike path and drifted into shallow, restless sleep. Dozens of people passed, some not noticing her in the dense foliage, some not realizing she was in trouble, some not wanting to get involved.

There she lay, her spirit waning, the strength draining from her emaciated body—and the people passed by.

CHAPTER NINETEEN

Breaking Point

The miles went by slowly. The drive was routine, but each more tiring than the last. My back ached after four hours on the road, and I spent the remaining two or three hours arching and shifting to help relieve the pressure. We were constantly on the road for one reason or another—a party for the kids, a birthday celebration for one of the siblings, an art festival with Jennifer's mom.

Steve usually drove to our house a few hours before we arrived, flipped on the air conditioner, and waited to greet us. It was a friendly gesture, and the cool conditions in the house were welcome, yet spending time with Steve was the last thing I wanted after a grueling drive. I wanted to unwind, go for a walk along the lake with Jennifer and the dogs, ride my bike—whatever. Instead, we watched television with Steve until I couldn't take the boredom any longer and retired to the bedroom.

Jennifer's family was welcome to visit anytime and stay as long as they wished. Some nights, one or more of them slept in our extra bedroom. It was usually noon by the time our guests departed or someone finally got around to picking up the kids. By then, it was either too hot or the traffic too heavy to safely walk the dogs. I couldn't understand the need for the slumber parties; her family lived only a few miles away. Our vacation time seemed to focus on and revolve around the needs and activities of my in-laws. The house, built as a retreat for the two of us, increasingly became a place for Jennifer to hang out with her family.

This trip would be different, I hoped. It was Memorial Day weekend—no family events that I knew of, just a few days of relaxation, and, more importantly, a detour to the St. John Parish animal shelter, where a litter of six puppies, each looking remarkably similar to Kelli, waited for me. I narrowed it to three based on their pictures, leaving personality and connection as the deciding factors. Saving one of those needy dogs, I hoped, might alleviate some of the guilt I carried. After six hours of driving, I was really looking forward to meeting the puppies.

"Those little stinkers? I gave the whole lot of them to a rescue organization Tuesday. I think they're planning to send them to Tennessee. I didn't know you were talking about those dogs."

"Yeah, don't you remember, I even described the pictures to you," I said, my spirit deflated.

"Well, I'm sorry. We've got another set of puppies in the back."

"Go ahead, hon, take a look," Jennifer encouraged.

I walked through the kennel area, looking at the fall-back dogs.

"Can you let these two come out?" I asked halfheartedly, pointing to one jet black puppy and one with tiger stripes.

"Sure, go wait around the side, and I'll bring them to you."

The two puppies waddled across the small dirt-covered yard and, every so often, clumsily charged one another.

I played with them for a few minutes, hoping something would click. Nothing did.

"No, I don't think these guys are what I'm looking for," I said.

"I'm real sorry about the other puppies. I'll call the rescue organization for you. They're in Lake Charles."

"I appreciate it—that's right on the way home."

A few minutes later she returned.

"They won't let the puppies go. They apparently all have mange and need to be treated before they can adopt them out."

I walked back to the Yukon, frustrated, disappointed, and stressed from the long drive.

"Damn it, Jennifer. You really screwed up this time. I asked you to call last week and remind them we were coming. I had my heart set on getting one of those puppies. This shit-hole was two hours out of our way."

"How dare you blame me for this? I never blamed you for what you..." Jennifer hesitated, realizing she kicked me incredibly hard. She blamed me all along, though hadn't admitted it until pushed.

I glared at her for a moment and said, "I really hate you. I can't even stand to look at you anymore." The words hung toxically in the air.

"Let me out of the car!" Jennifer cried. "Let me out! I can't take it anymore."

"I'm not going to let you out here; it's dangerous."

"What do you care, you *hate* me, remember? I'll call Shelly to pick me up!" she screamed, unbuckling her seat belt and wrestling with the locked door.

"Stop it!" I said, grabbing her arm to keep her from spilling out onto the roadway. "I'm sorry—I didn't mean what I said. I was angry."

"Let me go, I want you to drop me off," Jennifer cried, pulling her arm free.

"I'll take you to your sister's house. You don't need to get out here."

"I don't want to talk to you anymore. Just drive me home."

Things had been building for a while—the fights, the misunderstandings, the frustration. Each argument cut a little deeper than the last. We had both become people we wouldn't have recognized or thought possible a few years earlier. Where there was once affection, there was indifference. Where there was once love and respect, there was hostility and frustration. We were tolerating each other for the most part—neither of us with a plan to fix things, and neither of us with the desire or energy to try. I felt less than unimportant in her life, I felt like a nuisance. And I'm sure she felt the same way.

We spent the rest of the drive in silence. Both of us wondering how we got here—and how we could escape.

CHAPTER TWENTY

Behind Gray Walls

Lucas stirred from his deep sleep and waited anxiously for the door leading to the outside run to open. Taking slow, awkward steps, limping on his stiff right hind leg, he made his way to the far end of the enclosure and peed for a long time. Hours of lying on his side without much room to stretch caused his muscles to develop a little out of balance. He learned to hold his pee through the night because of the unpleasant treatment he received when he didn't. He knew an accident meant being leashed and dragged to the spray area and hosed down. He was always frightened by the ordeal.

The door closed behind him and he heard bowls clanking and jets of water spraying the inside portion of his kennel. Soon, the door reopened, providing access to a fresh bowl of food and small container of water. Lucas only received water at certain times of the day because he splashed his paws in the bowl if they left it for more than a few minutes. He was fascinated by the sensation and enjoyed watching the dish flip over.

He was accustomed to the daily pattern—two-thirds of his short life had been spent at the shelter. Following his morning meal, he usually laid down and stared blankly at the front of the cage. Every now and then, someone walked by. He got excited when he smelled or heard Jessica in the vicinity. He looked forward to the few times each week she took him to the playroom or the outside enclosure. Even the sound of her voice comforted him.

Something was different this day. Unlike the quiet mornings he usually enjoyed, the air was filled with sounds of people talking, kennel doors opening, and dogs barking. A young volunteer came to Lucas's kennel and gently slipped the temporary leash over his head. She pulled him along until he relented, and minutes later his body was clean. After drying his thick fur, she brought him to the van and loaded him into a cage next to five others.

He had experienced it before—maybe four or five times, he recalled. He knew he was in for a long day in front of the pet store. Strangers would look at him and poke their fingers through the small openings in his steel mesh enclosure. Occasionally, someone would take him for a short walk. Sometimes he enjoyed the attention, but most times he was frightened by it. He spent most of his time pressed against the back of the cage to limit his contact with strangers, a stark contrast to the other dogs who licked fingers and jumped with excitement when people approached. After what seemed like an eternity, they'd load him into the van and return him to the safety of his kennel.

It was actually the ninth adoption event for Lucas. The staff had been hopeful early on, but the weeks passed and more events concluded with no takers. They discussed leaving Lucas behind to make room for another dog with better chances. But, because he'd been through so much, they wanted to give him another chance to warm up to people.

Lucas was a good-looking puppy with golden-brown fur and a snout that appeared to have been dipped in black ink. Small black tufts above the inside corner of each eye gave the impression he was in deep thought or concerned about something. He received a lot of attention at the events because of his unique appearance. Yet his shyness was a deal-killer for any prospect. *He's not playful enough—he doesn't respond—there's no connection—he's just not the dog for us.*

It was the same story at the shelter. Every few days, he was taken to the playroom or the outside pen with some stranger. They talked to him and tried to play with him, but the more they tried to engage him, the more terrified Lucas became. Outside was a place of chaos and uncertainty. Inside the confines of his kennel, he felt safe.

It wasn't surprising Lucas was a bit wary of people. In the first two months at the shelter, he was poked, prodded, and manhandled constantly. He didn't realize all the effort was for his own good. He couldn't understand his alternative was to be euthanized. All he knew was when people came near him, he was usually in for something unpleasant. As time passed, Lucas pushed to the back of the cage in fear when someone, other than Jessica, approached.

He had arrived at the shelter at only two months of age, his coat covered with sarcoptic mange and his stomach filled with parasites. He had open, infected wounds on his skin where he chewed or scratched until they bled. At only eleven pounds, he was significantly underweight for his breed and age. He had so many problems, and there were so many healthy, well-adjusted dogs in need of kennel space. Ignoring the odds, the staff decided to help the little guy.

He spent weeks in isolation as the foul-tasting medicine slowly worked to eradicate the contagious mange mites. To control his infections, they pried his mouth open twice each day, placing a pill at the back of his throat, holding his snout and massaging his neck until he swallowed. They rubbed ointments on the wounds and placed a plastic cone around his neck to prevent his teeth or tongue from reaching his skin. The uncomfortable contraption made grooming impossible and sleeping difficult. They could only remove it at mealtime because, given the chance, Lucas would return to treating the wounds himself.

Once cured, there was more in store for Lucas. He was given shots, put under anesthesia, and had his testicles removed. Following surgery, the stitches and the whereabouts of his missing parts were of great interest to him, necessitating the return of the cone. A few weeks later, Lucas developed a persistent, deep cough, leading to more tests, more isolation, and two weeks of pill wrestling.

With the medical problems behind him, he was transferred to the general kennels. Spending so much time in isolation hadn't prepared him for the chaotic lifestyle. He had always heard the muffled barking of the big dogs, but now he was up close and personal, separated in the outside run only by a chain-link fence. Lucas was as big as some of the other dogs in his area, but he was still a puppy when it came to socialization. He didn't understand the rules or why the dogs barked aggressively at him.

He received very little stimulation during his time in isolation. It wasn't much better in the kennel, and his little brain wasn't developing at a normal pace. Two months to six months is the age puppies learn rapidly about the world around them and begin making connections in their brain. The simple, structured existence didn't provide much opportunity for exploration or learning. He figured out what he needed for survival in the first few weeks.

Lucas became lethargic and his reaction time slowed. Ironically, it was one of the keys to his survival. Even though most of his life was spent in a cage or a kennel, he didn't develop anxiety. The high energy of other dogs was both a blessing and a curse, making them more sociable and fun with prospective families, yet nervous and agitated when kept too long in the small space. Lucas's calm and simple nature kept him from worrying about his confinement. He didn't remember what it was like to be free. All his memories, all his experiences occurred within the dull, gray walls of the building. Each day came and went as the day before and, for as far into the future as he could comprehend, he saw the same existence. He was comforted by the thought.

Time was running out for Lucas—he'd reached the lanky stage, signaling the approach of adulthood. The cute puppies usually found a home quickly. If they missed their window of opportunity, it usually meant a lifetime in the cage. The less adoptable a dog became, the less he was taken to adoption events. There were neither enough volunteers nor room to bring all the dogs to the events. Decisions had to be made, tough decisions—they could only try to save some of them.

The ones left behind had to depend on walk-in traffic. Every now and then, someone came by the shelter, wanting to meet a few of the dogs. The ones craving human companionship, highly excited to get out of the cage, frightened the prospective parents. *He's too much dog, too powerful, too unpredictable. He has no discipline, no boundaries. The dog's going to be a problem.* Back to the cage. Maybe next time.

It was a warm, sunny morning in Mandeville for the opening of the new dog park. Four Humane Society volunteers pitched a tent and stationed the prospective dogs in the flow of maximum foot traffic. It promised to be a good day to find a match for some of the dogs; lots of visitors meant lots of opportunity. The six dogs were the lucky ones—they made the cut. The volunteers displayed pictures of the adult dogs left behind at the shelter. It was a long shot—maybe someone would feel a connection. But it was the only chance those dogs had.

Lucas settled in for another long day.

CHAPTER TWENTY-ONE

Free

The morning after our argument we, like so many times before, tried to forget the ugliness. Yet, behind the smiles, I could sense something had changed. There was less emotion than normal—almost a sense of detachment.

We gathered the dogs and headed to the opening of a new dog park a mile from our house. Once there, Kodi and Buddy did their normal routine of sprinting and wrestling. As they met each new dog, it was chase or be chased. It would have been the perfect place for Kelli—a vast enclosed area—a place to let it all loose. Running as fast as her legs could carry her with no risk of getting hurt, no risk of catching a scent and running off. I imagined the high-energy battle Kelli would have initiated with Kodi and Buddy. Three months had passed, yet each time I thought of her, the pain and guilt came flooding back.

After an hour or so, Jennifer encouraged me to look at a dog named Snickers at the Humane Society tent. I could see why Jennifer liked her. She was lean, spirited, and play-ful like Kelli. A woman was already engaged with the dog when I arrived, so I looked at the others. All were ener-getic and friendly—all but one. He was a lanky dog with unique markings and a sad expression. Jennifer held the leashes for Buddy and Kodi while I knelt down beside him. Stretched out on the cool grass, he wagged his tail slightly as I approached. He didn't bother to get up; he'd found a cool, shady spot and was enjoying the sensation of soft grass under his belly.

He didn't react much as I stroked his head and back. Still, something about him attracted me. I caressed him for a while then leashed and walked him through the nearby stand of trees. After three or four minutes, he was ready to head back. We returned to the tent where he drank a little water, found a fresh patch of grass and laid down, not really noticing I was still near him. The other dog, Snickers, was no longer at the tent. Well, no big deal. I had my heart set on the dogs from the other shelter. All these guys would probably get a home. Maybe not the lanky one, he was too skittish, too somber, and didn't appear to crave human affection. It was just as well I didn't find the right dog. I really couldn't take on any more problems. We loaded up our dogs and headed home.

A few hours later, Jennifer left to spend the day with Cathy and the boys while I headed to Lisa's small hair salon in the nearby city of Covington. On the way, I thought about the dogs I'd seen at the park. I wasn't ready for another dog, but the desire to save something, to give another dog a chance, kept gnawing at me. I took a small detour and pulled into the Humane Society shelter lot. At the desk, I was met by a cheerful, slender woman with a gentle smile.

"I was wondering if I could take a look at some of your dogs."

"Sure, give me a couple of seconds," Jessica replied. "A few of the puppies still haven't made it back from the adoption event we held today. If you'd like to come see, we have some older dogs in the back who really need a home."

"I think I'm going to need a puppy. We already have an established pack."

"Let's take a look and see which ones are back."

"I was at the adoption event earlier. How'd it go?" I asked, following Jessica to the kennels.

"We got one placed," she said, her mood brightening. "A two-year old named Snickers—a lady fell in love with her. We had a few people look at the others, but no takers."

"I remember seeing Snickers. I knew someone would take her—she had a sweet personality. Only one?"

"It's tough to find homes for these dogs. People don't want to take on the expense when the economy is slow. And, because a lot of people are dumping their animals, all the shelters are running at capacity."

I spotted a two-year-old that, except for his cropped tail, greatly resembled Clyde.

"Can I meet this one? He reminds me of a dog I used to have."

Jessica hooked him up and led me to the outdoor pen.

"I'll be back in a few minutes. I've got to take care of some things in the office."

The dog ran tight circles in the small yard, barely noticing I was in the enclosure with him. After retrieving the ball a few times, the beautiful, heavily muscled animal laid down, panting heavily, waiting for Jessica to return.

"I feel bad for him, but it won't work," I said. "Our dogs won't do well with an adult—I need to get a puppy." It was hard to make the walk back to the kennel and leave the big guy, knowing he'd probably spend the rest of his life there.

"How do you handle working around these guys all day long? It would break my heart."

"It's hard. I've got one at home, and I'm always tempted, but I wouldn't be able to give my dog the attention she needs. I have to keep reminding myself I'm doing the best I can."

We made one more pass of the kennels and the lanky, sad dog had returned. They had him doubled up with another cute puppy in a large dog run.

"What's this guy's name?"

"That's Lucas. He's a sweet dog, but he's a little shy."

"Yeah, he was pretty scared when I tried to walk him at the event. I'm late to meet my sister—maybe I'll come back and take another look at him and a couple of the other puppies."

At Lisa's shop, I was met at the door by a creature with short, silky, golden-brown fur stretched tightly across a thick, muscular frame. With jaws borrowed from a small shark, young Wally appeared more menacing than his namesake. Within seconds, his inspection was complete and his tail began to wag. Wally joined me on the couch, seeking a full body rub from his new best friend. Lisa told me about the dog prior to my visit, but the verbal description paled in comparison to the meaty, bone-crusher leaning against me.

It was odd how the young dog came into Lisa's life shortly after Walliford died. Bonnie and Clyde's dad lived to the age of sixteen, surviving his mate, Pepper, and all his children, except Tango. Lisa came home from work one day and, like always, Walliford and Tango eagerly waited to greet her. Walliford hobbled to her, wagged his tail slightly, stumbled to the ground, and drew his last breath.

Six months later, a malnourished Pit Bull showed up at the gate several days in a row. Not ready for a new dog, Lisa put food over the fence each day and often checked the papers in a futile attempt to find his owner. When she finally decided to let him in, he, after a brief introduction to Tango, went directly to Walliford's grave and laid down. Whether it was destiny or coincidence, Wally had found a new home.

Though Tango accepted the new addition, the grief of losing his father, friend, and companion accelerated his physical decline. With mobility greatly impaired by his bad hips and old injuries, he struggled to hang on despite the intense pain of late-stage cancer. When Lisa couldn't bear to watch him suffer any longer, she had Tango euthanized and buried next to Walliford's grave.

"The shop's looking nice," I said. "Are you getting any new clients?"

"It's slow. I need to get a few more customers soon or I'll have to rent out one of the chairs to help pay the bills. What do you think of Wally?"

"He's a cool dog. I guess you don't have to worry about any trouble with him around." Years earlier, a giant Pit Bull like Wally would've frightened me. Now, I could see him for what he was—just a big, lovable dog.

"That's why I bring him with me. He's friendly when he should be and mean when he needs to be."

Lisa got down to business and began cutting my hair. She didn't ask how I wanted it—she never did. She just did what she felt like doing, and, because I was starting to lose quite a bit of hair, I didn't much care.

"I'm thinking about getting another dog. I saw one at the shelter that looked kinda pitiful."

"Are you crazy? You already have four. Why would you want to do something like that?"

"I need to do something. I can't get what happened to Kelli out of my mind."

"You need to get over that, Jason. You didn't cause it; it was an accident. Is Jennifer going to let you bring home another dog?"

"Yeah, she's fine with it—she thinks it might help bring me out of my funk. It's strange though. I think something's going on with Jennifer."

"What do you mean?"

"Something's changed. All we do is fight. And instead of trying to fix things, we just blow it off." I added half-seriously, "I think we might be splitting up."

"Are you kidding? You guys are always together. You're probably overreacting, like always."

"I don't know if I'll be coming back this way for a while. I'm really starting to hate coming in town—every time it gets worse."

"I noticed something was weird between you two at Thanksgiving. I told Rob it looked like Jennifer was acting different. She used to be so attentive toward you. At the dinner, you were doing all the work. Her family wasn't very friendly either."

"No, I don't think anything was going on then."

I changed the subject back to the adoption and told her more about the sad dog and the puppy in the cage with him. Lisa gave a few other reasons why I shouldn't do it, but I wasn't really listening. I was going to do something—I just didn't know what.

On the way home, I called Jennifer.

"I'm thinking about adopting one of the dogs at the Humane Society—remember the one I walked at the park this morning? There's another puppy that looks a bit like him—she's a female. Maybe you could come help me pick one out."

"I'm going to dinner with Cathy and the boys. You should get the dog you want," she said. "I'll be fine with whatever you decide."

Whatever you decide? It wasn't the way she normally reacted. In the past, she was excited to help save an animal. Now, she didn't seem to have feelings either way. I ended the call unsure of what to make of her new attitude.

I detoured again at the road to the Humane Society.

"Hey Jessica, I'd like to see the sad dog—I think you said his name is Lucas."

She led me to the small playroom and went to retrieve Lucas. When he came in, it was much the same reaction as the park. He slowly approached me, wagging his tail slightly as I caressed him. After a few seconds, he turned and began looking for an escape route. He jumped on the far couch and looked through the window adjoining the offices, beyond which a female was doing paperwork at her desk. Lucas's tail wagged furiously as he scratched at the window, then ran to the door and barked. Though he came back to me, he was clearly trying to enlist my help in his escape. Next, he jumped on the other couch and scratched at the outside window. When he approached me, his head turned back every other step to see if help was on the way. Once he realized the futility of getting out through the walls or windows, he sat down facing the crack between the door and the wall, longing for it to open.

I felt sad that he yearned for his kennel. I imagined how his life would play out. The dog I took to the outdoor enclosure earlier—that was his future. He had no personality and no affection. Two big strikes against getting adopted. He was already forty pounds and heading for a hundred based on the size of his paws—still huge compared to the rest of his body. The size coupled with the personality would make him completely unmarketable.

I thought about all the bubbly, energetic, affectionate dogs I'd seen over the past month. Lucas wasn't even in the running. He needed me. He needed a pack of good dogs to show him how much fun life can be. Maybe his shyness would be a blessing, I thought. Once he built trust and formed a bond, it would be incredibly strong.

For the first time, I noticed he had light cream-colored patches on his shoulder blades. They were in the same place and roughly the same shape as the ones Kelli had. He looked nothing like Kelli, yet the patches were enough. When Jessica came back, I told her I wanted the dog.

"Oh, that's great! If you're not sure about it, you could do a trial weekend." She was thrilled Lucas might have found a home.

"No thanks, I'm sure it will work out. This is the dog—he's even got the same patches on his shoulders one of my dogs had."

"Those are called 'angel wings.'"

I signed the papers, paid the nominal adoption fee and noticed something odd in the records. Lucas arrived at the kennel in the middle of February; the same week Kelli died. Maybe the angel wings and the timing were nothing more than coincidences, but they removed any doubt he was the right dog. I loaded Lucas into the front seat for the drive to his new home. Lucas sat quietly for a while, then began to investigate his surroundings. He settled on top of a stack of mulch and fell asleep.

The dogs barked wildly as I carried the terrified animal into the backyard. They sniffed the newcomer curiously, then tried to engage him in play. Each time Buddy initiated a friendly wrestling bout, Lucas offered no resistance and fell to the ground. He really didn't know what Buddy and the others were trying to do. Fearing the worst might befall him, his muscles tensed and his legs struggled to keep his body upright. His reaction to Buddy was understandable, but even Buster made him cower. Lucas was wondering who we were, why he was here and, more importantly, how he could get back to his kennel.

Our socialization experiment was interrupted when a strong thunderstorm rolled in. We went inside and Lucas immediately took a squat and began to poop. He ducked and ran from me as I yelled and tried to corral him.

"Hurry up, Lucas. Hurry up," I encouraged after dragging him out into the heavy rain. He sat quietly, shivering with fear, staring blankly at me. I brought him back in and he soon peed on the floor, initiating the same unpleasant routine. By now, Lucas was not only afraid of Buddy, he was afraid of me. After the storm passed, things calmed down quite a bit. I was able to keep all the dogs outside and give Lucas praise whenever he went to the bathroom.

That night, I didn't sleep much, waking every hour to take Lucas outside and give him the command to pee. The first few times he looked at me, sat down, and wondered why he was being awakened so frequently. Eventually, Buddy lifted his leg on a small oak tree, setting an example for Lucas to follow. Lucas stretched forward, keeping all four paws on the ground, and relieved his bladder.

"Good boy, Lucas!" I shouted, thrilled he had made the connection so quickly.

Instead of encouraging him, my praise made him duck and cower. I felt so bad for the little guy. He was completely overwhelmed with confusion and fear.

A little after sunrise, Jennifer left to visit her cousin, and I continued to work with Lucas. He made the connection on peeing pretty quickly, often going on command out-side, or at least making it to the back door when he became confused. Pooping was a different story As soon as I was the least bit distracted, Lucas stole away to a corner of the room and unloaded a pile the size of Buster. The first time, I shouted and chased him outside, but soon dialed it back, realizing I was only reinforcing his fear.

Kodi instinctively began to provide guidance like a sur-rogate mother. It was the same thing I'd seen Haley do when Kelli and Kodi were puppies. Now, it was Kodi's turn to train the puppy and keep him in line. She was very gen-tle with him during play, giving him the time he needed to build trust. It was going to be quite a project to transfer her expert combat skills to him, given his lack of coordination, slow reflexes, and intense fear. Buddy, on the other hand, just wanted another wrestling partner. Even after Lucas understood Buddy was only trying to play, he was unable to do anything but fall over, fearing one wrong move would lead to serious consequences.

Lucas, easily fatigued by the combination of heat, activ-ity, and poor conditioning, often retreated to the kitchen, plopping down in front of the water bowl, dipping his snout, taking a few gulps, then flipping the bowl with his paws. Once the bowls were moved outside, he sometimes stood with his front paws in the bowl or dunked his snout in pursuit of an imaginary salmon. The result was always the same—the bowl upside down and its contents saturat-ing the patio. I let it slide a few times because it was nice to see him finally trying to play. It was going to be a delicate balance between solving his bad habits and scaring him half to death.

After lunch, the dogs, ready to catch some much-needed sleep, settled on their beds while I set off on a long bike ride. During the rides, my mind usually drifted back to the events of the day Kelli died. Over and over, the images haunted me. That day, however, my thoughts were on more immediate concerns—Lucas was going to be a challenge. It was clear at the shelter he was a very disturbed animal. And there was something wrong with his brain—too much time between stimulation and reaction—almost like he was high. The slow reaction and the confused look in his eyes was more like what I'd expect from a two-month-old. I violated my own rule—never take a problem dog from the shelter. There are just too many loving, well-adjusted animals waiting for a home.

Thoughts of Jennifer drifted through my mind. Oddly, I didn't mind her spending another day with family. In fact, I was relieved she was gone. The frustration and stress of our continual bickering left me physically and emotionally drained. I once looked forward to spending every waking moment with her, feeling like the center of her world and knowing she was the center of mine. Lately, I made excuses to skip our lunch visits and, on weekends, took the dogs places I knew she wouldn't want to go. Other times, I'd go bike riding while she attended church or shopped with friends.

Twelve years. Jennifer and I had been through so much together. Instead of pulling us closer, the challenges broke down the relationship bit by bit. The last couple of years, filled with so many heartaches, misunderstandings, arguments, hurt feelings, and apologies, left us numb to it all. No matter how many times we tried to break the cycle, each new bit of progress was wiped away with another senseless argument. The relationship, hobbled by arguments over the house, weakened by conflicts regarding family, and sabotaged by our own stubbornness, became so fragile that a careless word could lead to a huge blowup. I should have never agreed to build the damn house. I knew better—never do business with family—never.

Curiously, despite a litany of unforced errors, a cadre of fraudulent contractors, and months of living in continual mess and chaos, we made it through the home renovation in Metairie. We didn't just endure it, we enjoyed it. We were on the same team—we celebrated together as tasks were accomplished, supported each other when mistakes were made— it was always us against them. We laughed, we played, we washed dishes in the bathtub, ate po' boys on the front lawn. Nothing seemed to faze us.

Maybe it was the lack of boundaries in Mandeville that made the difference. In Metairie, though we saw Jennifer's family frequently, there were no sleepovers, no drop-ins, no marathon visits. I didn't mind having her family around from time to time. In truth, I enjoyed feeling part of a close family for once in my life. Jennifer had as much contact as she desired without infringing on our time together—visiting at their houses, meeting for lunches, or chatting on the phone. She didn't have to, and usually didn't want to, interrupt our time together.

With each passing trip to Mandeville, it became more and more obvious I was no longer the center of her world—not even close. Her family members, each happy to monopolize her time or take advantage of her kindness, became a wedge between us. As I felt less important in her life, I began to resent not only her family, but Jennifer as well.

CHAPTER TWENTY-TWO

Too Much to Handle

Caught up in my thoughts, I didn't notice the ride was almost over. Over an hour had elapsed—*how many intersections did I blow through without looking?* I saw something moving to the left of the path about a hundred yards ahead. It crawled slowly out of the ditch and into the tree line.

I stopped and spotted a creature hiding behind a pine tree about ten yards off the trail. As it moved a little, I realized it was a dog—a dog with exaggerated features due to starvation. I called to it. It studied me and began to shake nervously. I stripped off my helmet and sunglasses and called to it again.

The dog lurched forward and stumbled toward me, tail wagging more with each step. She lunged and hit me in the chest, nearly knocking me from my squatting position. She licked my face while her body wiggled and pressed against mine. She rolled over to get a belly rub and peed all over herself—and me. It took several minutes for the excited puppy to calm down.

By the looks of her razor-sharp, white teeth, I estimated she was barely four months old. It appeared she hadn't eaten for quite a while—her stomach completely caved in and ribs clearly visible under her thin skin. Her hips jutted out abnormally, leaving gaps that allowed my fingers to follow the contours of the bones. She had dozens of open sores on her belly and reeked from the grime caked on her body. Her short black coat was dull and completely bare in a number of areas.

Miles from the nearest neighborhood, she didn't look like she could've traveled very far under her own power. I let the thoughts go. The puppy was very hot and thirsty. It was about three o'clock in the afternoon and the temperature was still hovering in the nineties.

I poured some water into my cupped hand. She licked at it excitedly, drinking some, but splashing most to the ground. I removed the top and tilted the bottle to bring the water close to the rim. She quickly lapped up half the contents before I stopped her. We needed to save some—I wasn't sure what I was going to do with this poor mess. No food, one water bottle, no cell phone—I wasn't prepared to help this little puppy.

I couldn't think of any good alternatives. We had already exceeded our capacity by taking on Lucas. Five dogs—and it was clear Lucas was going to be a challenge. It was the last thing our fragile marriage needed. I thought about coming back with the SUV and taking her to the shelter. But, realistically, who'd want the dog? Even after she was cleaned up and treated, she'd still be an awkward-looking thing— and black. For some reason, black dogs weren't adopted as readily as cream or gold-colored dogs. When I was at the Humane Society, Jessica told me one of the local shelters was running a five-dollar black dog special. Five bucks to adopt a dog—their cost is in the hundreds between shots and neutering.

We took a number of strays to shelters over the years. One time, there was a dog living on the bank of the canal in our neighborhood. We tried on a number of occasions to approach the dog, but it always ran from us and it ran from several of our neighbors who tried to help it. Animal Control tried to capture him, yet he always escaped to the opposite bank of the canal. The dog grew thinner each time we saw him, but refused to allow anyone near. One morning, he saw Kelli and Kodi off leash in the park and joined in the play. He was a cute puppy and had great chemistry with my crew, but we already had four dogs at the time. After a few more encounters, he followed us home. The next day, I brought him to the Citizens for Animal Protection shelter, donated two-hundred dollars and asked them to give extra effort in finding him a home. I never checked back to see if he was adopted or was euthanized. I was afraid to find out the answer. For weeks, I wondered if I did the right thing.

Another time, I called Jennifer to help me rescue a stray at my office. It took a couple of hours and a few hamburgers before the dog could be enticed to get into the SUV. I needed to get back to work, so I asked Jennifer to take it to the shelter. Because the dog snapped at a worker when they tried to take it in the back, they told Jennifer they'd probably euthanize the animal. They'd give it another day and see if they could work with him, but they couldn't adopt out dogs displaying aggressive behavior. Jennifer was upset by the ordeal and told me the next time I wanted to get involved, I needed to take the dog in myself.

I was faced with the choice again: intervene and take the dog to an uncertain fate at the shelter, or leave the dog and hope someone else helps it. I decided to ride the area and look for signs, thinking someone must be missing her. I gave the puppy a little more of my water and got back on the bike. The puppy screamed and stumbled after me as I began to ride away. I slowed down to allow the puppy to follow at a slow trot. Each step sounded hollow, like a horse galloping on a dirt track. She had abnormally large wrists—perhaps the source of the strange sound.

I unclipped my right foot and used it to keep the dog, who was joyfully looking up at me and clumsily weaving toward my pedal, at a safe distance. I kept us moving slowly forward with my left foot and we made our way down a few deserted streets nearby. Realizing it might be kind of dangerous to aimlessly wander the area, we returned to the trail, sat down and the puppy drank the last of the water. The short walk had really worn her out.

Our rest was short-lived as a swarm of mosquitoes provided sufficient motivation to get moving again. I took off my cycling shoes and stuffed them in the pockets of my jersey. I picked up the dog and slung her over my left shoulder, then picked up the bike with my right hand and balanced it by the handlebars. Excitedly, the puppy licked my face and peed on me again. We were in for a nice, long walk.

Man, it was hot. Walking in the stifling heat and humidity with the dog pressed against my soaked, sticky, polyester-covered body was beyond miserable. I flagged down a passing cyclist and borrowed his cell phone. Jennifer didn't answer. I tried to remember her cousin's number, but, after four wrong tries, I returned the phone. We kept moving. The bike was quite unwieldy as I attempted to steer it with only one hand. Every few minutes, I lost control of it and my leg whacked the pedal.

Despite her emaciated condition, the thirty-something pound dog seemed to grow heavier with each step. I switched her from side to side every few minutes as fatigue set in. Each time, I had to lay the bike down, set her down, walk around the bike, hoist the dog up and then squat to retrieve the bike—an extra minute, repeated dozens of times, greatly slowed our progress.

As we inched forward, I recalled the time I carried Kodi home. She was probably ten pounds heavier than this pitiful, smelly creature, but the weather was cooler, the distance was shorter and my endurance was better. Many months before Kelli and Kodi discovered the coyote field, we frequented a secluded levee behind our neighborhood. Though it was only a half-mile long, the grassy area was close enough to visit every evening. The north side of the levee was bound by fenced yards and the south by a quarter-mile wide swath of dense foliage and tall trees, beyond which flowed the Brazos River. Initially, we ran the course tethered together, but, as the weeks passed, I felt more comfortable with the security of the long trail. Once off-leash, the dogs wrestled and played joyfully, running like the wind and then sprinting back to check on me as I lumbered behind.

As had happened before in other venues, following dozens, perhaps hundreds of uneventful visits, Kelli spotted something and the two puppies quickly disappeared into the dense woods. Despite frantic pleading, screaming, and shouting, the dogs did not return. If they went a mile to the right, they'd end up on a major divided highway. If they went left, they'd find Interstate 59 a half mile away. If they went straight, they'd eventually get to the river, then could travel for miles along the bank in either direction. I decided to run toward the interstate and, as I closed in on the busy road, had all but given up hope.

About a hundred yards from the highway, Kelli bounded out of the woods, smiling and panting heavily. Kodi soon followed, limping on three legs, her front right dew claw pulled back and bleeding. I picked her up and slung her upper body across my shoulder, held her legs and butt with my left arm and held onto Kelli's leash with my right. After an hour or so, I finally made it home, covered in mud and dead tired.

The puppy was thirsty again, so I flagged down a guy passing on a mountain bike. Unable to hear what I was saying, he removed his ear bud and simultaneously grabbed the front brake handle a little too hard. With only one hand on the bar, it was all over quickly. He catapulted face first into the pavement, hitting it pretty hard. Despite a good patch of road rash on his chin, he sprang quickly to his feet, acting as if nothing happened. I knew it had to hurt, but I remembered the unwritten rule from my years of cycling—when you pull something uncoordinated, never let others know you hurt yourself. He gave me the rest of his water bottle and let me try a few more numbers on his cell phone. No luck.

We kept walking. After another hour or so, I finally remembered the number. By then, it was getting toward the end of the day and there wasn't much traffic. Another half hour passed before I found a cyclist with a cell phone.

The dog laid in my arms for the drive home in Cathy's car, completely exhausted from the ordeal. It was 6:30—we'd been walking for over three hours. At Cathy's house, Jennifer met us in the driveway with food and water for the dog. The dog quickly ate the food, licked the bowl and pushed it around the driveway, strategically drawing attention to her desire for more food. Jennifer brought another helping from the house and the dog quickly finished it off. Moments later, the dog vomited the undigested food, then quickly devoured it. She wasn't going to let anything go to waste.

We checked the paper and the internet for any lost dog ads. Nothing. Because it was a holiday and everything was closed, we'd have to either take her to the vet or to the shelter in the morning. I was too tired to make the decision and relieved I had more time to think about it. Jennifer named the dog Daisy. I wasn't thrilled with the name, but I didn't have any better ideas.

By the time we returned to our house, Kodi and the rest of the crew were pretty glad to see us. They must've been a little worried because they knew my rides were usually much, much shorter. As I approached the gate, I could see they were even more confused, wondering why I was bringing home another dog. I carried Daisy into the backyard and set her down. The dogs all swarmed and sniffed the scared little animal. Then Kodi dropped down into the normal dog play position. Daisy understood and started to wag her tail. As exhausted as she was, she found the energy to play for a little while. Even Buddy didn't worry her—she could tell he was a sweet dog underneath his brutish exterior. Buddy seemed to be quite relieved he had found a dog able to stay upright when he approached.

Before bringing her in the house, I gave her a thorough bath on the patio. Once the dirt was removed, I could see she was painted with the same colors as Kodi—except in more attractive patterns. She was solid black on the body and had brown hair around her snout and two small brown patches above the inside corners of her eyes. A small meandering river of snow white fur flowed from beneath her chin and splayed into a broad delta on her chest. The fur was only a quarter inch long, making the extent of her starvation more obvious. Her giant paws looked as though they belonged to a Great Dane and her oversized wrists to a Basset Hound.

Jennifer and I talked for a while at the patio table while the dogs got acquainted. She was certain if we took Daisy to the pound, they'd euthanize her. We couldn't keep her—five dogs was already looking like a bad idea. Well, it was really four if you excluded Cricket—so old and quiet he required very little effort. Maybe three, if you discounted Buster who, at only five and a half pounds, wasn't even a dog really.

We had to keep her. Unfortunately, that was bad news for Lucas. Though he'd only been with us a day, I still felt bad for him. It was a tough choice, but the only logical one—six dogs was not going to happen. The next morning we'd take Daisy to the vet and Lucas to the Humane Society.

We spent the rest of the evening training both puppies on the peeing commands and teaching them how to use the doggie door. That night, like the one before, we visited the yard each hour. Unlike the previous though, my heart was heavy. Each time I looked at Lucas and praised him, I thought about the poor guy living his life in a kennel. I kept trying to focus on Daisy—her life saved through his sacrifice. If only I wasn't so impulsive—if I waited another day to adopt Lucas—he wouldn't have to go through this disappointment.

Early the next morning, I made the call to the Humane Society.

"I adopted a dog a couple of days ago named Lucas. I found another stray yesterday, and I need to return him," I said sheepishly.

"I'm sorry. We already gave his kennel away," the voice on the other end replied. "We've got a waiting list—your only option is the Parish Shelter. They're running at full capacity too. He'll have seventy-two hours to find a home or they'll have to euthanize him."

I was a little surprised by her bluntness. I didn't rescue him just to have him destroyed. It wasn't going to happen. We would have six dogs—at least for the time being.

The next morning, Daisy received her vaccinations and was treated for the skin infection and parasites. By the time we returned to the house, Jennifer had us pretty well ready to go. We loaded the six dogs for the long ride home. It was a fairly tight fit, yet the dogs didn't seem to mind.

I had no idea how we could possibly manage life with a half dozen dogs. We'd been in violation of the neighborhood's three-dog rule on and off for ten years. Now, we'd be so far outside the bounds we'd surely be caught. I knew Lucas's good fortune earlier in the day only delayed the inevitable. Our only hope was to get him placed with a good family in Sugar Land and get our lives back to normal.

CHAPTER TWENTY-THREE

Going Home

Jennifer went along with and, in some ways, encouraged the expansion of our pack, yet the constant chaos in the house soon overwhelmed her. I wondered what she expected—two large-breed puppies added to three very active dogs—then throw in Cricket, a small yard and Lucas's learning disability. We were constantly trying to manage the rough play, control the barking, and stop the accidents in the house. It was more stress at a time neither of us could handle it well.

Jennifer was frustrated on walks with the two energetic young animals, and Buddy had the ability to pull her down if he decided to chase something. The four dogs always tried to walk together, tangling the leashes, tripping the humans, and dragging whoever didn't keep pace. It didn't help to walk them in shifts. Those left behind cried for a while, then destroyed anything within reach. The challenge of walking the pack of wild dogs necessitated finding an off-leash area to let them work off some steam.

The small, muddy Sugar Land dog park with its chocolate-colored pond became our favorite evening destination. There, the four dogs entertained each other and found a few friends along the way. Despite the uninspired surroundings, it took the edge off their energy and calmed their mood.

One weekend, we decided to try the mountain bike trails at Monument Park. During the drive, Daisy began to scream as if she was in intense pain. Jennifer leaned over the seat, assuming the dog snagged one of her dew claws, yet couldn't see anything that might be causing the pain. She unhooked her seat belt and crawled in the back, instantly calming the ailing dog. Daisy wasn't injured; she was merely frightened. It wasn't the first time she'd been in a vehicle, nor the first time on the interstate, but it was the first time she was heading east on the interstate. Maybe she thought we were bringing her back to Mandeville—back to the life she had before I found her. I guess I'd be screaming too.

We made the rest of the drive in peace, and the young puppies had a great time once on the trails. They stuck to Kodi and Buddy like ducklings following a mother duck, running and walking for two hours. I enjoyed it as well, but knew the trails wouldn't be a long-term solution for us.

As the two puppies grew bigger, stronger, and more confident, they'd likely venture off-trail, making it impossible to keep them together and safe.

Three weeks after our last trip to Mandeville, Jennifer returned to watch Dillon and Josh while Cathy was out of town. She went a few days earlier than planned because we had another fight about who knows what. The slightest mistake, the wrong tone of voice, even the way I looked at her—anything could set it off.

Jennifer took Buster and Cricket and left the big dogs with me. Surprisingly, the four dogs were pretty easy to handle once Buster was gone. Buster, it seems, was the cause of a lot of the chaos—barking continuously and chasing, lunging and biting at the big dogs. Buddy and Kodi tolerated him, often enjoying the attention. The new dogs looked at Buster as if he was some sort of alien creature, and, because he harassed them from sunup to sundown, I imagined we'd eventually see a replay of the Bonnie and Sandy situation.

With four canines and only one person, the dog park was a poor solution. It was only a matter of time before we ran afoul of the two-dog rule and received the $97 fine times two. Instead, we set our sights on the large open field across the parking lot. The area was bound by dense, six-foot-tall weeds resembling sugar cane and a stand of pines that lined the Brazos River. A dirt path made a three-quarter-mile loop, hugging the trees and surrounding knee-high grass and wildflowers. The dogs ran and wrestled playfully, then switched gears to a serious hunting mode when they smelled or heard something, their tails quivering as their snouts hugged the ground. Soon, birds were flushed from hiding, or a rat was killed and consumed. The two puppies were glued to Kodi, watching and learning as she led the hunting expeditions. Buddy, indifferent to Kodi's lesson plan, trotted happily by my side until the others decided to play again.

The dogs hardly noticed the people who infrequently crossed our path, interested only in catching, killing, and consuming mice, or, of course, wrestling and running with each other. One glaring exception was Daisy's affinity for cyclists. Upon seeing a bike, any bike, she sprinted toward it with her tail wagging and chased for a few dozen yards. She clearly wanted to play, perhaps fondly remembering the day we found each other, but the person on the receiving end of her affection usually wasn't amused by the ambush.

On one of our outings to the field, I met a woman who volunteered with a dog rescue organization. After I recounted the story of Lucas and Daisy, lamenting the fact we were one dog heavy, she suggested I bring Lucas to an adoption event they were holding in a few hours. It was the right thing to do. Nearly a month had passed and Lucas continued to have accidents in the house. He fit in well with the other dogs, yet still hadn't bonded with me. Forget bonding, I would've been happy if he stopped running each time I approached. We needed to find someone who could devote more time and attention to him.

When it was time to take Lucas to the adoption event, I grabbed the leash and called him. Most dogs willingly follow when you pick up the leash. Not Lucas—he ducked and ran, sensing something was up. After corralling him, I had to slip a choke collar over his head to encourage him to come with me. The fear in his eyes was depressing. Even after a month, he was still terrified of me.

Leaving Lucas in the Yukon, I entered the pet store and saw two ladies seated at a table next to three large dogs in cages. Instead of approaching them, I walked the aisles reflecting on what I was about to do. I was planning to take a poor, disturbed animal who had lived most of his life in a cage and completely break his spirit. I thought about the pain he'd feel as I closed him in the cage and walked out of the store. I couldn't do it. I grabbed a chew toy, paid for it and brought it to Lucas. For all he knew, he'd been on a special trip to get the toy. I was disappointed in myself for even letting it get that far. Lucas was part of the family.

On trips home, Jennifer usually called several times a day to check in. When the phone failed to ring for a few days, I began to leave messages. When she finally returned my calls, she didn't have much to say, seeming even more distant and disengaged. She told me she felt free and happy—and might stay longer than planned. After ten days, she returned home.

"I think we need some time apart," she said.

"What? Why?" I asked, knowing the answer. We were becoming meaner and more distant each day. A little cooling-off period might be a good thing.

"I'm going to make an appointment for us to meet with a Christian divorce lawyer."

"We don't need a lawyer to separate. Why don't you just pack a few suitcases and stay in Mandeville for a while?" I asked, slightly confused. *What the hell is a Christian divorce lawyer anyway?*

"No, I want to talk to the lawyer in case we want to get things moving."

"Look, I'm not happy either, but we've always gotten past these things before."

"I'm renting a truck and I'm taking my things with me," she said calmly.

"Jennifer, we have a furnished house there. Why do you need to take all your stuff if you plan to come back?"

"I want my things with me. You'll get mad and break them."

"Why would I break your stuff? You're talking crazy."

None of it was making any sense. Jennifer wasn't renting a small trailer; she reserved a real moving truck. She was planning to take everything she valued—family furniture, lamps, clothes, paintings, scrapbooks, you name it. Once I realized we weren't really talking about separation, I was crushed. All my big talk was now coming back to haunt me—*if you aren't happy here, why don't you just leave?* I never imagined she'd actually do it.

"When are you leaving?"

"Friday."

"You just got here—you've been gone for almost two weeks. What's the rush?"

"I can't stand to be here anymore. In Mandeville, I felt free for the first time in a long time. I feel smothered here."

"Smothered? You have all day, every day, to yourself while I'm at work. I don't monitor you—I don't even know what you're doing most days."

"You don't understand. I'm tired of being ignored. All you care about is the dogs."

"That's not true. You're the only person in my life. How can you say I ignore you? We do everything together."

"You don't want me. You keep telling me to leave."

"I never told you to leave. I told you if you weren't happy, you should leave. What's really going on?"

An hour later, in the sent mail folder of our joint e-mail account, I found a couple of notes from Jennifer to friends in Mandeville. One had the words "…can't wait to come back, and I look forward to being your permanent neighbor. Do you know of anyone that's hiring?" The word "permanent" kicked me in the chest. Another had the words "…things are miserable here, I can't wait to leave." I printed the e-mails and walked back to the room to find Jennifer organizing her belongings.

"Are you planning to get a job when you get to Mandeville?" I tested her.

"I haven't thought about it."

"Well, then how do you explain this?" I asked, tossing the paper evidence on the bed.

"What are you doing reading my personal e-mails?"

"It's our joint account. Look, you're lying to me. What's really going on? Why do you want to leave?"

"It's everything."

"What do you mean?"

"You're always picking on me."

"What are you talking about? I don't pick on you."

"You criticize what I wear, how much I drink, what I watch, what I listen to. It seems like I can't do anything right."

"How can you say that? What am I supposed to do when you ask my opinion? We're supposed to be honest with each other, aren't we?"

"You're not honest, you're just mean. You think you're so great—you need to take a good, long look in the mirror."

"So that's it? I just need to sit here like a dummy and keep my mouth shut?"

"It's more than that. I don't like how you treat my family. I'm tired of all your rules. I don't want any boundaries."

"No boundaries? That's funny—they don't have any boundaries now. They can come over any time, no need to call ahead, and they stay as long as they want."

"I don't want to hear you complain about it anymore. When we're in Mandeville, I'll let you know what the plans are, and you can either come along or stay at home."

"I might as well stay in Sugar Land."

"You do nothing but complain about my family."

"I just don't want them around me all the time. Maybe if we had some privacy, we could act like a married couple—instead of roommates. This one I won't be able to change and, honestly, I don't want to. I really can't stand your family anymore. In fact, I hate your family—every last damn one of them."

"That's your problem, they all love you and you don't appreciate it. You don't deserve them."

"Fine, what else is bothering you?"

"I don't like our social life."

And the list went on: go to church more, be more affectionate, smile when I see her, take vacations without the dogs, learn how to dance, and another dozen or so helpful suggestions. I stared blankly at Jennifer for a few moments while I tried to digest the litany of grievances. I had never been kicked so hard in my life. The ease with which she highlighted my failings made it seem as if I hadn't mattered to her at all.

"A lot of these things are unrealistic. There's not much chance I'll ever be able to make you happy." Feelings of rejection overwhelmed me and my voice began to crack, "How can you just throw all this away?"

"I'll stay if you ask me to," she offered, half-heartedly.

"No, go ahead and leave." I couldn't do it. I could see how miserable she was and how much she disliked me—*how else could she leave this lifestyle, her friends, her church, her dogs—especially her dogs?*

The next day, I called a friend at work and got the number of a divorce attorney. I made an appointment for the first available slot—Thursday afternoon, the same day the moving truck was scheduled to arrive.

I arrived at the law firm a half hour early and waited anxiously in the lobby. To pass the time, I reread the letter I had composed over the last few days.

"...I am devastated that our relationship has deteriorated this far. I know many of the things that brought us to this point are not your fault. ...I can only imagine how unhappy you must be to walk away from a life of security and wealth, from the close friends you have made over the years here, from the connection to your church and, most of all, from your dogs..."

How could she leave the dogs?

"...But even if I could do the things you asked, it is irrelevant. You have already been hardened to the point that the spark and the love are gone and you are no longer kind towards me."

Ms. Archer's assistant offered me something to drink and let me know the lawyer was running a little behind schedule. I picked up the letter again.

"...I have a world of regrets that will always be with me. I regret not figuring out a way to communicate more effectively with you. I regret not accepting you as you are. I regret not getting counseling early in our marriage. I regret letting my pride stand in the way of being happy—I should have let it all go. Most of all, I regret letting the love we shared erode bit by bit over the years..."

"...I filed for divorce today. I don't know if this news will bring you feelings of despair or relief. You've been so cold, and things have been so strange between us lately, I don't really know how you'll react to this..."

"...even if I have some of this wrong, it doesn't matter. I don't have the desire, the strength, the patience, and, more importantly, the forgiveness left in my heart to try to fix things…"

I had trouble managing more than a shallow breath, feeling as though someone was standing on my chest. The assistant led me to Ms. Archer's office and I handed over the stack of bank statements, mortgage information, and other requested documents. I described the situation, my voice cracking and tears welling, feelings of failure, rejection, and sadness overwhelming me.

"Are you ready to file?" she asked. "You can get an injunction today that will prevent Mrs. Phinney from withdrawing money from the accounts—and it will protect her from you doing the same. It's standard practice."

"I trust her. She wouldn't do anything like that."

"That's a huge mistake. You'd leave yourself wide open."

"What if we were legally separated?"

"There is no legal separation in Texas. Your only option is to file for divorce. If enough time goes by, she could declare residency in Louisiana and file there. I think that might be a bad outcome for you. A sympathetic judge might award more than the Texas standard."

The word "permanent" from her e-mail came to mind. *Why did she use that word?*

"OK, let's do it." Even though the last few years had been miserable, filing for divorce was the hardest thing I had ever done. I had thought about and sometimes threatened divorce at other low points in our marriage—never serious about following through. This time, I felt like I really had no other choice.

"I wrote her this letter to explain my reasoning."

She read the two pages quickly and looked up with disbelief. "I don't recommend you give this to her. You'll be seeing it again in court, and all your admissions of fault will be used against you."

"She needs to know why I'm doing this. I can't just walk in and say I'm divorcing her."

"Tell her if you think you need to, but do not give her a copy of the letter. Why don't you let me have her served when she gets to Mandeville?"

"No, I have to face her when I do it. I owe her that much."

"OK, we could have her sign a waiver of service so she won't be surprised by a process server. It's another standard form that saves money and is easier to handle for some people."

"All right, let's draft up what I need to sign."

"First thing we'll need is five thousand dollars and your signature on the retainer agreement."

Later that day, I nervously waited for Jennifer to come home. She had packed her belongings, loaded the heavy items in the truck, and then left. The house still had a number of pieces of furniture in it, but all the things that made it feel like a home were already stowed away.

As the hours passed, my anxiety increased as I wondered how she would react. Maybe she'd tell me it was all a big misunderstanding and never intended it to go so far. Cathy called, looking for her, and I blurted out what I had done. She said she was going to call Jennifer's cell phone so she wouldn't be surprised. Shortly thereafter, around eight in the evening, Jennifer came home.

"You really messed up now," she said. "You're going to be very sorry you did this." She was incredibly angry—yet there was no sadness. "Why did you file without telling me?"

"I wasn't the one who started all the talk about meeting with the Christian divorce lawyer. I needed to protect myself. I had no idea what you were going to do."

"Well, you're going to pay for it now," she said, texting on her phone.

"Who are you writing to?"

"It's none of your business anymore. You're going to be very, very sorry you did this."

She went into the bedroom and began gathering the last of her things. Every few minutes returned to the living room, shouting insults and throwing things at me as I sat dumbfounded on the couch.

"You need to wear this hat," she said, flinging a blue beret with a hammer and sickle insignia. "You're a Nazi."

"That's not a German beret—it's Russian," I corrected her reflexively.

"You think you're so smart! Always have to prove a point, don't you? You're going to be sorry!" she screamed.

I stayed on the sofa that night, unable to sleep, worried about what might happen next. I had never been afraid of Jennifer before, but that night I truly was. I never had a chance to break the news to her with my letter. It wouldn't have mattered in her state of mind—the outcome would have been the same.

By morning, Jennifer had already moved on from the events of the previous evening and calmly readied her belongings for the trip. I moved a few things I wanted to keep into the office—the photo album of Bonnie and Clyde's life and their ashes, the sculpture that reminded me of Kelli, the carved bear from our trip to Glacier National Park. Everything else was fair game—except the dogs. The four big dogs were mine. Period. I wasn't going to break up the pack. If she was going to leave, it was going to be without them.

Outside the office, box by box, our shared life was disappearing onto the moving truck. What seemed so clear a few weeks before—that I'd be happier if she left—didn't seem so any longer. She was so cavalier about it. Like she just got tired of an old pair of shoes. After all our years together, I wondered how she could do it. The real question I was asking was how could she do it *so easily?*

CHAPTER TWENTY-FOUR

On Our Own

I spent the rest of the day wandering through the quiet, cavernous house in a daze. The emotions were overwhelming—betrayal, rejection, anger, sadness, fear, loneliness, and, oddly enough, relief. Through all the pain, I was relieved the fighting, hostility, misunderstandings, and frustration had finally come to an end.

For the first few weeks, I received odd text messages from time to time and an occasional e-mail related to our divorce proceedings. Jennifer didn't call and rarely answered when I did. With each passing day, the reality of it all sunk in a little more, and the crushing loneliness settled upon me.

Most of the people I knew were either "couple friends" or work associates. My friendships disappeared over the years and I hadn't tried to replace them, depending on Jennifer to build and maintain our social network. In the days and weeks that followed, a few of our neighbors and friends called to check on me; however, most of the people we shared time with didn't feel comfortable picking up the phone. I was upset at first, then realized I hadn't put much effort into the relationships.

At least worrying about the dogs distracted me from the personal situation. Without Jennifer to supervise during the day, the pups needed to be completely exhausted before I left for work. Otherwise, they'd surely expend their energy destroying the house and its few remaining pieces of furniture. The field near the Brazos became our destination for predawn outings similar to those at the lakefront with Bonnie and Clyde. This time, however, we had half the people and twice the dogs.

Seconds after the back of the Yukon opened, only the strobe lights on their collars were visible—flashing lights floating and dancing in the distance. I jogged after them, nervously watching the lights separating, converging, pairing off, disappearing into the woods then suddenly reappearing. In the secluded darkness, a half mile off the main road down a rutted gravel path, there was no one to help us if we found trouble.

A few weeks into our new routine, the dogs chased down a skunk and Kodi took a direct hit. Instead of stopping the game, the pups were invigorated by the challenge of tracking the noxiously-armed creatures. Every week or so, one was sprayed, and I washed the unlucky pup with tomato juice to neutralize the smell and stop the burning sensation. Without the aid of the miracle juice, I'd have been quite a topic of conversation at work. Well, maybe I was and just didn't know it.

I often came across evidence of foraging hogs and occasionally saw a dozen or so deer moving along the opposite bank. Sometimes, the sky was filled with large cumulus clouds glowing a pinkish hue toward the break of dawn. When thunderstorms loomed in the distance, I could see dozens of lightning strikes that never left the clouds. I counted the time between the flash and the sound to make sure we were at least a few miles from the storm. I'm sure we weren't far enough, but with all the things going on in my life, it didn't seem to matter.

Daisy was, by far, the best hunter in the bunch, exhibiting great instincts in locating prey, having successfully tracked and consumed six rats during the morning missions. On one of our excursions, perhaps having been sprayed one time too many, Daisy came bounding toward me carrying a dead skunk. Convinced and concerned she'd decimate the remaining skunk population in short order, I ended our predawn visits.

Daisy became especially fond of Kodi, shadowing her and licking her face in a very submissive, though relentless manner. When she grew tired of the attention, Kodi locked her jaws on the large puppy's head and dominated her to the ground with a frightening growl, causing Daisy's bladder to lose control. Kodi was only doing what Haley had done to her. Maybe it was instinct. Daisy already matched Kodi's size and was adding five pounds of muscle each week. Kodi had to establish her superiority early and often, or she faced a lifetime of domination by the rapidly growing puppy.

Daisy also bonded quickly with Lucas. Despite spotting him ten pounds and two months, she was a good match for him. She learned mock combat quickly from Kodi and gave poor Lucas a tough time. To make matters worse, Buddy and Kodi ganged up on him when he already had his hands full with Daisy. Always on the losing end of the engagements, he nevertheless seemed to enjoy himself.

When Daisy wasn't following Kodi or playing with Lucas, she looked to me for affection. Not realizing the size of her rapidly growing body, she often crawled onto my lap or laid on top of me, constantly yearning to be touched. She became so attached that, when left alone for any length of time, she developed horrible separation anxiety. Suffering from an adrenaline-boosted panic attack, she leaped and grabbed at me upon my return, raking her razor-sharp dew claws down my back or arms. Despite knocking her down numerous times, she kept coming, unable to control herself. Other times, when her mood was a little mellower, she only peed from the excitement of our reunion.

Lucas was another story altogether. The weeks passed and he continued to poop in the house, leaving his presents in the far corners of the upstairs bedrooms. He knew he needed to get it as far away as possible, as he did in his kennel, but didn't see much difference between carpeting and grass. Sometimes, he peed right in front of me, knowing full well I would yell and chase him outside. I had to break him of his habit, but still couldn't approach without him cowering in fear or running away.

A month after leaving, Jennifer returned to retrieve her remaining belongings and, unfortunately, claim Buddy. I tried to talk her out of taking the dog, even offering to pay her, hoping to hang on to the life I traded for Kelli. I relented partly because I didn't want the court to decide which dog she was entitled to and partly because it was becoming very difficult to manage the four big dogs—especially Buddy. Sometimes on our weekend visits to the Brazos, Buddy charged within a few yards of a petite woman, standing motionless except for his rapidly wagging tail, staring momentarily before returning to the pack. Though he didn't mean any harm, his heavily muscled body and bear-pig appearance usually frightened his target. I guess from his vantage point, the ladies looked a bit like Jennifer and he had to get within a few feet before he could recognize who it was—or who it wasn't.

The dogs were extremely excited to see Jennifer, nearly knocking her down as she entered the gate. While the big puppies battled for attention, Kodi gently leaned against Jennifer as she sat on the staircase step. I hardly recognized her. Beyond the different makeup, hairstyle, hair color, and clothes—it was how she behaved. There was no emotion about the separation or about seeing me again. She drank wine, laughed, and chatted with the two friends, Alex and Margie, who accompanied her on the drive. The feelings of rejection that had dissipated over the past few weeks came back with a vengeance.

After dinner, we retrieved my belongings from the pickup truck and loaded the rest of Jennifer's things. A short while after retiring to bed, Alex tried to come down the staircase for a glass of water. Though he was petting Buddy only a few minutes earlier, the dog charged at him. There was no doubt, the dog needed glasses. I worried it might end badly for him in Mandeville, perhaps attacking someone because he became confused.

The next morning, they had breakfast and made some excuse why they had to get on the road. Even if there was more time to talk to Jennifer, we really didn't have anything to say. Buddy dutifully jumped into the backseat of the truck and headed to his new home. I loaded Kodi, Daisy, and Lucas into the Yukon and we headed to the Brazos to help them forget the day's events.

For the next few days, the dogs ran to the back gate and wagged their tails when they heard the slightest noise. They'd come get me in the house and run back to the gate. I wanted to explain they'd probably never see Jennifer or Buddy again. I let Tiger and Bailey come over each day to help cheer up the distraught trio. The neighbor dogs soon lost interest, as Kelli and Buddy had been their favorites. Kodi often sat by the back fence, looking through the gap, her tail wagging each time the neighbor dogs moved. I knew she missed the old days.

I finally accepted our relationship was over. If I had any doubt, it vanished when I learned she adopted another dog two weeks after taking Buddy. Even if we wanted to get back together, seven dogs made it impossible. I became angry she was putting me through the pain, believing she was intentionally trying to hurt me. The negative emotions made it easier to handle the divorce proceedings. Every time there was a misunderstanding, it reinforced why it had to end.

I should've been glad she was gone. But I wasn't. I knew she hadn't always been like this.

CHAPTER TWENTY-FIVE

Destruction, Again

"Brian, do you want another beer?" I offered.

"Sure, I'll take a St. Arnold's this time," Brian said, draining the last few ounces of his tepid Red Stripe and beginning anew with the cold bottle.

"What's wrong with your TV?" he inquired. "It looks fuzzy."

"There's nothing wrong with it," I answered confidently. "It's a high-def set."

"No, it's blurry. Can't you see? Look at the names on the jerseys." Brian walked closer and crouched to look at the cable box. "This isn't a high definition box. You have a regular box. That's why it's not working." Brian began to laugh and added, "Man, you're killing me."

"I never noticed there was anything wrong before. Shows you how much attention I pay to things. I remember Jennifer had it cut off a while back after getting into an argument with the cable company. I didn't know I had to ask for anything special when I reconnected the service."

"Well, you need to go get a high definition box. Just take this one in, and they'll swap it out. You won't believe the difference."

"Now that you've pointed it out, I'm surprised I didn't notice before."

"It's a good thing we like you. You had to pick the LSU-Auburn game, didn't you?"

"Maybe once you down enough beer, you won't notice the blurriness as much."

"Sounds like an interesting experiment," he joked. "I'm guessing it'll take at least four."

"Hey, what do you think is wrong with my backyard? For some reason it feels smaller than yours. They're about the same size."

"It's the holly tree," Brian said, pointing to the fifteen-foot, red-berry tree planted near the corner of the patio. "It blocks the rest of the yard."

"I think you're right. You know, every time I look at it, I'm reminded of Jennifer," I commented, emptying my third beer since kickoff. We had planted a number of trees close to the patio in a desperate attempt to get some relief from the intense Texas heat. But, like everything else in the yard, the trees grew poorly due to the impermeable soil. While Brian and his son-in-law, Jerome, watched the blurry second quarter of the football game, I stumbled to the garage and grabbed a bow saw.

"What do you think? Opens it right up, doesn't it?" I asked Jerome, who walked out as the tree fell.

"Are you crazy?" Jerome laughed. "What are you doing?"

"I hated the tree. Come to think of it, I hate this tree too," I said, pointing to the bottlebrush growing between the patio and garage. The tree blocked the sprinkler from reaching a good portion of the yard, creating a sloppy mess right off the patio. Within a few minutes, the bottlebrush joined the holly on its side.

"You know what, Jerome—all these damn trees remind me of Jennifer."

"Maybe you ought to think about it a few minutes," Jerome cautioned in a less than serious tone.

"What are you doing?" Brian asked, joining us in the yard as the second quarter came to an end.

"I'm opening it up, like you suggested."

"I didn't tell you to cut your trees down. I only said it made the yard look smaller."

"Well, the trees have pissed me off long enough. It's time for this one to go too," I said, pointing to a scraggly ten-foot oak off the west side of the patio. Another few minutes of effort left the tree on its side. Within twenty minutes, two drake elms and another bottlebrush met their end. Satisfied with the progress on the backyard renovation, I put the saw away, grabbed another beer, and rejoined my friends to watch the remainder of the game.

The tree-felling story became a favorite topic for Brian. Each time I met any of his friends or family, they already knew me—the drunk guy who cut down all his trees. Everyone got a good laugh out of the story, whose details were embellished with each recollection.

Needing something monumental to keep my mind occupied and work out my anger, I turned my attention to the source of much frustration—layer upon layer of rotting clay sod. I spent every spare moment working in the yard, digging out stumps, stripping away and cursing each shovelful of sod. Each day, the pile of excavated mud expanded, eventually reaching the size of a small boat—four feet high, eight feet wide, and thirteen feet long. Thousands of pounds of crushed granite, laid in areas of high traffic, finally solved the mud problem.

Inside, Lucas became the epicenter of escalating chaos. The hunting trips, combined with his continual interaction with Daisy and Kodi, led to a surge in Lucas's cognitive abilities. Rather than devote this improved mental capacity to noble pursuits, he developed a penchant for destruction.

The green couch that survived three years of small-scale attacks by Kelli and Kodi became his initial target. Of course, he had help—the other two dogs were on exactly the same page when it came to this type of demolition. I'm certain Kodi shared the techniques she honed to perfection in the years with Kelli and Buddy. When the new destruction began, I realized Kelli wasn't the instigator of past damage as I had assumed. I should've known better—Kodi always had the guiltiest reaction each time I returned home.

The damage done by Kelli and Kodi had been largely cosmetic and confined to the throw pillows. This crew was determined to systematically dismantle the beleaguered couch. They started out small, shredding the two remaining pillows. Weeks later, they moved on to the large, soft back cushions. From there, they attacked the hard bottom cushions, then the cushioned arms, and, finally, chewed all the way to the springs. With the springs exposed, I had to put the couch out of its misery. The puppies had accomplished in four months what Kelli and Kodi failed to do in three years. I kept the sofa around long after it was no longer functional, because it still served a purpose as a decoy. If they were chewing on the old worthless couch, they weren't chewing on something else. Eventually, I reluctantly sawed the giant couch into pieces and dragged them to the curb. I was sad to see it go. So many good memories.

As expected, they moved on to other targets. They pulled up carpeting, chewed windowsills, gnawed door casings, ate the fabric on the chairs, and chewed the legs of some wood furniture—everything was fair game.

Lucas learned another thing quickly—the way to get food off the kitchen counter. If I left the room for even a minute, it was a good bet whatever food was being prepped was going to be either on the floor or partially devoured by Lucas. After I found him attempting to eat hot ground beef out of the frying pan, I began cooking on the rear burners of the stove. Even then he found a way to get at it. One time, he managed to reach a burger-filled skillet, quietly lowering the pan and its contents to the floor. Luckily for Lucas, it wasn't hot at the time.

He didn't limit his counter-surfing to the stove. He ate my vitamins off the table if I walked away before breakfast. He routinely fished spatulas and food containers out of the sink and shredded them in the yard. In the early days, it was easy to stay one step ahead of him. Now, he had become a worthy adversary.

Lucas also invented the sport of couch surfing. It was a variation of the game Bonnie and Clyde used to ravage my father's couches. With our smooth tile floors, the heavy leather couches could move with a bit of effort, and effort is what Lucas provided. Once he and Daisy became sufficiently worked up, he punched through the doggie door and hit the back couch cushions as Daisy slammed into him with the force of a freight train. He leaped across to the other couch and redirected it several inches the other way. Soon, he was running back and forth at full speed until the couches wedged against the far walls of the house. I thought it was harmless fun until his mass and speed increased to a level where the impact left dents in the walls. When several gaping holes appeared, I moved the couches against the walls for good.

Though the right reaction would have been to punish him, Lucas still became spooked by the slightest change in my demeanor or body language. Soft words were no match for his intuition, as he could discern any departure from my normal behavior. Even if I concealed medicine in my pocket, he scooted out the doggie door as I approached, believing it better to run first and ask questions later.

Lucas wasn't the only problem child. Daisy began patrolling the house for any unattended footwear. Within seconds of locating her prey, both she and the shoe were in the backyard. By the time her absence was noticed, she might have consumed a quarter or more of it. She routinely snatched bedroom slippers, sandals, tennis shoes, and, after an unfortunate oversight on my part, the cycling shoes purchased to replace the pair Kelli and Kodi destroyed. She reminded me of a shark with her vigilance and destructive ability—always circling, waiting for the next opportunity. I warned guests not to leave their shoes unattended—to lock them in the closets—or else. The last time my sister visited, she almost lost a very expensive pair of alligator sandals to the land shark.

Even in the best of circumstances, it's difficult to correct the destructive behavior of large-breed puppies. When you're going through a divorce, you don't have the mental energy to try to work with the dogs. At least I didn't. The dogs were my one source of happiness. The last thing I wanted to do was yell at them. I decided to enjoy the antics and not worry about the money. I laughed during the times I should've corrected them and ignored their behaviors when I should've punished them. Emotional exhaustion—the same reason I couldn't bring myself to break Kelli. She was the embodiment of everything Clyde couldn't be due to his illness. With Lucas and Daisy coming into my life on the heels of Kelli's death and the added trauma of the divorce, I didn't want to squander even a moment of happiness. With so many issues to deal with, I couldn't worry about the destruction of the house, or even potential behavioral problems down the road.

It was ironic. I was back to living like I did when Bonnie and Clyde were a year old. Though the house was newer, the furnishings were about the same. A couple of old couches, a table, a lamp, a few pictures on the walls. I had come full circle.

At least the dogs were having fun, and I could live vicariously through them. Dogs focus on the here and now, never missing an opportunity to enjoy themselves. We live most of our lives thinking about the past or the future. Dogs instinctively know today is all you really have.

CHAPTER TWENTY-SIX

Reflections

After several months, the feeling of loneliness was as acute as the day she left. The hole in my life was immense, and I had trouble filling even a portion of it. During our marriage, I spent every free minute of every day with Jennifer. Breakfast, walking the dogs, hanging out at the house, running errands, working in the yard, going to the gym—whatever. She was a part of every aspect of my life. I didn't develop separate hobbies or interests—only the things we could do together. Maybe it was too much pressure for the relationship. I spent a lot of time trying to unravel what had gone wrong in our marriage, trying to understand how it could have deteriorated so quickly. I wondered what could have triggered such deep resentment and hostility. Maybe the conflicts were always there and we just had more patience in the beginning.

Dogs instinctively know how to sustain good relationships. From the moment Daisy and Lucas met they began to bond. Within days, they were good friends and, within weeks, inseparable. Often, Daisy laid next to Lucas and gently licked his ears and face. Other times, Lucas gnawed gently on Daisy's head and neck. They played with each other almost every waking minute.

At first, Kodi was involved in all the play, but, as the puppies bonded, Kodi often became the third wheel. When she tried to engage them in play, they'd comply for a few moments, then quickly became distracted with each other. She was experiencing the same rejection Haley felt when Kelli bonded with Kodi. Like Haley, Kodi instinctively took on the mother role at the expense of the playmate role.

Despite the love Daisy and Lucas felt for each other, a boundary was occasionally overstepped and a skirmish ensued. Resolved in seconds, they were back to being friends—no hurt feelings, no simmering hostilities, no clinging to how one was wronged by the other, no frustration a similar fight occurred over the same bone the day before. They settled their differences in real time.

Day by day, each tested the other. One was destined to be in charge and the other would accept it, knowing there can be only one leader in the pack. And, beyond the leader, there is a need for each to understand his or her place and role in the pack. Clyde was the leader, and Bonnie was fine with that. Kelli was the leader, and Kodi was fine with that as well. Buddy and Kelli were jockeying for position when she died, yet she seemed willing to hand the reigns over to him, playfully letting Buddy gnaw on her neck without reprisal. Daisy and Lucas will eventually figure it out and, once they are older, I expect the dominant one will challenge Kodi for the alpha role. Despite a thirty- to forty-pound advantage, I don't think either of them will be successful for quite some time.

Some people think dogs are happy only because they live in the moment. I think their happiness stems from something more. I believe it's because they go "all in" with their emotions. Nothing is held back. They don't calibrate their attachment to their mates to limit the sorrow they might feel when one dies. Even after experiencing a series of heartbreaking losses, Kodi has pushed all her chips in on me and the two puppies. Based on her experience, she knows each time she falls in love with another dog or person, it ends in heartbreak. Despite that knowledge, she loves deeply and completely, unwilling to worry about the losses that may come.

Jennifer and I could've learned a lot from the dogs. Instead, we hung on to our hurts, lived in the past, didn't resolve issues when they arose, and, unfortunately, both wanted to be in charge. While we compromised on some things, it was usually a battle until one of us gave up.

As I was getting ready to ride one day, I pulled out the cycling shoes Daisy attacked months before. The tongues of both shoes had been partially ripped out, and the buckle on the left shoe was missing, leaving only the Velcro strap to hold the shoe together. The strap, barely doing its job without the buckle's reinforcement, was worn out after being ripped apart hundreds, maybe thousands of times. The hook side, weakened by dozens of broken barbs, was further hampered by lint and other foreign matter between the healthy hooks. The fabric side, once a uniform bed of hoops, was frayed and thin. Both sides of the Velcro were damaged, neither able to compensate for the weaknesses of the other. Kind of like our marriage—bonds so weak at the end it wasn't hard to pull apart. Each time we peeled the relationship back with an ugly fight, we snapped the barbs, ripped the fabric, and allowed trash to get in the way. After pulling apart hundreds of times, we were left with little or no connection. If we had one big issue—an affair or some other big mistake, we might've worked through it and, possibly, repaired the damage. Instead, we had hundreds of small conflicts that we never resolved—or if we did, the resolutions didn't last.

Of course, it was all Jennifer's fault, wasn't it? She was more than difficult; she was impossible at times, I often reminded myself. Yet, when I began to look at my own role, I didn't like what I saw. We didn't wake up one morning and decide to fall out of love with each other. It took a lot of effort from both of us. I thought about the fights over meaningless things—the music we played for a party, the location of the couch, how much time the sprinklers ran, how many treats the dogs received. The more the fighting continued, the more we both chose to be disagreeable. There was no reasoning behind it, sometimes it was pure spite. There were so many opportunities along the way to take a different path, to resolve things, to compromise. So many times, one of us could have just let go.

Over time, Jennifer came to see any suggestion, any attempt to help, as an effort to control or criticize her. The more I tried to "help," the more her defenses went up. The pattern went on for years, until I finally grew tired of feeling like a nuisance. The only way I could cope with the stress of keeping silent was to harden my heart and detach from her. It was ironic she felt smothered and controlled when she left. By that time, I rarely asked what she was doing, and I didn't really care.

I guess we both got worn out over the years—so many conflicts about so many issues, each seemingly important at the time, though, in retrospect, many of them meaningless. Hundreds and hundreds of little things over the years, adding up to an overwhelming force that drove two people apart. Did she provoke me sometimes with the things she said and did? Sure. Yet, no matter how much I dissected her actions, I couldn't find anything excusing my behavior. Maybe I should've tried to get us help. I could've been big about things instead of digging in my heels. If nothing else, I should've ended the relationship years ago when it became clear we'd never resolve our conflicts.

Once I recognized the role I played in the destruction of our marriage. I forgave her for the painful things she did in its waning days and during our separation. My anger and resentment quickly dissipated. All that remained was the horrible feeling of being despised by the person who once loved me more than anything.

CHAPTER TWENTY-SEVEN

Changing Venues

The morning sun rested on the horizon, filtering its golden rays through branches of the towering trees lining the Brazos River. A layer of heavy fog drifted on the surface of the slow-moving water. The dogs wrestled along the bank, splashing playfully in the shallows of the river. Soon, they were on the move, bounding through the tall wildflowers lining the wide canal draining into the river.

Upstream of a small dam, Lucas noticed a few ducks on the calm water. With Daisy and Kodi in his wake, he pursued the fowl upstream, flushing them repeatedly, until abandoning the chase. The dogs came charging back through the shoulder-high grass, their prey shifting to mice. Before long, Daisy captured and consumed one as Lucas watched enviously. The dogs wrestled and ran through the wet grass, making several more circuits of the open field. The small droplets of dew sparkled in brilliant colors as the sunlight hit them at precisely the right angle. Though I wanted to rest and soak in the peace and beauty of our special place, the arrival of joggers and other visitors necessitated our departure.

I needed to find a safer place to take the dogs on the weekends. It was just a matter of time before they ventured too close to the road, happened upon a moccasin, or came across an alligator. Sure, it was pretty unlikely we'd run across one of the ancient creatures, but I sometimes awoke from a dream where Kodi struggled for her life in the jaws of an alligator while I watched helplessly from the bank. Maybe it wasn't that crazy. The small inlet was a popular fishing destination, providing a steady stream of bait and attracting plenty of fish. And, of course, a hungry alligator wants to be where the dining is good.

The area still worked for us in the evenings, because hundreds of small birds congregated in the grassy field near dusk. The three dogs sprinted through the field, relentlessly flushing the birds from their hiding places. Daisy, always in the lead, instinctively knew where the next flock of birds lay hidden.

It was time to return to the dog park scene, but Sugar Land was no longer an option. After enjoying the freedom of the open field, the dogs had little interest in the meager amenities of the park. Instead, they spent their time walking the perimeter, yearning for the adventure that beckoned just beyond the parking lot. Thankfully, we found a park fifteen miles away with perfect amenities for the dogs—seven times the open space, large trees, a nice swimming pool, and, most importantly, a number of mud lakes to play in and, unfortunately, drink from.

Daisy was terrified on the first few visits, relentlessly jumping and hugging me with her paws, raking her dew claws down my sides. I had to push her off at least a half dozen times before she calmed down. Larger than most of the dogs, she was still very much a puppy in her mind. She spent a lot of time sitting between my legs—seeking protection from the other dogs.

At the house and in the open field, Daisy and Kodi gave poor Lucas hell. They attacked him constantly and worked as a team to take him down. I just assumed he'd be frightened and passive at the park. Yet Lucas didn't have a problem with the park—Lucas was the problem. Assuming the worst upon meeting each new dog, he lifted his lip to expose a few razor-sharp teeth and growled. All it took was a stern "No!" for Lucas to back off. Four months into his rehabilitation, he still ducked and ran when I raised my voice. He knew his actions were wrong, yet months at the shelter ingrained some bad habits. Surprisingly, when Lucas growled at a friendly dog, Kodi lunged at him, quickly putting an end to his unacceptable behavior. He dutifully accepted the correction, unwilling to test her patience.

Sometimes, he approached dogs and lost control in the other direction. He cowered and licked the underside of the dog's mouth and rolled onto his back, apparently unprovoked. Perhaps these dogs, mostly German Shepherds or Rhodesian Ridgebacks, reminded him of a parent or a dominant dog at the shelter. Whatever the story, his puppyhood left an indelible impression on his psyche.

Once Daisy gained some confidence, the dogs ran and played until they were completely spent. Kodi enjoyed being the rabbit, initiating the chase, allowing Daisy and Lucas to tear at her like she was a wounded animal. Every now and then, a new dog tried to join in the attack on Kodi. Because their play fights were invitation only, the new dog immediately became the target and the chase was on. With two seventy-plus-pound dogs chasing one, it wasn't a fair match. Daisy usually rode the dog to the ground like a cowboy taking down a steer. Or she rolled it and ran right over it. Lucas barked incessantly, jealous Daisy was playing with another dog. Despite appearances, the chase was all fun and games, with the target dog usually coming back for more.

Daisy also loved to play with puppies and small dogs. Unaware of the disparity in size and strength, she often whacked them with her massive paws to "encourage" the dog to play. As a result, we were quickly wearing out our welcome.

By late fall, a group of male dogs began harassing Daisy. She quickly sat or ran between my legs when the dogs tried to engage her. It didn't take long for me to realize Daisy hadn't been fixed like I had assumed. The dog park was out of the question for the next few weeks.

It was time to try walking the neighborhood on the leashes again. After a few outings, a lot of things began to make sense—like why I used choke collars to walk Bonnie and Clyde. With Daisy and Lucas attached by chest harnesses, the pressure on the leashes was relentless. I returned from the walks completely exhausted, and my hand a little numb for a while afterward. Without choke collars, the powerful animals were almost unmanageable. It was only a matter of time before they caught me off guard and either ripped free, knocked me down, or dragged us all into traffic. Still, the collars were not workable with three dogs. One of the dogs was always getting choked accidentally—usually when one stopped to pee and the others kept going. None of them was doing anything wrong, yet they all suffered the consequences.

Daisy's habits made the walks even more challenging. Every four or five steps, she lunged from excitement and snapped the leash against my wrist. More troubling, she pulled toward the street as each loud vehicle passed, lifting her head and peering into the car. No matter how many times I yanked on the leash and corrected her, she continued the habit. She wasn't trying to chase the car in an aggressive manner. Rather, she was apparently looking for something—or someone—perhaps looking for whoever dumped her. Sadly, after all this time, she still thought they might be looking for her.

They did better in the mornings when there was very little traffic, fewer people, and only the occasional dog. Still, when we came across something unexpected, the battle was on. I was pulled through a neighbor's garden in pursuit of a cat, nearly plunged into the lake as they chased a few ducks, and had to straddle a tree one time to avoid being dragged into the street.

On these predawn walks, we reconnected with an old friend we hadn't seen since the last time Kodi and Kelli walked the levee. For weeks, Kodi pulled hard as we came within a few blocks of the house where the head once appeared. She stopped, sat, and searched the crest, waiting for her friend. I pulled her along and she resisted in her normal fashion—by falling over. Then, she popped to her feet and scanned the wall again.

"Come on girl, the old guy has probably moved—let's go." After a few minutes, she dutifully came along.

One morning, the sound of the huffing and puffing old dog became audible as we made our approach to the wall.

He ran back and forth along its length before springing his aged body to the top where he latched his arms into position. Barely able to get his nose across, it was enough for Kodi, who excitedly leaped up to greet him. On his next attempt, the two startled puppies joined in the greeting. Two was all he had in him that morning. In the old days, it was five or six times, and he could've easily done a dozen, had I not pulled them away. We finished our walk, Kodi radiating happiness and contentment all the way home.

We only went that way once or twice a week. I enjoyed letting Kodi see him, but I also wanted to let the old guy recover. And, once the puppies knew where he lived, they relentlessly pulled from a block away. My body could only take so much of the abuse.

On the weekends, we returned to the levee that had served us well with Kelli and Buddy. The usable section had shrunk even further, as they had completed a road bisecting the levee and canal. Before giving up, we ventured off into the fifty-acre open field. They ran like a herd of antelope in the half-foot tall grass as I struggled to keep up. The best I could do sometimes was just keep them within shouting distance.

One day, we visited the place where the coyote den once was. From a distance, their home seemed exotic and secluded, but it was little more than a piece of corrugated tin, angled off the ground, surrounded by scrub trees and bushes. All those years they had survived—through extreme droughts and bitter cold. Finally, when their food supply was decimated by development, they couldn't hang on any longer.

Lucas somehow located a fresh pile of human feces. Apparently, he channeled some of Kelli's spirit as he immediately decided to wear it as both a beard and a sweater. Thankfully, neither of the other dogs joined in the festivities. After wrestling him into the shower and washing and rewashing for a half hour, the nauseating smell dissipated. He hid from me for hours after the ordeal. I didn't have to punish him—the shower was enough.

I drove to the levee on future visits and the dogs sprinted as soon as the hatch lifted. Kodi was always in the lead, the cold weather setting her on fire. They sprinted to the pond and flushed the ducks and other birds. We ran toward the coyote den, then sprinted off to a stand of trees, and then to the brush-covered hill. Sometimes, they added a detour to the canal and hunted along the water's edge. After a few circuits, we were all dead tired.

Kodi became obsessed with a portion of the pond on the far bank. She frequently swam across and splashed around as the two puppies watched intently. After ten minutes or so, I called her back, and we ran toward the other sites. Sometimes, Kodi turned abruptly and sprinted back toward the pond. We could be a half mile away and she'd take off. Kodi's obsession provided a chance to catch my breath and relax because I always knew where to find her.

One morning, after a few minutes of splashing, Kodi yelped, causing Daisy and Lucas to come to her aid. Daisy bumped her out of the way and dunked her head under the water. When Daisy's head reappeared, she had what looked like a twenty-pound nutria rat attached to her face. Daisy screamed as the animal fought back with its sharp teeth and claws. Lucas and Kodi quickly grabbed the creature and pulled it away. Within seconds, the dogs had the animal by three limbs and mercilessly ripped it apart. Once the animal was dead, Kodi chased off the puppies. They swam toward me with a look of fear I hadn't seen before. From across the pond, I could see Kodi's fur was up across the entire width and length of her back. The kill was hers.

Daisy returned with a little blood coming from a slice on her lower jaw and two long scratches on her chest. Lucas had a cut dangerously close to his right eye. When Kodi finally returned, she was unhurt. Unwilling to find out if other rats lived in the area, I ended our visits and the pups had to settle for the backyard again.

In a few weeks, Daisy was out of heat. I was relieved we could return to the relative safety of the dog park. There was always the risk they'd pick up fleas, parasites, or a contagious disease. And, with Lucas's unpredictable nature, it was possible he'd get into a fight with an aggressive animal. Out of alternatives, we found a place that met most of our needs. Though it was too far away, not wild enough for me, and not big enough for the dogs, it was the best game in town.

And we were glad to have it.

CHAPTER TWENTY-EIGHT

Changed Hearts

A few weeks after Christmas, Jennifer asked if she could visit, hoping, if things went well, we might be able to reconcile. It was easier when I felt I didn't have a choice in the separation and divorce. Though I forgave her words and actions, the trust we once shared had been lost. I'd always doubt her sincerity, no matter how much therapy we endured. But one thing about Jennifer—she was relentless when she had her mind set on something. After weeks of discussion and soul-searching, I invited her to bring Buddy for a visit.

Arriving nearly six months to the day she left, the dogs were understandably excited to see her again. Daisy lost control of her bladder then almost knocked Jennifer to the ground as she tried to hug her repeatedly. Each time she recovered from the onslaught, Lucas leaped from the other side. Kodi wiggled and waited impatiently for a chance to reconnect with Jennifer.

Lucas and Buddy's relationship had changed during their separation. In the intervening months, Lucas had gained strength and, more importantly, confidence. Lucas no longer fell over when Buddy approached him. In fact, he went paw-to-paw with Buddy during their rough play and peed on everything Buddy marked. It was now Lucas's yard.

We took the dogs to the big park and the four of them tore the place up. It was two hours of running and wrestling—dogs tumbling end over end, dogs being chased, and the dogs bonding with each other. Jennifer and I walked the loop, talking about our lives and what we'd been up to. There was no anger, no simmering hostility—just two people enjoying each other's company.

The days passed spending time with the dogs, visiting old friends and, surprisingly, sharing some romantic moments. As I drank in the affection, I began to wonder if filing for divorce had been a mistake. The thought had no sooner occurred when a simple misunderstanding escalated to an argument as suppressed feelings surfaced.

The fragile trust we built during our time together was quickly extinguished. I could see what lay ahead if we tried to get back together. She'd always see me as trying to control her—her persecutor rather than her ally. And I'd always feel the frustration of trying to help someone who really didn't want it.

The argument was so senseless, so avoidable, it made me wonder if Jennifer, despite initiating the visit, really didn't want things to work out. Maybe it was her way of clearing her conscience—I drove her out and refused to take her back. I thought of Fletcher Christian in *Mutiny on the Bounty* burning the ships upon landing at Pitcairn Island. Without the temptation to go home, they had to make it work in the new land. I think Jennifer probably felt she could never break free unless there was no possible way to come home. Otherwise, she might be tempted to return to the security of the relationship if things got tough. Perhaps, the adoption of more dogs and a needlessly antagonistic legal strategy was her way of burning the ships.

Two months later, I stood in front of a judge, answered a few questions and, within minutes, our marriage of twelve years ended.

In the months following the divorce, I tried desperately to make some friends. I joined a church and attended the singles events—dances, lunches, divorce recovery classes, Bible study meetings—anything and everything they offered.

Despite the friendliness of the people, I felt isolated in the midst of the large congregation. Isolation was only part of what I was feeling. Mostly, I felt guilt. I had shut down in the last years of our marriage and made excuse after excuse to not attend. And now I was spending more time than I could have ever imagined in church—hoping for healing, longing for acceptance, attempting to fill the hole in my life.

One weekend, the singles group met for country dance lessons. I left after only a few minutes, memories weighing heavily on my mood. "Let's take lessons, I want us to dance together," Jennifer often said. She loved to dance, sometimes breaking into a made-up routine while watching a Fred Astaire movie, gliding gracefully across the living room while we laughed together. I remember her donning a thirty-year-old dress and discoing as soon as the movie *Saturday Night Fever* came on. And the tap dancing—every now and then she put on the shoes and started tapping to the music in her head.

One Sunday morning, I sat restlessly in the pew as the pastor began to preach on the topic of forgiveness. I looked at my watch with a bit of impatience. My thoughts drifted to the morning run with the dogs—such a great time running in the field of tall grass. Daisy, Lucas, and Kodi were all in high spirits because of the chilly April weather.

The pastor spoke of the traumas that are often at the root of grudges—the crumbling marriage, the painful childhood, the parent who was an alcoholic. We often hang on to the hurts like a person holding a rope that connects to a large bell, each ring echoing loudly and keeping the ancient grievances alive in our mind. The wrongs occurred long in the past, yet they rush into the present each time the rope is pulled. By holding on, you are only punishing yourself.

My eyes scanned the crowd as the pastor spoke. I always looked around when I was at church—searching for something or, more likely, someone. Kind of like Daisy peering into the car windows as they passed. Maybe somewhere in the sea of people, there was one person who could lift me from my loneliness.

The hurts are real, the preacher said, but we can chose to either hang on to the anger and become its prisoner, or deliver it into God's hands and be set free. He ended with the phrase, "...all you have to do is let go of the rope."

I thought about all the years I held on to my anger toward my father. How I judged him so harshly—so mercilessly, never missing an opportunity to heap a little more guilt onto his shoulders, reminding him of the lousy things he had done. I suddenly realized the hypocrisy of my long-simmering hostility and resentment. I was better educated, had more opportunities and was more intuitive than my father, yet I did some of the same things I hated him for—the criticism, the stubbornness, the pride and, unfortunately, the emotional combat with Jennifer.

A few weeks after the sermon, I called my father on the phone.

"Hey Dad," I said, projecting an upbeat voice.

"Hello son! This is a pleasant surprise. I've called you a few times and left messages. You never return my calls—I thought you were mad at me."

"I've been busy dealing with a lot of things. I haven't been in the mood to talk to anyone. And you keep going on about Jennifer trying to get more money."

"Well, she's taken you for everything you've got, hasn't she?"

"You don't even know what the settlement terms were. It's frustrating you can argue about something you know nothing about. The law is pretty clear; she gets half of what we accumulated together."

"I remember years ago, my friend's son kept being harassed by his barfly ex-wife. She kept coming after him—for more than twenty years. Each time, she got more money, and she finally got a big chunk of his pension."

"Well, I don't care. Jennifer's not going to do that—and even if she tried, the law is the law," I said, my irritation increasing.

"Well, all I know is, she kept coming after him."

"Look, can we just drop this? Even if she does one day, there's nothing I can do about it now."

"I just know how those shyster lawyers are. If you were a blind man they wouldn't quit until they took your tin cup and pencils."

Now why did I call him again? It was so easy to get derailed when talking to my father. "Hey, I wanted to let you know I forgive you for the things you did when I was a kid."

The phone was silent for a moment, and then he said, "I know I must have been a rotten dad sometimes." He continued with resignation in his voice, "I have so many regrets about the past. Everyone is gone—your mother is gone, my sisters, your aunt Peggy, your granddad—all the good ones. I used to be in the Lion's Club, we had friends, and we had parties all the time, now I'm alone. Every day, I think about how I let your mother down."

"Well, I finally understand what it's like to live with regret. I look back at my own life and think about all the things I screwed up. There's no way to go back and make things right."

We talked for a while about the old days and I kept the discussion from getting back on the subject of my divorce.

"Are you still writing the book about the dogs?" he asked.

"Yeah, why?"

"It occurred to me you ought to put some sort of fact in there most people don't know so they'll tell their friends about the book. That's how you get on the best seller list. People tell their friends about it."

"What are you talking about?" I laughed.

"I remember forty or fifty years ago reading a book where the author talked about why New Yorkers are better than other people. I don't remember the name of the book or what it was about, but all these years later I still remember his story about New Yorkers. It was about how they ate their salad. He said people from Los Angeles eat their salad before their meal and people from the Midwest eat their salad with their meal. New Yorkers, on the other hand, are better than others because they eat their salad after their meal—like they do in five-star restaurants in Europe."

"That was the best case he could make for New Yorkers?"

"It gives people something to talk about."

"Well, I'll have to think about what fact to throw into the book."

"Maybe you could write something about the lasagna dinner I took your brother to when he was in town. How I didn't realize, as smart as I am, you probably aren't going to get freshly made lasagna when you go to a place that doesn't do a lot of business. When you told me how long it takes to make fresh lasagna, I realized they had to be serving frozen most of the time."

"Yeah, sounds great. I'm sure a lot of people don't know that." *And don't care.* "It was good talking to you. I need to get going."

"I appreciate you calling. And remember, son—I care about you."

"I...uh, take care of yourself. I'll talk to you later."

During the last few years of my marriage, I didn't have the energy or patience to spend much time with my brother. I worried about what he might say to set Jennifer off or might do to push me beyond my limit. Like my father, he could always find the tender spot and then persistently, and relentlessly, poke at it.

Once Jennifer moved away, he checked in frequently, showing a level of concern I hadn't seen since my mom died. Most weekends, he came by to watch a movie and have dinner. Though leading up to the weekend, Rob often provided unsolicited feedback on the quality of his previous dining experience. *I didn't get enough vegetables. It wasn't very heart-healthy. I need less fat and more fiber in my diet. What do you have against vegetables?* Ironically, he subsisted on fast-food restaurant fare—his menu selections based solely on the coupons he received in the mail.

Initially, we didn't talk about my issues much during his visits. Either he became engrossed with television, talked about his latest trip to Sam's, discussed the progress on his nine-month car search, or droned on about his nonsensical discussions with my father. Over time, we sparingly began to have conversations about the challenges in my life. Ironically, the brother I had nearly written off years earlier was the only one I could turn to for support.

Each time Rob arrived, the dogs punched through the doggie door as the engine of his car became audible to their sensitive ears. Two minutes later, the vehicle was parked, the sun shade meticulously installed, transported items retrieved from the trunk, the doors locked, checked, and rechecked, and Rob walked slowly, with a hobbling gait similar, if not identical, to my father's, toward the backyard. The time-consuming ritual allowed the dog's excitement level to build.

"Hello!" Rob said in a Kermit-the-frog voice, reminiscent of his father. He pushed his way into the gate, beyond which the dogs formed a writhing, furry gauntlet. The dogs leaped and lunged for his attention and affection while Rob's arms hung uselessly by his sides.

"Rob, use your hands to fend them off," I encouraged. Rob turned his back instead, opening a new area of attack to the dogs.

"Ouch! Damn it!" Rob yelled as Daisy raked a dew claw down his hand. "What's wrong with your retarded dog? She's always doing this."

"I told you to use your hands to push her off, not just stand there like an old man. You know how she is, why don't you react?"

"I'm going to wear my ski gloves next time."

"It's ninety degrees out—you're going to look ridiculous."

"I don't care, your stupid dog is impossible."

"Well, I'm sorry she hurt you. Thanks for coming over, Rob. I didn't want to hang out here alone again," I confided.

"You need to quit moping, little Jason crybaby. No wonder the dogs are depressed when I'm not around. When are you going to get over this?" Rob inquired, stopping briefly in the kitchen to put his water bottle in the freezer and a bag in the refrigerator.

"What do you know about it? You've never been married—there's no way you can imagine what it feels like to have fifteen years with someone and then lose it. What's in the bag?"

"It's Marie's blue cheese salad dressing—I brought five jars that still have some leftovers to use on my salad." Rob moved to the couch and plopped down in the center, placing his feet on the leather hassock that was somehow left unscathed by the canines during their many destructive escapades. Kodi crawled between Rob's legs and nestled her head on top of his large gut.

"I wasn't planning on making any salad. I was only going to make pasta. I don't feel up to a big dinner project this time."

"I need both—you don't ever give me enough vegetables. I don't know what's wrong with you. You have an issue about eating healthy."

"That's funny coming from a guy who eats most of his meals at crap-hole restaurants. Why don't you get your vegetables during the week instead of expecting them here?"

"Unlike you, I want to be healthy. I want some vegetables with my dinner."

"Fine, I'll make salad too."

"I don't know what's wrong with you. You had your divorce class and were making progress. You were dating, and now you're just sitting around, getting isolated again."

"I don't feel like going out anymore. The women I've met have way more problems than Jennifer, without any of her good qualities."

"What good qualities?" he said derisively. Daisy, competing with the television for Rob's attention, swatted him in the face. "Ouch! She's like a retarded horse—a retarded horse-dog. That's your new name, 'retarded horse dog.'" Daisy persisted with the paw strikes as Rob feebly tried to defend himself. Lucas kept his paws down, wagged his tail rapidly, and leaned his face toward Rob's.

"She was a good person—she just changed near the end," I said.

"Are you kidding? She was always like that. You never saw it because you were so in love."

"Look, I caused a lot of problems in the marriage early on. It wasn't all her."

"Yeah, right. What did you do that was so bad?"

"I told her I wanted a divorce two days after we got married—that I had made a mistake. How do you think it made her feel?"

"She got over it. You guys had a lot of good years after that. If she was so devastated by what you did, why didn't she leave?"

"I don't think she could handle the thought of failing again; she got out of a lousy marriage a few years before we met. It was probably easier to put up with the humiliation."

"It's funny, you always say I'm like Dad—you're the one who's really like him. You both suck at investing, and you both carry around every mistake you made throughout your life. You probably treated her better than her ex did—and probably better than most would've."

"You don't understand—it was more than that. All she wanted was to be accepted as she was. I never left her alone, constantly pointing out the things she did wrong—I couldn't let anything go."

"You never could let anything go—just like the old man."

"Why did I invite you over again? Oh yeah, you were going to cheer me up. Here's a thought, you probably shouldn't volunteer at the suicide hotline."

"You're just a wuss. She craps all over you, and all you can think about is what you did wrong. Maybe you should hand over another pile of money to alleviate your guilt. You're like a woman. Maybe we should get you a dress."

"Rob, let's not start insulting each other. I don't want to go back to the way we used to get along."

"Oh, that's right. You're like Gandhi since your religious transformation," he mocked.

"Gandhi wasn't a Christian, you dumbass."

"'Little Gandhi'—that'll be your new nickname. Hey, 'Little Gandhi!'"

Here we go again. It was like we were back in our teens.

"Rob, I'm not up for this." I shifted the discussion to the dogs and the adventures we had. It was amazing they were so fond of him. He never really bonded with any of my dogs after Clyde. He came over and largely ignored the canine residents, and they pretty much returned the favor. However, these dogs somehow got to him. Kodi became especially fond of Rob, seeming distraught if he didn't come over for a few weeks. On weekends, she approached and leaned her body toward me, pulled her ears back, and stared into my eyes. I had the impression she was asking me to make "Uncle Rob" appear.

"Dinner's ready in five minutes. You might want to begin your decontamination procedure, Howard," I said, referring to his Hughes-like hand-washing routine.

"There's never any hot water in your house. There's something wrong with your crappy hot water."

"Rob, you say that every time. The water heaters are in the attic—there's thirty feet of pipe between there and the bathroom. I've told you a hundred times, it takes a little while."

"I think there's something wrong, it takes too long. I have hot water instantly at my apartment."

"There's nothing wrong, Rob, it's the way the house is designed."

After four minutes of scrubbing, he exited with hands scalded beet-red from the water that failed to meet his temperature requirements. A trail of water followed him to the kitchen where he grabbed a paper towel and dried his hands. He rescued the bag of bottles from the refrigerator and joined his salad at the table.

"Did you wash your hands when you made this?" Rob inquired with concern.

"Of course."

"Can you hand me the balsamic vinegar? I need to rinse the dressing out."

"There's nothing in those bottles. Why the hell do you keep an eighth of an inch of residue—why don't you throw them away after you use them?"

"There's still stuff in there. Unlike you, I don't waste food." Rob swished a few ounces of vinegar into the jar, stirred vigorously and drained the contents into his salad. After repeating the procedure four more times, his salad floated in a pool of milky-brown dressing.

"Your salad isn't as good as last time," he complained.

"What do you expect when you add a pint of vinegar to an ounce of blue cheese? Here's your pasta," I said, serving a bowl with contents appropriate for a family of five.

"Yum. It smells great. What's in it?"

"Goat cheese, Romano, olive oil, and buffalo meat."

"Oh, so you're sharing your expensive buffalo meat with me this time. What did I do to deserve that?"

"Nothing, I just ran out of the cheap stuff and didn't feel like going to the store. You can't tell the difference anyway, so I don't like to waste it on you."

Rob drained the vinegar-rich remnants of his salad dressing onto the freshly prepared pasta.

"What the hell are you doing?" I asked.

"I had some left over. I didn't want to waste it."

"You've ruined it now."

"What do you care? I'm the one eating it. Stop being such a fussy little chef."

Forgetting my audience for a moment, I continued to seek validation of my feelings. "Look, part of it is I keep reliving all the pain and the mistakes each time I pick up the manuscript. It brings back all the good times and bad. Worst of all, it dredges up all the mistakes I've made."

"Oh, that's right—little Jason Hemingway's Pulitzer prize-winning novel," he again mocked.

"Well, you wouldn't know; you've never read it," I said defensively.

"I don't need to read it. It's probably a bunch of nause-ating stuff about Jennifer—what a wonderful woman she was."

"Rob, that's the difference between you and me. If you wrote something, I'd read it—no matter what it was about or how crappy it was. You—you can't be bothered."

"Admit it; you just don't want to cut the cord. Trust me—once she moves on, she won't be concerned about you at all. You still jump every time something goes wrong in her life. You're probably still paying her bills."

"Don't worry. I'm not going to get back with her. We've had plenty of opportunities to try to fix things. I don't want to go back to the relationship. I was just hoping I could hang on to her friendship."

"Nobody can be friends after a divorce. You're just living in a dream world."

CHAPTER TWENTY-NINE

Just Smile

"Oh my God, he's smiling at me!" the tall, pretty brunette exclaims.

"He started doing that a few minutes ago—you're the third woman he smiled at this morning," I reply.

Lucas has a thing for some women. He senses something from a few yards away, and his whole body begins swaying. His ears tuck and his tail wags furiously as he weaves his way toward them. Sometimes he jumps up on them, and other times he dances around, convulsing with excitement. Lucas has always been quick to show off his teeth, though, in the past, it was a display of dominance around other dogs. This is different—he's really trying to smile, pulling his lip above his front teeth like a chimpanzee does, trying to communicate his feelings in a way we can understand. These types of things catch me by surprise with Lucas. Such a project in the beginning—it seems he's finally hitting his stride.

Why wouldn't he smile? His life is filled with joy and love, his intense fear has abated, and he finally feels he can trust me. I can correct him or give him medicine without his entire world collapsing. He's moved his sleeping location from the dog beds to a spot next to me. In the morning, he follows me, wagging his tail continuously and, when I come home from work, he dances around for a few seconds, vying for my attention at the gate. Every now and then, I catch him smiling, and it makes my day. After a quick trip to the fence to bark at Bailey and Tiger, he and his mates sprint back to welcome me, punch through the doggie door, leap over the back of the couch, and wait impatiently for me to get in the door. They stand against the back, wiggling and wrestling for position—like Kelli and Kodi did a few years earlier.

Lucas has developed into an imposing and handsome animal. The puppy features are gone and have been replaced with a serious, confident look. Not yet two years old, he sports a touch of gray on the underside of his snout—likely from the stress of his days at the kennel. With nearly ninety pounds of pure muscle, he's a good match for his best friend, Daisy.

Yes, Lucas is smiling. But then again, I guess we all are.

Daisy is nothing but smiles. Though she still has baggage from the events in Mandeville, she only knows she is loved. In time, she'll forget about the abandonment, the fear, and the loneliness she felt in the beginning. Thankfully, she's stopped her habit of lunging when I come home. It's been a steadily improving situation, from the full sprint ending with a leap toward my chest—to now where she only pops up a little. Maybe someday I can have company over without fearing they'll leave with a broken hip.

Daisy has also grown into a beautiful animal. The abnormally large head and paws are now perfectly proportioned. Her eyes have changed from a deep, dark brown to include a beautiful green ring between the pupil and the outer brown edge. At nearly one-hundred pounds, she's slightly bigger than Lucas and towers over Kodi, yet still cowers and licks Kodi's face for each perceived transgression. After particularly strong corrections by Kodi, she comes to me for reassurance.

At night, she worms her way across my body like an army recruit belly-crawling under barbed wire, her elbows providing the necessary leverage to inch her massive body forward. A few minutes before the alarm each morning, she begins to gently exfoliate my face with a tongue capable of cleaning a frying pan faster than a wire brush. Sometimes, she adds a clumsy swat of her paw on my face to ensure I wake up, the rough underside of her pad providing additional exfoliation. I softly tell her no and move the paw away. She gently places the paw in the same spot, as if the problem was the force and not the positioning. After another correction, she gently touches another spot on my face. Another correction, another spot, and then another. I think she believes we're playing a game. In the evenings, she locks onto a massive cow bone and holds it inches from my face, sometimes adding a robust swat of the paw to ensure I appreciate the treasure she's discovered. After showing off her catch for a few seconds, she goes about the business of obliterating it.

Daisy has become my new friend for the hammock. She can't get enough of it, and definitely makes her presence known. She lies across my abdomen or next to me, with one of those sharp elbows propping her up on my stomach. Lucas usually gets in second and slides between my legs. Kodi is content to lie on the dog bed next to us. I haven't been able to fall asleep yet, because the puppies are still too restless. Quite a bit more crowded than it was in the old days, it feels nice to have some company again.

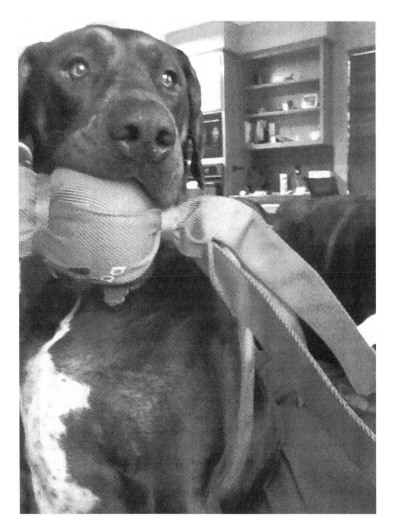

Despite the many losses Kodi has endured, she is still very happy. The other night, she initiated a running battle with Daisy and Lucas in the backyard, diving at them and clacking her jaws—like she used to do with Kelli. Then, she was off, and they chased after her—around bushes, across gardens—tumbling over one or the other, and then sprinting away again. I don't know if it's the start of a more playful time for her, or if something just clicked.

Kodi has taken the place of Kelli as my closest companion, and she can sense it. Kodi's freedom to run and explore on our weekend excursions wouldn't be possible if Kelli was still here. She would have lived much like Bonnie—always second, always limited by the number one dog's abilities or bad habits.

Kodi has chosen Daisy as her protégé, perhaps because she's more playful than Lucas, or because she has more wrestling aptitude and desire. Kodi constantly drills her in mock combat, and, like Kelli did when she was being ignored, Lucas barks relentlessly from the perimeter of their battles. After several minutes of his barking, they turn their attention to him and provide the beating he's asking for. Kodi's also trained her in the game of hide-and-seek; however, Daisy hasn't quite worked out the "hide" part of it. In the backyard, she stands behind a small bush or even a tall weed, ducks her head, and stares at Lucas. A good ninety percent of her body is still visible—so she crouches a bit, dropping the percentage to eighty-five. Lucas lowers his head, tucks his ears, and cautiously approaches her position. He stops every few steps looking a bit fearful—though something draws him forward. When he gets a few feet away, she springs out of "hiding," and the chase is on. Within a few seconds, she's riding him down to the ground or pinning him against the fence.

For a long time, I thought Daisy would be the dominant one in the relationship because of her vastly superior strength and agility. Yet Daisy quickly backs down when Lucas has had enough. In the dog world, attitude makes up for a lot of gaps on the physical side. Kodi is still firmly in control of the pack, though it's clear Lucas will one day be the alpha.

The three dogs have begun to engage in the same group howling I last heard with Bonnie, Clyde, and Haley. Daisy, always the instigator, sits on the bed, uttering a single bark every ten or fifteen seconds, while the others lay nearby. Soon, Kodi adds a plaintive, intermittent cry, causing Lucas to sit up and take notice. As the frequency of Daisy's barking increases, Kodi begins to howl, and Lucas begins to bark. Soon, all three are howling together, heads arched skyward, creating a deafening symphony. As suddenly and randomly as it apparently begins, the harmonious music ends and the choir lies down. Curiously, they won't begin until I leave the room, and they stop immediately when I'm insensitive enough to return before they're finished. And, unless Kodi is in the mood to perform, it doesn't get beyond Daisy's suggestive bark. I often wonder what drives them to perform such a strange ritual. Are they crying out for lost comrades, paying tribute to Kodi—or is it simply for fun?

The destruction of the house has abated somewhat. The stuffing has been pulled out of both arms of the leather sofa and a carpeted piece of wood has replaced the ripped seat cushions of the other. They still dig up a bush or two a month and destroy the occasional dog bed, but it's nothing like the devastation that once occurred. And Lucas never misses an opportunity to couch surf when I forget to move the pieces against the walls. Every now and then, I leave something on the counter, and Lucas consumes it by the time I return. The theft of half a gallon of olive oil was a bit unexpected—and a bit unpleasant to clean up after it had run its biological course. Kodi has her usual guilty reaction when I get home, yet she knows I'll always forgive her and, within moments, we'll be playing again. Often, she wags her tail before the scolding ends.

And we still have the unexpected events—like the time Lucas saw a cat in the front yard and pushed hard enough on a small window to shatter it. Before I was out of my chair, Lucas squeezed his body through the tiny, ten-inch-wide window frame and spilled onto the front porch. Luckily, he froze when I yelled at him, and I was able to get him back in the house. If I was at work when it occurred, he surely would have chased the cat with Kodi in close pursuit. If Daisy tried to follow, her giant body might have become wedged in the small window frame. With a busy street a half block away, it wouldn't have ended well. More times than not, the bread lands with the butter side up. And, with big, powerful, spirited dogs, the bread gets dropped a lot.

Most of our favorite places have disappeared under the relentless development in our area. The levee now has a busy street dividing the nutria pond from the old coyote den. All that remains of our special place is a small grassy area around the old shack and a few trees beyond. The spot where Kodi found the nutria has been covered with a concrete walking trail that follows the perimeter of the pond. At the Brazos, they paved the old gravel trail leading to the grassy field and built a major road crossing the canal where the tall weeds stood and the skunks once lived. And we're no longer welcome at the dog park due to Lucas's "snap first, ask questions later" attitude.

When I was about to give up on the search, a friend told me about a huge wilderness area ten miles from our home. There, we discovered a hundred acres of pasture reminiscent of Lisa's ranch, surrounded by dense woods, and separated into small meadows by long stands of tall trees. Each meadow has a different character—some have yellow flowers, another has tall purple grasses that sway gently in the breeze, another is filled with tall white flowers, and still others with green, lush grass. Every free day, the dogs and I run for nearly an hour in the new oasis. It's similar to the place I always imagined—the place I've been searching for since Bonnie and Clyde. Sometimes, when we are out there, I think of how much Clyde would have enjoyed it.

Memories are everywhere for me in this house and neighborhood—the tile floors we worked on for six months, the kitchen walls we textured and painted five times before calling in a professional, the patio still without shade, the front garden she designed and planted, the neighbors we shared so much time with and no longer know, the small park where Jennifer and I took Bonnie and Clyde for afternoon picnics, the island, the outer loop walk. Everywhere I turn, I'm reminded of what we once shared.

I don't want to remember our marriage for what it turned into. I remember the affection we shared, the special way she made me feel in the early years, and the way she showered me with love I didn't think I deserved or would ever find. I'm glad we didn't leave with hatred in our hearts—only compassion, regret, and sadness. Over time, I hope we'll remember the good times, and the bad times will drift away.

The other day, I awoke with Lucas and Daisy pinning me on either side. As I lay there unable to move, my mind drifted back fifteen years to the days with Bonnie and Clyde at my dad's house. One light-colored, one dark, both eighty-plus pounds and each full of love, spirit, and need. Just me and the dogs. I wondered how it could be so similar. First Bonnie and Clyde, then Kelli and Kodi, and now Daisy and Lucas—each time I picked out one and the other unexpectedly came along for the ride.

I know it can't be just coincidence these dogs came into my life when I needed them most.

And knowing that is reason to smile.

Epilogue

A kind girl I did meet
As we sat upon a seat
And talked of my book for a while
She'd help me to edit
Without pay or credit
A novel in need of some style

"I'm not an author myself
But I've read a full shelf
Of books written by those good and great"
I'm sure you'll do well
It's quite easy to tell
You'll be able to help me relate

While reading the book
She took a fresh look
At the big-headed dog by her side
Four years he'd been with her
Alone, Deep did miss her
When long hours at work she applied

A Thousand Sunny Days

Such stories of bonding!
Of swimming and ponding!
Of love, adventures, and thrills!
Yet alone Deep must lament
A house still and silent
While she worked to pay off the bills

Though he wasn't forgotten
She began to feel rotten
For his single life lived day by day
So she went to the pound
And there he was found
A puppy picked up as a stray

He looked like sweet Kelli
Right down to his belly
The same angel wings, color, and size
He looked like he's splattered
With mud if it mattered
Might be why none had thought him a prize

She took the boy home
And there he did roam
Followed by Deep's menacing growl
But he soon made amends
And they fast became friends
Once apparent he meant him no foul

The dog known as Freight Train
Would help her to regain
The joy she for so long had missed
The touch of his soft head
As he snuggled in her bed
Felt as though her soul had been kissed

The dogs soon did tether
Their heartstrings together
Closer two dogs couldn't be
They'll be friends all life long
With kinship as strong
As those born of family

About the Author

F. Jason Phinney earned a degree in engineering and works as a management consultant with an international energy company. Over the past twenty years, Jason adopted nearly a dozen shelter dogs, sharing in their joy and pain as the dogs formed lasting friendships and grieved for those who were lost. The untimely death of a beloved companion inspired Jason's debut novel, *A Thousand Sunny Days*.

24879478R00176

Made in the USA
Charleston, SC
06 December 2013